HEALTHY *Smoothie* RECIPE BOOK

180+ Quick and Easy Nutritious Blends for Longevity, Wellness, Weight Loss, Detox, and Energy. Perfect for Beginners and Busy People to Create a Happier and Healthier You

ROSEMARY BROOK

When I first got into nutrition, I thought healthy eating was all about strict meal plans and counting every calorie. Turns out, most people—including me—don't want to live like that. We want ease, enjoyment, and a way to nourish ourselves without feeling like we're constantly working through a never-ending to-do list. Enter smoothies—the elegant, efficient answer to modern nutrition.

Lately, foods that pack a lot of benefits into small servings—like high-protein yogurts—are trending. Mushroom and algae proteins are also gaining popularity, proving that nutrition science is evolving fast. But one thing remains constant: longevity without health is meaningless. No one wants to live long but feel terrible. What really matters is healthspan—staying strong, energized, and thriving for as many years as possible.

A good smoothie is more than just blended fruit—it's a stealthy full meal, a turbo boost for your day, a burst of energy that doesn't come with a crash, and a wellness ritual that fits into the chaos of everyday life. But not all smoothies are created equal. Some are nutrition-packed powerhouses, and others are basically melted ice cream in a slightly more respectable form. The trick is knowing how to make a smoothie work for you, and that's where this book comes in.

Inside, you'll find 180+ smoothie recipes designed for real life—whether you want to feel more energized, support your gut, lose weight, or sip on something that makes you happy. But this isn't just a recipe collection; it's a masterclass in blending with purpose. You'll learn how to make smoothies that sustain you, avoid common pitfalls (yes, too much of a good thing is a thing), and craft blends that aren't just healthy but taste incredible.

I wrote this book for everyone—the total beginner, the time-crunched professional, and the health enthusiast who wants their smoothies to do more. My goal? To make sure you never blend another boring drink again.

You've probably noticed that the paperback version features black-and-white photos, while the hardcover edition is full color. Why the difference? It's simple—I wanted to make this book affordable for everyone. But don't worry — you won't miss out! You'll find full-color photos of every recipe in your BONUS digital book. Just go to page 144, scan the QR code, and enjoy a gorgeous gallery of smoothies right on your screen.

And hey, if you love this book, let me know! Scan this QR code:

Your review helps others find it, and it makes my day. Seriously. So, when you whip up a smoothie that makes you do a happy dance, take a second to share your thoughts. I'd really appreciate it.

Happy reading,
Rosemary Brook

CONTENTS

INTRODUCTION

WELCOME TO SMOOTHIES: A SIMPLE PATH TO WELLNESS

Let me start by sharing something personal: I wasn't always a fan of smoothies. For years, they seemed like the domain of hyper-disciplined health enthusiasts—those kale-and-spinach devotees who somehow thrived on minimalism. But then I realized something: smoothies aren't about rules, virtue, or perfection. They're about practicality—offering a flexible, low-pressure way to nourish yourself, even when life feels chaotic.

Smoothies work because they meet you where you are. Whether your pantry is bursting with fresh produce or you're down to a slightly squishy banana and some frozen spinach, there's always a way to make it work. Don't have almond milk? Water will do just fine. Found yourself with a blend that's slightly off? A splash of lemon or a dash of cinnamon can fix it in seconds. They're forgiving, adaptable, and refreshingly judgment-free.

I can't tell you how many mornings I've stood in my kitchen, staring at an empty fridge, a ticking clock, and a cup of cold coffee that's somehow supposed to pass for breakfast. That's when smoothies shine. In just 60 seconds, a banana, some frozen berries, a scoop of protein powder, and a dollop of peanut butter can become something delicious, filling, and energizing. It's not just food—it's a small, meaningful act of self-care.

And let's be honest: we could all use more of that. There's something grounding about blending whole, recognizable ingredients—foods you can identify—and knowing exactly what's going into your body. There are no cryptic labels. No hidden sugars disguised under clever names. Just fruits, vegetables, and the occasional indulgent twist. Eating well doesn't have to mean giving something up.

The beauty of smoothies lies in their endless possibilities. Sure, you can stick with classics like bananas and berries. But why not branch out? Have you ever tried pineapple with avocado? It's creamy, refreshing, and slightly unexpected. Think of this book not as a rulebook but as a guide. Smoothies aren't about getting it "right"; they're about discovering what works for you—a zingy tropical blend to brighten your morning or a decadent chocolate peanut butter smoothie that feels like dessert.

If you're new to smoothies, keep it simple at first. Start with one fruit you already love, a liquid you have on hand, and maybe something creamy like yogurt or nut butter. Blend, taste, and adjust as you go. Don't worry about fancy blenders or obscure ingredients—just bring your curiosity and a willingness to experiment. The beauty of smoothies is that they forgive.
Will they solve all your problems? Of course not. But they'll make your mornings easier, your meals more satisfying, and your body a little happier. And isn't that a good start? So, let's skip the pressure and focus on what's practical and enjoyable. Eating well can be simple—and you deserve that much.

WHY CHOOSE SMOOTHIES?

Healthy eating often feels like an endless checklist: deciphering labels, planning meals, and avoiding takeout traps. It's enough to make anyone feel overwhelmed before they even start. That's where smoothies come in. They're not a fleeting health trend or a complicated commitment—they're a practical, adaptable way to nourish yourself without adding stress to your life.

Smoothies thrive on simplicity. Got a browning banana you forgot to eat? It's perfect. Some spinach looking a little past its prime? Toss it in. Running on fumes after a week of late nights and takeout?

Blend some frozen berries, a scoop of protein powder, and a splash of almond milk, and you've just reset your day with minimal effort. Smoothies don't require perfection; they adapt to your time, ingredients, and energy.

What makes smoothies truly remarkable is the control they give you. Unlike store-bought options loaded with hidden sugars and preservatives, homemade smoothies are entirely yours. Want more energy? Add matcha or greens. Craving something indulgent but still wholesome? Blend cocoa powder with frozen banana and almond butter. The choices are endless, and the power is yours.

At their core, smoothies make healthy eating easier. They focus on real food, flavor, and benefits without the guilt or complication. They simplify wellness in a way that feels approachable, achievable, and even enjoyable. And that's why they're worth a place in your life.

HOW TO GET STARTED

Stepping into the world of smoothies can feel a little daunting—especially if words like "spirulina" and "adaptogen" sound like something out of science fiction. But getting started is much simpler than it seems. Think of smoothies as a creative experiment with no wrong answers—just a few guiding principles to help you build blends that work for your taste, routine, and goals.

1. Start Simple
Your first smoothie doesn't need to be groundbreaking. Stick to three key components:
- A **fruit** you love (e.g., banana, berries, or mango).
- A **liquid** you have on hand (e.g., almond milk, coconut water, or plain water).
- An optional **creamy element** (e.g., yogurt, nut butter, or avocado).

For example:
- *Banana + almond milk + peanut butter.*
- *Frozen berries + Greek yogurt + water.*

2. Layer Smartly
Blending is smoother—literally—if you layer ingredients strategically:
- Start with **liquids** to help the blades move freely.
- Add **soft ingredients** like bananas or yogurt next.
- Finish with **frozen or tough** items like ice or spinach.

If your blender struggles, don't panic. Add a splash of liquid or shake the container to help things along.

3. Taste, Adjust, Repeat
No smoothie is perfect on the first try. If it's **too thick**, add liquid. **Too thin?** Blend in frozen fruit or oats. The flavor feels off? Adjust it:
- **Too sweet?** Add lemon juice or a handful of greens.
- **Too tart?** A banana, Medjool date, or drizzle of honey can balance it out.

Smoothie Challenge: Start with ingredients you already have at home and see what you can create. How inventive can you get?

4. Prep Ahead
Make your mornings easier by prepping ingredients in advance. Portion fruits, greens, and add-ons nto freezer bags or jars. You can even freeze liquid bases like almond milk or green tea into ice cubes for an extra-cold, flavorful smoothie.

Smoothies aren't about perfection—they're about discovery. They're a creative, adaptable way to nourish your body while fitting seamlessly into your life. Whether you're blending for breakfast, a post-workout boost, or an afternoon pick-me-up, the best smoothie is the one you enjoy making and drinking. So grab your blender, get curious, and start experimenting. This is your chance to make healthy eating feel genuinely good—because it should.

INGREDIENTS AND TOOLS FOR SMOOTHIE SUCCESS

Creating a great smoothie doesn't require a pantry full of obscure powders or a blender with more horsepower than your car. It's about working with what you have, choosing a few key ingredients, and having the right tools to bring them together. Whether you're a minimalist or a kitchen gadget enthusiast, smoothies are refreshingly low-maintenance. Here's how to set yourself up for success.

Essential Ingredients: Building Blocks of Great Smoothies

Think of these as your smoothie MVPs—versatile ingredients that balance flavor, texture, and nutrition:

1. Fruits (Fresh or Frozen):
- Sweet: Bananas, mangoes, and peaches create creaminess and natural sweetness.
- Tart: Pineapple, berries, or citrus fruits brighten your blends.
- Frozen: Keep a stash of frozen fruits—they're convenient, cost-effective, and chill your smoothie without diluting it.

2. Vegetables:
- Leafy Greens: Spinach and kale are classics, blending seamlessly into fruit-forward smoothies.
- Mild Veggies: Zucchini, cauliflower, or cucumbers add fiber and bulk without altering flavor.
- Underrated Stars: Try beets for natural sweetness or watercress for a peppery kick.

3. Protein:
- Dairy: Greek yogurt or cottage cheese for creaminess and 10-15g of protein per cup.
- Plant-Based: Silken tofu, hemp seeds, or protein powder (pea, rice, or hemp).
- Bonus: A dollop of nut butter adds protein and healthy fats.

4. Healthy Fats:
- Avocado for a velvety texture.
- Seeds like chia, flax, or hemp for omega-3s.
- Tahini or almond butter for a nutty richness.

5. Liquid Base:
- Creamy: Almond, oat, or coconut milk.
- Light: Coconut water or brewed teas like chamomile or green tea.
- Probiotic-Rich: Kefir or plain yogurt thinned with water.

6. Flavor Boosters:
- Spices: Cinnamon, nutmeg, ginger, or turmeric for warmth and complexity.
- Citrus: Lemon or lime juice/zest brightens any blend.
- Sweeteners: Medjool dates, honey, or maple syrup (start small—natural sweetness from fruit often suffices).

Must-Have Tools: Keep It Simple

You don't need a high-tech kitchen to make incredible smoothies, but a few reliable tools can make the process easier:

1. Blender:
- High-Speed Models: Great for silky, creamy textures.
- Basic Blenders: Perfectly functional—just blend longer or layer strategically (liquids first, frozen last).

2. Measuring Tools:
- For beginners, measuring cups and spoons help you nail proportions.
- Once you're confident, eyeballing works just as well.

3. Freezer Bags/Containers:
- Pre-portion ingredients for quick, stress-free mornings.

4. Ice Cube Trays:
- Freeze leftover coffee, tea, or coconut water for flavorful liquid bases.

5. Reusable Straws:
- Not essential, but they make sipping more fun—and eco-friendly.

Setting Yourself Up for Success

Smoothie-making thrives on simplicity and preparation. Here's how to stay ready for whatever your day throws at you:
- **Stock Smart:** Keep your kitchen stocked with staples—bananas, frozen berries, spinach, and almond milk are great basics. Build from there as you get more adventurous.
- **Prep Ahead:** Save time by prepping ingredients in batches. Portion them into freezer bags or jars so you can grab and blend in seconds.
- **Experiment Slowly:** Introduce one new ingredient at a time—like matcha, spirulina, or watercress—and see how it transforms your blend.

Interactive Challenge: This week, try blending a smoothie using only ingredients already in your kitchen. Can you create something delicious without a grocery run?

Smoothie Hack: Got leftover greens, herbs, or fruit? Blend them with water or coconut water, pour into ice cube trays, and freeze. Toss a few cubes into your next smoothie for a boost of flavor and nutrients without waste.

With these essentials and tools, you're well-equipped to make smoothies that fit your taste, schedule, and nutritional goals. Now let's dive deeper into how to fine-tune your blends and make them truly unforgettable.

HOW TO CREATE THE PERFECT SMOOTHIE

Crafting the perfect smoothie is less about following strict recipes and more about understanding the balance of flavors, textures, and nutrition. Think of it as an art form with a touch of science—one that adapts to your taste, mood, and goals. Here's your ultimate guide to building a smoothie that hits all the right notes every time.

MASTERING SMOOTHIE FLAVORS

The right balance of flavors transforms a smoothie from average to exceptional. Here's how to get it right every time:

1. Sweet vs. Tart
- Sweet Fruits: Bananas, peaches, or jackfruit.
- Tart Fruits: Pineapple, citrus, or berries.

Guideline: Start with a 2:1 ratio of sweet to tart and adjust as needed.

2. Contrast for Depth
- Too Rich? Brighten with citrus or herbs like mint.
- Too Light? Add creamy elements like avocado or yogurt.

3. Layer for Complexity
- Spices: Cinnamon, ginger, or turmeric for warmth.
- Herbs: Mint or parsley for freshness.
- Zest: Lemon or lime zest for an aromatic lift.

Quick Challenge: This week, experiment with one unexpected ingredient—like a pinch of cayenne or fresh cilantro—to discover new flavor combinations.

ACHIEVING NUTRITIONAL BALANCE

Smoothies can be a full meal or a light snack, depending on how you structure them. Balance your macronutrients for a blend that's as functional as it is delicious.

Blueprint for Balance:
- **Carbohydrates (Energy):** 1 cup of fruit or veggies.
- **Protein (Satiety):** 10-20 grams from protein powder, Greek yogurt, or tofu.
- **Fats (Sustained Energy):** 1-2 tablespoons of avocado, seeds, or nut butter.
- **Fiber (Digestive Health):** Berries, chia seeds, or oats.

Interactive Challenge: Craft your "signature smoothie" by experimenting with one ingredient from each category above. Start with a favorite fruit, pair it with an unexpected liquid base, and finish with a unique flavor booster like ginger or turmeric. Share your creation with friends or family and invite them to try their hand at making their own.

Creating the perfect smoothie isn't about following a rigid recipe—it's about exploring flavors, balancing textures, and having fun with the process. With these principles in mind, every blend becomes an opportunity to nourish your body and delight your taste buds. So grab your blender and start experimenting—the possibilities are endless!

DRINK SMARTER: WHAT WORKS, WHAT DOESN'T, AND WHY

Smoothies are like a Swiss Army knife for nutrition—versatile, efficient, and sometimes a little too easy to misuse. They're the shortcut to getting more fruits and veggies into your day, the stealthy way to sneak greens past picky eaters, and the liquid fuel for busy mornings. But not all smoothies wear the cape of health they claim. Some can power you through the day like a well-oiled machine, while others set you up for a mid-morning energy crash that feels like a cosmic betrayal. The secret? Knowing how to blend with purpose, not just enthusiasm. Let's break it down.

The Good, the Bad, and the Overblended

We all know that smoothies help us eat more fruits and veggies—something 90% of Americans fail to do, according to the CDC. That's a big win! But here's the catch: blending breaks down the fiber structure of fruits and vegetables, which makes nutrients easier to absorb—good!—but also makes sugar hit your bloodstream faster—not so good.

The fix? Balance. Pair fruits with healthy fats (avocado, nut butters, chia seeds) and proteins (Greek yogurt, plant-based protein powders). This slows sugar absorption and keeps your energy steady rather than sending you on a blood sugar rollercoaster.

The Antioxidant Paradox: Too Much of a Good Thing?

Antioxidants are like an enthusiastic guest at a dinner party—fantastic in moderation, but chaotic if they dominate the conversation. They neutralize free radicals, which is good, but overloading on them can actually interfere with your body's natural defense systems. Research published in *Free Radical Biology and Medicine* suggests that excessive antioxidant intake can suppress the body's adaptive response to stress. Another study in *The Journal of Physiology* indicates that high-dose antioxidant supplements may blunt the benefits of exercise by disrupting cellular adaptation processes.

Does this mean you should stop adding blueberries to your smoothie? Nope. Just don't overdo it. Rotate ingredients. Let kale take a break once in a while—maybe swap in some parsley. Trust that your body thrives on variety, not just a single "superfood."

The Fiber Factor: Why It Still Matters

One big knock against smoothies is that they don't require chewing, which means you're missing out on the digestion-stimulating benefits of, well, using your teeth. Chewing produces saliva, which kickstarts digestion and helps you feel fuller longer. Gulping down a smoothie? Not so much.

So, what's the fix? **Texture and timing.** Don't overblend. Leave a little thickness to slow down consumption. And instead of chugging, sip mindfully. Better yet, grab a spoon and eat it like a smoothie bowl with some crunchy toppings. That way, you engage digestion and actually feel like you had a meal.

Timing Is Everything

When you drink your smoothie matters. A sugar-heavy fruit smoothie first thing in the morning can lead to an insulin spike, followed by a mid-morning crash. Not ideal. Instead, **front-load your smoothie with fiber, protein, and healthy fats** to keep energy levels stable. After a workout? That's when a mix of carbs and protein can help with muscle recovery. Replacing a meal? Make sure your smoothie includes all three macronutrients—carbs, protein, and fat—to avoid feeling hungry an hour later.

The Cold Truth About Nutrient Absorption

Blending doesn't just change texture—it affects how nutrients interact. Vitamin C, for example, degrades quickly when exposed to light and oxygen. A study in *The American Journal of Clinical Nutrition* found that vitamin C content in fruit juice drops significantly within minutes of exposure to air. Meanwhile, fat-soluble vitamins (A, D, E, K) need dietary fat to be properly absorbed. That means your virtuous kale-celery-cucumber-lemon smoothie might be loaded with vitamins, but without a fat source, your body won't absorb them efficiently.

Simple fix: add a splash of coconut milk, a spoonful of almond butter, or even a drizzle of olive oil. Your body will thank you.

The Verdict: Smart Smoothie Strategies

1. Balance your macros – Include fiber, fat, and protein to slow sugar absorption and keep energy steady.
2. Rotate ingredients – Don't overdo one type of antioxidant; mix it up to diversify nutrients.
3. Be mindful of fiber – Keep smoothies slightly thick and try smoothie bowls for a digestion-friendly texture.
4. Time it wisely – Adjust your smoothie ingredients based on when you drink it: pre-workout, post-workout, meal replacement, or snack.
5. Optimize nutrient absorption – Pair fat-soluble vitamins with healthy fats and drink fresh to avoid nutrient loss.

Smoothies are an incredible tool for getting the nutrients you need—if you make them wisely. Think of them as an orchestra: each ingredient should play its part in harmony, rather than one overpowering the rest. Keep it balanced, mix things up, and use smoothies as a supplement to a well-rounded diet, not a crutch. Now go blend something amazing—but maybe, just maybe, chew a little while you're at it.

HOW TO BOOST SMOOTHIES WITH ADD-ONS

Once you've mastered the basics of smoothie-making, it's time to elevate your blends with thoughtful add-ons. These extras can transform your smoothie into a full meal, pack it with nutrients, or introduce new and exciting flavors. The key is balance—each addition should enhance the smoothie without overwhelming it. Let's explore how to customize your smoothies like a pro.

TURNING SMOOTHIES INTO MEALS: SMOOTHIE BOWLS

Smoothie bowls are a more indulgent, spoonable version of your classic smoothie. They're thicker, heartier, and topped with a variety of textures that turn a simple drink into a satisfying meal.

Building the Perfect Base:
- Use less liquid for a thick, soft-serve consistency.
- Blend frozen fruits like bananas, mangoes, or berries with minimal liquid. Add yogurt or avocado for extra creaminess.

Topping Inspiration:
- **Fruits:** Fresh slices of kiwi, strawberries, or pomegranate seeds.
- **Crunch:** Granola, crushed nuts, or cacao nibs.
- **Superfoods:** Chia seeds, hemp seeds, or bee pollen.
- **Creaminess:** A drizzle of nut butter or a dollop of Greek yogurt.

Smoothie Hack: Freeze your toppings—like banana slices or berries—before adding them. This keeps your bowl cool while maintaining a satisfying crunch.

HOW TO USE PROTEIN POWDERS EFFECTIVELY

Protein powders can transform your smoothie from a snack into a meal or a post-workout recovery drink. However, they require a bit of finesse to avoid overpowering the flavor or texture.

Choosing the Right Protein Powder:
- **Whey Protein:** Ideal for quick muscle recovery.
- **Plant-Based Options:** Pea, hemp, or rice protein for vegans or those avoiding dairy.
- **Collagen Peptides:** A neutral-flavored option that supports skin, hair, and joint health.

Blending Tips:
- Use one scoop (15-20 grams of protein) to start—too much can dominate the flavor.
- Pair the protein's flavor with complementary ingredients:
    - *Chocolate protein + peanut butter + banana = Decadent and rich.*
    - *Vanilla protein + berries + almond milk = Light and fruity.*

Insider's Secret: To avoid clumping, add protein powder after the liquid or blend it separately with a small amount of liquid before combining with other ingredients.

ADDING SUPERFOODS AND SUPPLEMENTS

Superfoods are nutrient-dense ingredients that bring specific health benefits to your smoothie. They're small but mighty, so use them thoughtfully.

Top Superfoods:
- **Chia Seeds:** High in omega-3s and fiber, they thicken smoothies and add a subtle nutty flavor.
- **Flaxseeds:** A great source of omega-3s and fiber—use ground flaxseeds for better absorption.
- **Spirulina:** A protein-packed algae that's rich in antioxidants. Start with ¼ teaspoon and build up.
- **Maca Powder:** An adaptogen with a caramel-like flavor that pairs well with bananas and cacao.
- **Cacao Nibs:** Perfect for a chocolatey crunch and a dose of antioxidants.
- **Baobab Powder:** Rich in vitamin C and fiber, with a tart, citrus-like flavor.
- **Lucuma Powder:** A naturally sweet Peruvian fruit powder with a caramel note.
- **Goji Berries:** High in antioxidants, they add a chewy texture or can be blended for natural sweetness.

Supplements to Consider:
- **Turmeric:** Anti-inflammatory and subtly earthy. Pair it with black pepper to enhance absorption.
- **Probiotics:** Powdered probiotics or kefir support gut health.
- **Ashwagandha:** Helps combat stress and promotes relaxation.

Quick Challenge: Add one new superfood to your smoothie this week—experiment with maca, spirulina, or even turmeric.

CHOOSING CREATIVE NATURAL SWEETENERS

Sweetness is essential for balance, but it doesn't have to come from refined sugars. Natural sweeteners enhance flavor while adding their own nutritional benefits.

Best Sweeteners for Smoothies:
- **Ripe Bananas:** Add both sweetness and creaminess.
- **Medjool Dates:** Caramel-like and rich, they're perfect for deeper flavor profiles.
- **Honey or Maple Syrup:** Dissolve easily and work well in most blends.
- **Coconut Sugar:** Adds a subtle caramel note without overpowering the smoothie.

EXPLORING LIQUID BASES BEYOND MILK

Your liquid base is more than just a blender lubricant—it's a canvas for flavor. While almond milk is a go-to option, branching out can add depth and unexpected twists.

Creative Liquid Bases to Try:
- **Coconut Water:** Hydrating, lightly sweet, and ideal for tropical smoothies.
- **Herbal Teas:** Brewed and chilled teas like chamomile, hibiscus, or green tea bring subtle complexity.
- **Fresh Juices:** Orange, carrot, or grapefruit juice adds brightness—just use sparingly to avoid too much sugar.
- **Kefir:** Probiotic-rich and tangy, it supports gut health and enhances creaminess.

Smoothie Hack: Freeze liquid bases in ice cube trays. They'll chill your smoothie without watering it down and intensify the flavor.

Interactive Prompts to Inspire Your Creativity

- **Challenge Yourself:** Create a smoothie using only ingredients you already have at home. How resourceful can you get?
- **Try a New Liquid Base:** Swap almond milk for green tea, kefir, or coconut water in your next blend.

- **Experiment with Toppings:** Make a smoothie bowl and test out unconventional toppings like cacao nibs, shredded coconut, or even granola clusters.

Add-ons are where smoothies truly come to life. They're the difference between a simple drink and a tailored, nutrient-packed experience. Whether you're looking to turn your smoothie into a meal, add a superfood punch, or explore bold new flavors, remember: the best smoothies reflect your preferences, goals, and creativity. So, experiment boldly and have fun with every blend—you're crafting something uniquely yours, not just making a smoothie; you're crafting something uniquely yours.

MORNING
BOOSTERS

01 Coffee Banana Energizer

🕐 **Total:** 5 mins 🍴 **Servings:** 2 📶 **Level:** 1/5

Nutritional Info *(Per Serving, based on brewed coffee and no optional additions)*: 160 kcal; 25g carbs; 4g protein; 6g fat; 4g fiber.

Ingredients

- **Liquid Base (Choose One):** 1 cup brewed and chilled coffee, 1 cup unsweetened almond milk, or 1 cup low-fat dairy milk
- **Main Ingredients:** 1 large frozen banana, 1 tablespoon almond butter, 1 tablespoon unsweetened cocoa powder
- **Optional Sweetener:** 1 teaspoon honey, maple syrup, or agave syrup
- **Optional Superfood Additions:** 1 tablespoon chia seeds, 1/2 teaspoon ground cinnamon

Optional Variations:
- **Diabetic-Friendly:** Replace banana with 1/4 avocado. Use unsweetened almond milk and avoid additional sweeteners.
- **Vegan:** Avoid honey as a sweetener, avoid low-fat dairy milk, and choose almond milk or coffee.
- **Keto:** Replace banana with 1/4 avocado. For an energy boost, use unsweetened almond milk and add 1 teaspoon of MCT oil.
- **Pregnancy-Safe:** Use decaffeinated coffee or replace it with almond milk.
- **Protein-Packed:** Add 1 scoop of unflavored protein powder.

🍳 **Serving Tip:** Top with a sprinkle of cocoa powder, a few chia seeds, or a banana slice. Pair with fluffy whole-wheat pancakes topped with caramelized bananas and a dusting of espresso powder for a balanced morning treat.

Instructions

1. Brew coffee in advance and allow it to chill in the refrigerator. Slice and freeze the banana for a creamier texture.

2. Add the liquid base to the blender first for easier blending. Add the frozen banana, almond butter, and cocoa powder. Sprinkle in any optional superfood additions, such as chia seeds or protein powder.

3. Start blending on low speed to break down the banana and mix ingredients. Gradually increase to high speed and blend for 1–2 minutes until creamy and smooth. Add a splash of liquid if the consistency is too thick. Taste the smoothie and, if desired, add honey, maple syrup, or agave syrup for sweetness.

4. Pour into glasses and enjoy while chilled.

02 Matcha Green Tea Awakener

Total: 5 mins | **Servings: 2** | **Level: 1/5**

Nutritional Info (Per Serving, based on almond milk and no optional additions): 140 kcal; 20g carbs; 4g protein; 5g fat; 3g fiber.

Ingredients

- **Liquid Base (Choose One):** 1 cup unsweetened almond milk, 1 cup coconut water, or 1 cup low-fat dairy milk
- **Main Ingredients:** 1 teaspoon matcha green tea powder, 1/2 frozen banana, 1/4 avocado
- **Optional Sweetener:** 1 teaspoon honey, maple syrup, or agave syrup
- **Optional Superfood Additions:** 1 tablespoon chia seeds, 1/2 teaspoon ground cinnamon

Optional Variations:
- **Diabetic-Friendly:** Replace banana with 1/4 cup frozen zucchini. Use unsweetened almond milk and avoid additional sweeteners.
- **Vegan:** Avoid honey as a sweetener, avoid low-fat dairy milk, and choose almond milk or coconut water.
- **Keto:** Replace banana with 1/4 avocado. Use unsweetened almond milk and avoid sweeteners. Add 1 teaspoon of MCT oil.
- **Pregnancy-Safe:** Use a high-quality, low-caffeine matcha or replace matcha with spirulina.
- **Protein-Packed:** Add 1 scoop of unflavored protein powder.

Serving Tip: Garnish with a sprinkle of matcha powder or chia seeds. Pair with a handful of almonds or a slice of whole-grain toast for a balanced breakfast.

Instructions

1. Freeze the banana in advance for a creamier texture.

2. Add ingredients to the blender. Start with the liquid base, followed by matcha powder, banana, and avocado. Sprinkle in any optional superfoods.

3. Start blending on low speed and gradually increase to high for 1–2 minutes until creamy. Adjust consistency with more liquid if needed. Taste the smoothie and, if desired, add honey, maple syrup, or agave syrup for sweetness.

4. Pour into glasses and serve immediately.

---

03 Raspberry Almond Recharge

Total: 5 mins | **Servings: 2** | **Level: 1/5**

Nutritional Info (Per Serving, based on almond milk and no optional additions): 180 kcal; 22g carbs; 6g protein; 8g fat; 6g fiber.

Ingredients

- **Liquid Base (Choose One):** 1 cup unsweetened almond milk, 1 cup coconut water, or 1 cup low-fat dairy milk
- **Main Ingredients:** 1/2 cup frozen raspberries, 1/2 frozen banana, 1 tablespoon almond butter
- **Optional Sweetener:** 1 teaspoon honey, maple syrup, or agave syrup
- **Optional Superfood Additions:** 1 tablespoon chia seeds, 1/2 teaspoon ground cinnamon

Optional Variations:
- **Diabetic-Friendly:** Replace banana with 1/4 avocado. Use unsweetened almond milk and avoid additional sweeteners.
- **Vegan:** Avoid honey as a sweetener, avoid low-fat dairy milk, and opt for almond milk or coconut water.
- **Keto:** Replace banana with 1/4 avocado. Use unsweetened almond milk, and avoid sweeteners. Add 1 teaspoon of MCT oil.
- **Pregnancy-Safe:** Ensure all ingredients are fresh and thoroughly washed.
- **Protein-Packed:** Add 1 scoop of unflavored protein powder for an extra boost.

Serving Tip: Garnish with a few whole raspberries or a sprinkle of chia seeds. Pair with almond butter spread on crispy rice cakes, topped with fresh raspberries and a dusting of cinnamon for sustained energy.

Instructions

1. Freeze the banana in advance for a creamier texture.

2. Add ingredients to the blender. Pour the liquid base first, then add raspberries, frozen banana, and almond butter. Sprinkle in any optional superfoods.

3. Start blending on low speed and gradually increase to high for 1–2 minutes until creamy. Adjust consistency with more liquid if needed. Taste the smoothie and, if desired, add honey, maple syrup, or agave syrup for sweetness.

4. Pour into glasses and serve immediately.

04 Spiced Chocolate Morning Bliss

Total: 5 mins **Servings:** 2 **Level:** 1/5

Nutritional Info (Per Serving, based on almond milk and no optional additions): 180 kcal; 24g carbs; 6g protein; 7g fat; 5g fiber.

Ingredients

- **Liquid Base (Choose One):** 1 cup unsweetened almond milk, 1 cup low-fat dairy milk, or 1 cup oat milk
- **Main Ingredients:** 1 large frozen banana, 1 tablespoon almond butter, 1 tablespoon unsweetened cocoa powder, 1/2 teaspoon ground cinnamon
- **Optional Sweetener:** 1 teaspoon honey, maple syrup, or agave syrup
- **Optional Superfood Additions:** 1 tablespoon chia seeds, 1/2 teaspoon ground nutmeg

Optional Variations:
- **Diabetic-Friendly:** Replace banana with 1/4 avocado. Use unsweetened almond milk and avoid additional sweeteners.
- **Vegan:** Avoid honey as a sweetener. Avoid low-fat dairy milk. Choose almond or oat milk.
- **Keto:** Replace banana with 1/4 avocado. Use unsweetened almond milk and avoid sweeteners. Add 1 teaspoon of MCT oil.
- **Pregnancy-Safe:** Ensure all ingredients are fresh and high quality.
- **Protein-Packed:** Add 1 scoop of unflavored protein powder.

Serving Tip: Garnish with a sprinkle of cocoa powder or a dusting of cinnamon. Pair with a slice of whole-wheat toast with ricotta, honey, and almonds for sustained energy.

Instructions

1. Freeze the banana in advance for a creamier texture.

2. Add ingredients to the blender. Pour the liquid base first, then add banana, almond butter, cocoa powder, and cinnamon. Sprinkle in any optional superfoods.

3. Start blending on low speed and gradually increase to high for 1-2 minutes until creamy. Adjust consistency with more liquid if needed. Taste the smoothie and, if desired, add honey, maple syrup, or agave syrup for sweetness.

4. Pour into glasses and serve immediately.

05 Plum Vanilla Booster

Total: 5 mins **Servings:** 2 **Level:** 1/5

Nutritional Info (Per Serving, based on almond milk and no optional additions): 170 kcal; 26g carbs; 5g protein; 6g fat; 4g fiber.

Ingredients

- **Liquid Base (Choose One):** 1 cup unsweetened almond milk, 1 cup low-fat dairy milk, or 1 cup oat milk
- **Main Ingredients:** 2 ripe plums (pitted and chopped), 1/2 frozen banana, 1 teaspoon pure vanilla extract, 1 tablespoon almond butter
- **Optional Sweetener:** 1 teaspoon honey, maple syrup, or agave syrup
- **Optional Superfood Additions:** 1 tablespoon chia seeds, 1/2 teaspoon ground flaxseeds

Optional Variations:
- **Diabetic-Friendly:** Replace banana with 1/4 avocado. Use unsweetened almond milk and avoid additional sweeteners.
- **Vegan:** Avoid honey as a sweetener, avoid low-fat dairy milk, and choose almond or oat milk.
- **Keto:** Replace banana with 1/4 avocado. Use unsweetened almond milk and avoid sweeteners. Add 1 teaspoon of MCT oil.
- **Pregnancy-Safe:** Ensure all ingredients are fresh and high quality.
- **Protein-Packed:** Add 1 scoop of unflavored protein powder.

Serving Tip: Garnish with a sprinkle of chia seeds or a dusting of cinnamon. Pair with a handful of walnuts or a slice of whole-grain toast for a balanced breakfast.

Instructions

1. Pit and chop the plums. Freeze the banana in advance for a creamier texture.

2. Add ingredients to the blender. Pour the liquid base first, then add plums, frozen banana, vanilla extract, and almond butter. Sprinkle in any optional superfoods.

3. Start blending on low speed and gradually increase to high for 1-2 minutes until creamy. Adjust consistency with more liquid if needed. Taste the smoothie and, if desired, add honey, maple syrup, or agave syrup for sweetness.

4. Pour into glasses and serve immediately.

06 Lemon Ginger Charger

Total: 5 mins   **Servings:** 2   **Level:** 1/5

Nutritional Info *(Per Serving, based on coconut water and no optional additions)*: 150 kcal; 30g carbs; 3g protein; 2g fat; 6g fiber.

Ingredients

- **Liquid Base (Choose One):** 1 cup coconut water, 1 cup unsweetened almond milk, or 1 cup plain Greek yogurt thinned with water
- **Main Ingredients:** 1/2 frozen banana, 1/2 cup frozen mango chunks, 1 tablespoon freshly squeezed lemon juice, 1/2 teaspoon grated fresh ginger
- **Optional Sweetener:** 1 teaspoon honey, maple syrup, or agave syrup
- **Optional Superfood Additions:** 1 tablespoon chia seeds, 1/2 teaspoon ground turmeric

Optional Variations:
- **Diabetic-Friendly:** Replace banana with 1/4 avocado. Use unsweetened almond milk and avoid additional sweeteners.
- **Vegan:** Avoid honey as a sweetener. Replace Greek yogurt with coconut water or almond milk.
- **Keto:** Replace banana and mango with 1/4 avocado and 1/4 cup frozen zucchini. Use unsweetened almond milk and avoid sweeteners. Add 1 teaspoon of MCT oil.
- **Pregnancy-Safe:** Ensure fresh ingredients and limit ginger to mild amounts.
- **Protein-Packed:** Add 1 scoop of unflavored protein powder.

Serving Tip: Garnish with a lemon zest twist or a sprinkle of chia seeds. Pair with smoked salmon and cream cheese on whole-grain bread to enhance mental clarity.

Instructions

1. Freeze banana and mango in advance for a chilled, creamy texture.

2. Add ingredients to the blender. Pour the liquid base first, then add frozen banana, mango, lemon juice, and ginger. Sprinkle in any optional superfoods.

3. Start blending on low speed and gradually increase to high for 1–2 minutes until creamy. Adjust consistency with more liquid if needed. Taste the smoothie and, if desired, add honey, maple syrup, or agave syrup for sweetness.

4. Pour into glasses and serve immediately.

07 Cucumber Lemon Wake-Up

Total: 5 mins   **Servings:** 2   **Level:** 1/5

Nutritional Info *(Per Serving, based on coconut water and no optional additions)*: 120 kcal; 20g carbs; 3g protein; 3g fat; 4g fiber.

Ingredients

- **Liquid Base (Choose One):** 1 cup coconut water, 1 cup unsweetened almond milk, or 1 cup low-fat dairy milk
- **Main Ingredients:** 1/2 cup chopped cucumber (peeled if preferred), 1/2 frozen banana, 1 tablespoon freshly squeezed lemon juice, 1/2 teaspoon grated fresh ginger
- **Optional Sweetener:** 1 teaspoon honey, maple syrup or agave syrup
- **Optional Superfood Additions:** 1 tablespoon chia seeds, 1/2 teaspoon ground turmeric

Optional Variations:
- **Diabetic-Friendly:** Replace banana with 1/4 avocado. Use unsweetened almond milk and avoid additional sweeteners.
- **Vegan:** Avoid honey as a sweetener. Replace low-fat dairy milk with almond milk or coconut water.
- **Keto:** Replace banana with 1/4 avocado. Use unsweetened almond milk and avoid sweeteners. Add 1 teaspoon of MCT oil.
- **Pregnancy-Safe:** Ensure all ingredients are fresh and thoroughly washed.
- **Protein-Packed:** Add 1 scoop of unflavored protein powder.

Serving Tip: Garnish with a cucumber slice or a lemon zest twist. Pair with hummus and cucumber slices on rye toast to sustain energy throughout the morning.

Instructions

1. Freeze the banana in advance for a creamier texture.

2. Add ingredients to the blender. Pour the liquid base first, then add cucumber, frozen banana, lemon juice, and ginger. Sprinkle in any optional superfoods.

3. Start blending on low speed and gradually increase to high for 1–2 minutes until smooth. Adjust consistency with more liquid if needed. Taste the smoothie and, if desired, add honey, maple syrup, or agave syrup for sweetness.

4. Pour into glasses and serve immediately.

08 Tropical Sunrise Smoothie

Total: 5 mins   **Servings:** 2   **Level:** 1/5

Nutritional Info *(Per Serving, based on coconut water and no optional additions)*: 160 kcal; 35g carbs; 3g protein; 2g fat; 5g fiber.

Ingredients

- **Liquid Base (Choose One):** 1 cup coconut water, 1 cup fresh orange juice, or 1 cup unsweetened almond milk
- **Main Ingredients:** 1/2 cup guava (chopped), 1/2 cup frozen pineapple chunks, 1/2 cup frozen mango chunks, 1 tablespoon chia seeds
- **Optional Sweetener:** 1 teaspoon honey, maple syrup or agave syrup
- **Optional Superfood Additions:** 1 tablespoon ground flaxseeds, 1/2 teaspoon grated fresh ginger

Optional Variations:
- **Diabetic-Friendly:** Replace pineapple with 1/4 cup frozen zucchini for reduced sugar. Use unsweetened almond milk and avoid additional sweeteners.
- **Vegan:** Avoid honey as a sweetener.
- **Keto:** Replace pineapple and mango with 1/4 avocado and 1/4 cup frozen zucchini. Use unsweetened almond milk and avoid sweeteners. Add 1 teaspoon of MCT oil.
- **Pregnancy-Safe:** Ensure all ingredients are fresh and thoroughly washed.
- **Protein-Packed:** Add 1 scoop of unflavored protein powder.

> **Serving Tip:** Garnish with a slice of guava or a sprinkle of chia seeds. Pair with a handful of almonds or a slice of whole-grain toast for a balanced breakfast.

Instructions

1. Chop guava and freeze pineapple and mango for a chilled, creamy texture.

2. Add ingredients to the blender. Pour the liquid base first, then add guava, frozen pineapple, mango, and chia seeds. Sprinkle in any optional superfoods.

3. Start blending on low speed and gradually increase to high for 1–2 minutes until creamy. Adjust consistency with more liquid if needed. Taste the smoothie and, if desired, add honey, maple syrup, or agave syrup for sweetness.

4. Pour into glasses and serve immediately.

---

09 Strawberry Matcha Delight

Total: 5 mins   **Servings:** 2   **Level:** 1/5

Nutritional Info *(Per Serving, based on almond milk and no optional additions)*: 150 kcal; 28g carbs; 4g protein; 3g fat; 6g fiber.

Ingredients

- **Liquid Base (Choose One):** 1 cup unsweetened almond milk, 1 cup coconut water, or 1 cup low-fat dairy milk
- **Main Ingredients:** 1/2 cup frozen strawberries, 1/2 frozen banana, 1 teaspoon matcha green tea powder, 1/2 teaspoon vanilla extract
- **Optional Sweetener:** 1 teaspoon honey, maple syrup, or agave syrup
- **Optional Superfood Additions:** 1 tablespoon chia seeds, 1/2 teaspoon ground flaxseeds

Optional Variations:
- **Diabetic-Friendly:** Replace banana with 1/4 avocado for lower sugar. Use unsweetened almond milk and avoid additional sweeteners.
- **Vegan:** Avoid honey and opt for maple syrup or agave syrup.
- **Keto:** Replace banana with 1/4 avocado. Use unsweetened almond milk and avoid sweeteners. Add 1 teaspoon of MCT oil.
- **Pregnancy-Safe:** Ensure all ingredients are fresh and thoroughly washed.
- **Protein-Packed:** Add 1 scoop of unflavored protein powder for an extra boost.

> **Serving Tip:** Garnish with a sprinkle of matcha powder or chia seeds. Serve with whole-grain crackers topped with avocado slices and smoked salmon for an omega-3-rich breakfast.

Instructions

1. Freeze banana and strawberries for a creamier texture.

2. Add ingredients to the blender. Pour the liquid base first, then add frozen strawberries, banana, matcha powder, and vanilla extract. Sprinkle in any optional superfoods.

3. Start blending on low speed and gradually increase to high for 1–2 minutes until creamy. Adjust consistency with more liquid if needed. Taste the smoothie and, if desired, add honey, maple syrup, or agave syrup for sweetness.

4. Pour into glasses and serve immediately.

10 Banana Date Power

🕐 **Total:** 5 mins 🍴 **Servings:** 2 📊 **Level:** 1/5

Nutritional Info *(Per Serving, based on almond milk and no optional additions)*: 190 kcal; 35g carbs; 5g protein; 4g fat; 5g fiber.

Ingredients

- **Liquid Base (Choose One):** 1 cup unsweetened almond milk, 1 cup coconut water, or 1 cup low-fat dairy milk
- **Main Ingredients:** 1 large frozen banana, 2 pitted Medjool dates, 1 tablespoon almond butter, 1/2 teaspoon ground cinnamon
- **Optional Superfood Additions:** 1 tablespoon chia seeds, 1/2 teaspoon ground flaxseeds

Optional Variations:
- **Diabetic-Friendly:** Replace banana with 1/4 avocado for lower sugar. Use unsweetened almond milk and avoid additional sweeteners.
- **Vegan:** Avoid low-fat dairy milk and opt for almond milk or coconut water.
- **Keto:** Replace banana and dates with 1/4 avocado and a few drops of liquid stevia for sweetness. Use unsweetened almond milk and add 1 teaspoon of MCT oil.
- **Pregnancy-Safe:** Ensure all ingredients are fresh and thoroughly washed.
- **Protein-Packed:** Add 1 scoop of unflavored protein powder for an extra boost.

🧑‍🍳 **Serving Tip:** Garnish with a sprinkle of cinnamon or chopped almonds. Pair with a whole-wheat wrap filled with scrambled eggs, spinach, and feta cheese for a protein-packed morning meal.

Instructions

1. Freeze the banana in advance for a creamier texture. Remove pits from dates.

2. Add ingredients to the blender. Pour the liquid base first, then add frozen banana, dates, almond butter, and cinnamon. Sprinkle in any optional superfoods.

3. Start blending on low speed and gradually increase to high for 1–2 minutes untilcreamy. Adjust consistency with more liquid if needed.

4. Pour into glasses and serve immediately.

---

11 Avocado Lime Infusion

🕐 **Total:** 5 mins 🍴 **Servings:** 2 📊 **Level:** 1/5

Nutritional Info *(Per Serving, based on coconut water and no optional additions)*: 180 kcal; 18g carbs; 4g protein; 10g fat; 6g fiber.

Ingredients

- **Liquid Base (Choose One):** 1 cup coconut water, 1 cup unsweetened almond milk, or 1 cup low-fat dairy milk
- **Main Ingredients:** 1/2 ripe avocado, 1/2 frozen banana, 1 tablespoon freshly squeezed lime juice
- **Optional Sweetener:** 1 teaspoon honey or maple syrup
- **Optional Superfood Additions:** 1 tablespoon chia seeds, 1/2 teaspoon ground flaxseeds

Optional Variations:
- **Diabetic-Friendly:** To reduce sugar, replace the banana with 1/4 cup frozen zucchini. Use unsweetened almond milk and avoid additional sweeteners.
- **Vegan:** Avoid honey and opt for maple syrup or agave.
- **Keto:** Replace banana with 1/4 cup frozen zucchini. Use unsweetened almond milk and add 1 teaspoon of MCT oil.
- **Pregnancy-Safe:** Ensure all ingredients are fresh and thoroughly washed.
- **Protein-Packed:** Add 1 scoop of unflavored protein powder for an extra boost.

🧑‍🍳 **Serving Tip:** Garnish with a lime zest twist or a sprinkle of chia seeds. For a tropical morning treat, serve overnight oats soaked in coconut milk and lime juice topped with toasted coconut flakes.

Instructions

1. Freeze the banana in advance for a creamier texture.

2. Add ingredients to the blender. Pour the liquid base first, then add avocado, frozen banana, lime juice, and optional honey or maple syrup. Sprinkle in any optional superfoods.

3. Start blending on low speed and gradually increase to high for 1–2 minutes until creamy. Adjust consistency with more liquid if needed.

4. Pour into glasses and serve immediately.

12 Green Apple Spirulina Zest

🕐 **Total:** 5 mins   🍴 **Servings:** 2   📶 **Level:** 1/5

Nutritional Info (*Per Serving, based on coconut water and no optional additions*): 140 kcal; 28g carbs; 4g protein; 2g fat; 6g fiber.

Ingredients

- **Liquid Base (Choose One):** 1 cup coconut water, 1 cup unsweetened almond milk, or 1 cup low-fat dairy milk
- **Main Ingredients:** 1 small green apple (cored and chopped), 1/2 frozen banana, 1/2 teaspoon spirulina powder, 1 teaspoon freshly squeezed lemon juice
- **Optional Superfood Additions:** 1 tablespoon chia seeds, 1/2 teaspoon ground flaxseeds

Optional Variations:
- **Diabetic-Friendly:** Replace banana with 1/4 avocado for lower sugar. Use unsweetened almond milk and avoid additional sweeteners.
- **Vegan:** Avoid low-fat dairy milk and opt for almond milk or coconut water.
- **Keto:** Replace banana with 1/4 avocado. Use unsweetened almond milk and add 1 teaspoon of MCT oil.
- **Pregnancy-Safe:** Ensure all ingredients are fresh and thoroughly washed.
- **Protein-Packed:** Add 1 scoop of unflavored protein powder for an extra boost.

👨‍🍳 **Serving Tip:** Garnish with a sprinkle of chia seeds or a lemon zest twist. Pair with a handful of almonds or a whole-grain cracker for a balanced breakfast.

Instructions

1. Core and chop the green apple. Freeze the banana in advance for a creamier texture.

2. Add ingredients to the blender. Pour the liquid base first, then add green apple, frozen banana, spirulina powder, and lemon juice. Sprinkle in any optional superfoods.

3. Start blending on low speed and gradually increase to high for 1–2 minutes until creamy. Adjust consistency with more liquid if needed.

4. Pour into glasses and serve immediately.

---

13 Coconut Espresso Cooler

🕐 **Total:** 5 mins   🍴 **Servings:** 2   📶 **Level:** 1/5

Nutritional Info (*Per Serving, based on coconut milk and no optional additions*): 180 kcal; 12g carbs; 4g protein; 12g fat; 3g fiber.

Ingredients

- **Liquid Base (Choose One):** 1 cup unsweetened coconut milk, 1 cup coconut water, or 1 cup low-fat dairy milk
- **Main Ingredients:** 1/2 frozen banana, 1 shot (1 oz) brewed and chilled espresso, 1 tablespoon unsweetened shredded coconut, 1/2 teaspoon vanilla extract
- **Optional Sweetener:** 1 teaspoon honey, maple syrup, or agave syrup
- **Optional Superfood Additions:** 1 tablespoon chia seeds

Optional Variations:
- **Diabetic-Friendly:** Replace banana with 1/4 avocad. Use unsweetened coconut milk and avoid additional sweeteners.
- **Vegan:** Avoid low-fat dairy milk and choose coconut milk or coconut water.
- **Keto:** Replace banana with 1/4 avocado. Use unsweetened coconut milk and avoid sweeteners. Add 1 teaspoon of MCT oil.
- **Pregnancy-Safe:** Use decaffeinated espresso or replace it with chicory coffee. Ensure all ingredients are fresh and thoroughly washed.
- **Protein-Packed:** Add 1 scoop of unflavored protein powder.

👨‍🍳 **Serving Tip:** Garnish with shredded coconut or cocoa powder. For sustained energy, serve alongside a whole-wheat wrap filled with scrambled eggs, sautéed spinach, and feta cheese.

Instructions

1. Brew espresso in advance and allow it to chill. Freeze the banana for a creamier texture.

2. Add ingredients to the blender. Pour the liquid base first, then add frozen banana, chilled espresso, shredded coconut, and vanilla extract. Sprinkle in any optional superfoods.

3. Start blending on low speed and gradually increase to high for 1–2 minutes until creamy. Adjust consistency with more liquid if needed.

4. Pour into glasses and serve immediately.

14 Almond Mocha Fuel

Total: 5 mins **Servings:** 2 **Level:** 1/5

Nutritional Info *(Per Serving, based on almond milk and no optional additions)*: 180 kcal; 22g carbs; 6g protein; 7g fat; 5g fiber.

Ingredients

- **Liquid Base (Choose One):** 1 cup unsweetened almond milk, 1 cup coconut milk, or 1 cup low-fat dairy milk
- **Main Ingredients:** 1/2 frozen banana, 1 shot (1 oz) brewed and chilled espresso, 1 tablespoon unsweetened cocoa powder, 1 tablespoon almond butter, 1/2 teaspoon vanilla extract
- **Optional Sweetener:** 1 teaspoon honey, maple syrup, or agave syrup
- **Optional Superfood Additions:** 1 tablespoon chia seeds, 1/2 teaspoon ground flaxseeds

Optional Variations:
- **Diabetic-Friendly:** Replace banana with 1/4 avocado. Use unsweetened almond milk and avoid additional sweeteners.
- **Vegan:** Avoid dairy milk and choose almond or coconut milk.
- **Keto:** Replace banana with 1/4 avocado. Use unsweetened almond milk and avoid sweeteners. Add 1 teaspoon of MCT oil.
- **Pregnancy-Safe:** Use decaffeinated espresso or replace it with chicory coffee. Ensure all ingredients are fresh and thoroughly washed.
- **Protein-Packed:** Add 1 scoop of unflavored protein powder.

Serving Tip: Garnish with a sprinkle of cocoa powder or a few crushed almonds. Pair with a handful of nuts or a slice of whole-grain toast for a balanced breakfast.

Instructions

1. Brew espresso in advance and allow it to chill. Freeze the banana for a creamier texture.

2. Add ingredients to the blender. Pour the liquid base first, then add frozen banana, chilled espresso, cocoa powder, almond butter, and vanilla extract. Sprinkle in any optional superfoods.

3. Start blending on low speed and gradually increase to high for 1–2 minutes until creamy. Adjust consistency with more liquid if needed.

4. Pour into glasses and serve immediately.

15 Turmeric & Black Pepper Boost

Total: 5 mins **Servings:** 2 **Level:** 1/5

Nutritional Info *(Per Serving, based on almond milk and no optional additions)*: 160 kcal; 25g carbs; 5g protein; 6g fat; 5g fiber.

Ingredients

- **Liquid Base (Choose One):** 1 cup unsweetened almond milk, 1 cup coconut water, or 1 cup low-fat dairy milk
- **Main Ingredients:** 1/2 frozen banana, 1/2 teaspoon ground turmeric, 1/8 teaspoon ground black pepper, 1 tablespoon almond butter, 1/2 teaspoon cinnamon
- **Optional Sweetener:** 1 teaspoon honey, maple syrup, or agave syrup
- **Optional Superfood Additions:** 1 tablespoon chia seeds, 1/2 teaspoon ground flaxseeds, 1/2 teaspoon grated fresh ginger

Optional Variations:
- **Diabetic-Friendly:** Replace banana with 1/4 avocado. Use unsweetened almond milk and avoid additional sweeteners.
- **Vegan:** Avoid honey and opt for maple syrup or agave.
- **Keto:** Replace banana with 1/4 avocado. Use unsweetened almond milk and avoid sweeteners. Add 1 teaspoon of MCT oil.
- **Pregnancy-Safe:** Ensure all ingredients are fresh and thoroughly washed.
- **Protein-Packed:** Add 1 scoop of unflavored protein powder for an extra boost.

Serving Tip: Garnish with a sprinkle of cinnamon or a drizzle of honey. Pair with a handful of walnuts or a slice of whole-grain toast for a balanced breakfast.

Instructions

1. Freeze the banana in advance for a creamier texture.

2. Add ingredients to the blender. Pour the liquid base first, then add frozen banana, turmeric, black pepper, almond butter, and cinnamon. Sprinkle in any optional superfoods.

3. Start blending on low speed and gradually increase to high for 1–2 minutes until creamy. Adjust consistency with more liquid if needed.

4. Pour into glasses and enjoy while fresh.

WHY THESE SMOOTHIES ARE EFFECTIVE

Each smoothie in this collection is designed to provide sustained energy, mental clarity, and essential nutrients to fuel your body throughout the day. By combining natural sources of protein, fiber, healthy fats, and metabolism-boosting ingredients, these blends offer a functional and delicious way to enhance your daily nutrition. Whether you need a morning wake-up call, a mid-day refresher, or a post-workout recharge, these smoothies are carefully formulated to work with your body's natural rhythms.

Let's explore why each of these smoothies deserves a place in your daily routine:

1. Coffee Banana Energizer
This smoothie combines the natural caffeine of coffee with the slow-burning carbohydrates of banana, providing an immediate energy boost without the crash. Almond butter adds healthy fats to stabilize blood sugar, while cocoa delivers antioxidants that support brain function and mood.

2. Matcha Green Tea Awakener
Matcha is rich in catechins, powerful antioxidants that improve focus and support metabolism. Combined with avocado's healthy fats and banana's potassium, this smoothie helps sustain energy levels and maintain cognitive sharpness throughout the day.

3. Raspberry Almond Recharge
Packed with fiber and protein, this smoothie keeps you feeling full longer while supporting muscle recovery. The antioxidants in raspberries fight inflammation, while almond butter provides plant-based protein for sustained energy.

4. Spiced Chocolate Morning Bliss
Cocoa's flavonoids boost mood and cognitive function, while cinnamon stabilizes blood sugar levels. This smoothie is ideal for those who crave something sweet yet nutritious in the morning, with a balance of carbohydrates, protein, and healthy fats.

5. Plum Vanilla Booster
Plums are high in antioxidants that support cellular health, while vanilla adds a natural calming effect. This smoothie promotes hydration and digestion, making it a great way to start the day on a light, refreshing note.

6. Lemon Ginger Charger
Lemon and ginger work together to stimulate digestion, reduce bloating, and boost the immune system. Mango and banana provide essential vitamins and minerals, ensuring long-lasting hydration and energy.

7. Cucumber Lemon Wake-Up
Cucumber's high water content deeply hydrates the body, while lemon's vitamin C enhances metabolism. This smoothie is perfect for detoxifying the system and promoting a fresh, energized feeling in the morning.

8. Tropical Sunrise Smoothie
Mango, guava, and pineapple supply a potent dose of vitamin C, which supports immune health and skin vitality. The natural enzymes in pineapple aid digestion, making this smoothie both a refreshing and functional start to the day.

9. Strawberry Matcha Delight
Strawberries provide antioxidants that combat oxidative stress, while matcha delivers steady,

focused energy. This smoothie is a metabolism-boosting powerhouse that keeps cravings at bay and supports fat oxidation.

10. Banana Date Power
Dates supply natural sugars for a quick energy boost, while almond butter and cinnamon help regulate blood sugar. This blend is perfect for fueling workouts or replenishing the body after exercise.

11. Avocado Lime Infusion
Avocado's healthy monounsaturated fats support brain function and satiety, while lime adds a refreshing vitamin C boost. This smoothie is ideal for maintaining energy without spikes or crashes.

12. Green Apple Spirulina Zest
Spirulina is a nutrient-dense superfood that provides plant-based protein and essential amino acids. Green apple adds fiber to support digestion, making this smoothie a detoxifying and energy-boosting powerhouse.

13. Coconut Espresso Cooler
Coconut and espresso create a creamy, nutrient-packed alternative to traditional coffee drinks. The MCTs (medium-chain triglycerides) in coconut help fuel the brain, while coffee delivers a sustained focus boost.

14. Almond Mocha Fuel
This smoothie blends the richness of cocoa, the alertness of espresso, and the protein-packed benefits of almond butter. It's a great option for those who want a satisfying, nutritious alternative to high-calorie coffee shop drinks.

15. Turmeric and Black Pepper Morning Boost
Turmeric's curcumin fights inflammation, while black pepper enhances its absorption. This smoothie helps combat fatigue, supports digestion, and promotes long-term health benefits.

The Science Behind the Benefits
These smoothies are effective because they provide key nutrients that enhance energy, support digestion, and regulate blood sugar levels:
- **Steady Energy Release:** Ingredients like bananas, dates, and matcha provide long-lasting fuel without crashes.
- **Metabolism Support:** Green tea, ginger, and lemon stimulate digestion and fat oxidation.
- **Brain Function & Focus:** Healthy fats from avocado, almonds, and coconut oil nourish cognitive function.
- **Gut Health & Digestion:** Fiber-rich fruits and anti-inflammatory ingredients like turmeric and cinnamon promote a healthy digestive system.

A Smarter Way to Energize Your Day
These smoothies are more than just delicious—they're functional. By choosing natural, whole-food ingredients over processed energy drinks and sugar-laden snacks, you're giving your body the fuel it needs to perform at its best. Whether you're an early riser, a fitness enthusiast, or someone looking for a nutritious way to stay focused and energized, these blends offer the perfect balance of taste and health benefits.

BREAKFAST
SMOOTHIES

---

01 Pumpkin Spice Dream

Total: 5 mins **Servings:** 2 **Level:** 1/5

Nutritional Info (Per Serving, based on almond milk and no optional additions): 180 kcal; 30g carbs; 6g protein; 4g fat; 5g fiber.

Ingredients

- **Liquid Base (Choose One):** 1 cup unsweetened almond milk, 1 cup coconut water, 1 cup low-fat dairy milk
- **Main Ingredients:** 1/2 cup pumpkin purée, 1/4 cup rolled oats, 1/2 cup Greek yogurt, 1/2 teaspoon ground cinnamon, 1/4 teaspoon ground nutmeg
- **Optional Sweetener:** 1 teaspoon honey or maple syrup
- **Optional Superfood Additions:** 1 tablespoon chia seeds, 1/2 teaspoon ground flaxseeds

Optional Variations:
- **Diabetic-Friendly:** Reduce oats to 2 tablespoons and add 1/4 avocado. Use unsweetened almond milk and avoid additional sweeteners.
- **Gluten-Free:** Make sure to use certified gluten-free oats or replace oats with 2 tablespoons of cooked quinoa.
- **Vegan:** Replace Greek yogurt with coconut yogurt. Avoid honey and opt for maple syrup.
- **Keto:** Remove oats and replace with 1/4 avocado. Use unsweetened almond milk and add 1 teaspoon of MCT oil.
- **Protein-Packed:** Add 1 scoop of unflavored protein powder.

> **Serving Tip:** Garnish with a sprinkle of cinnamon or a few crushed pecans. Serve with warm quinoa porridge flavored with pumpkin purée and maple syrup for a high-protein alternative to oatmeal.

Instructions

1. Freeze pumpkin purée in advance for a colder, creamier texture (optional).

2. Add ingredients to the blender. Pour the liquid base first, then add pumpkin purée, oats, Greek yogurt, cinnamon, and nutmeg. Sprinkle in any optional superfoods.

3. Start blending on low speed and gradually increase to high for 1–2 minutes until creamy. Adjust consistency with more liquid if needed.

4. Pour into glasses and enjoy while fresh.

02 Sweet Potato Vanilla Shake

Total: 5 mins **Servings:** 2 **Level:** 1/5

Nutritional Info *(Per Serving, based on almond milk and no optional additions)*: 190 kcal; 30g carbs; 6g protein; 5g fat; 5g fiber.

Ingredients

- **Liquid Base (Choose One):** 1 cup unsweetened almond milk, 1 cup coconut milk, or 1 cup low-fat dairy milk
- **Main Ingredients:** 1/2 cup cooked and chilled sweet potato, 1/2 frozen banana, 1 teaspoon pure vanilla extract, 1/2 teaspoon ground cinnamon
- **Optional Sweetener:** 1 teaspoon honey, maple syrup, or agave syrup
- **Optional Superfood Additions:** 1 tablespoon chia seeds, 1/2 teaspoon ground flaxseeds

Optional Variations:
- **Diabetic-Friendly:** Replace banana with 1/4 avocado for lower sugar. Use unsweetened almond milk and avoid additional sweeteners.
- **Vegan:** Avoid low-fat dairy milk and opt for almond milk or coconut milk.
- **Keto:** Replace banana with 1/4 avocado. Use unsweetened almond milk and avoid sweeteners. Add 1 teaspoon of MCT oil.
- **Pregnancy-Safe:** Ensure all ingredients are fresh and thoroughly washed.
- **Protein-Packed:** Add 1 scoop of unflavored protein powder.

Serving Tip: Garnish with a sprinkle of cinnamon or a drizzle of maple syrup. Pair with a handful of walnuts or a whole-grain muffin for a balanced breakfast.

Instructions

1. Cook and chill the sweet potato in advance for a creamy texture. Freeze banana for a thicker consistency.

2. Add ingredients to the blender. Pour the liquid base first, then add sweet potato, frozen banana, vanilla extract, and cinnamon. Sprinkle in any optional superfoods.

3. Start blending on low speed and gradually increase to high for 1–2 minutes until creamy. Adjust consistency with more liquid if needed.

4. Pour into glasses and enjoy while fresh.

---

03 Celery Apple Breakfast Blend

Total: 5 mins **Servings:** 2 **Level:** 1/5

Nutritional Info *(Per Serving, based on almond milk and no optional additions)*: 170 kcal; 30g carbs; 5g protein; 3g fat; 6g fiber.

Ingredients

- **Liquid Base (Choose One):** 1 cup unsweetened almond milk, 1 cup coconut water, or 1 cup low-fat dairy milk
- **Main Ingredients:** 1 small green apple (cored and chopped), 1/2 cup celery (chopped), 1/4 cup rolled oats, 1/2 frozen banana, 1/2 teaspoon ground cinnamon
- **Optional Sweetener:** 1 teaspoon honey, maple syrup, or agave syrup
- **Optional Superfood Additions:** 1 tablespoon chia seeds, 1/2 teaspoon ground flaxseeds

Optional Variations:
- **Diabetic-Friendly:** Reduce oats to 2 tablespoons. Replace banana with 1/4 avocado. Use unsweetened almond milk and avoid additional sweeteners.
- **Gluten-Free:** Make sure to use certified gluten-free oats or replace oats with 2 tablespoons of cooked quinoa.
- **Vegan:** Avoid low-fat dairy milk and opt for almond milk or coconut water.
- **Keto:** Remove oats and replace banana with 1/4 avocado. Use unsweetened almond milk and and avoid sweeteners. Add 1 teaspoon of MCT oil.
- **Protein-Packed:** Add 1 scoop of unflavored protein powder.

Serving Tip: Garnish with a sprinkle of cinnamon or a few rolled oats on top. Serve with a hard-boiled egg and a slice of whole-wheat toast for a balanced and nutritious breakfast.

Instructions

1. Core and chop the apple. Chop the celery. Freeze the banana for a creamier texture.

2. Add ingredients to the blender. Pour the liquid base first, then add the apple, celery, oats, frozen banana, and cinnamon. Sprinkle in any optional superfoods.

3. Start blending on low speed and gradually increase to high for 1–2 minutes until creamy. Adjust consistency with more liquid if needed.

4. Pour into glasses and enjoy while fresh.

04 Peanut Butter Berry Crunch

Total: 5 mins   **Servings:** 2   **Level:** 1/5

Nutritional Info (Per Serving, based on almond milk and no optional additions): 200 kcal; 30g carbs; 7g protein; 8g fat; 5g fiber.

Ingredients

- **Liquid Base (Choose One):** 1 cup unsweetened almond milk, 1 cup coconut water, or 1 cup low-fat dairy milk
- **Main Ingredients:** 1/2 cup frozen mixed berries, 1/2 frozen banana, 1 tablespoon natural peanut butter, 1/4 cup rolled oats
- **Optional Sweetener:** 1 teaspoon honey, maple syrup, or agave syrup
- **Optional Superfood Additions:** 1 tablespoon chia seeds, 1/2 teaspoon ground flaxseeds, 1 teaspoon cacao nibs

Optional Variations:
- **Diabetic-Friendly:** Reduce oats to 2 tablespoons. Replace banana with 1/4 avocado. Use unsweetened almond milk and avoid additional sweeteners.
- **Gluten-Free:** Make sure to use certified gluten-free oats or replace oats with 2 tablespoons of cooked quinoa.
- **Vegan:** Avoid low-fat dairy milk and opt for almond milk or coconut water.
- **Keto:** Remove oats and replace banana with 1/4 avocado. Use unsweetened almond milk and avoid sweeteners. Add 1 teaspoon of MCT oil.
- **Protein-Packed:** Add 1 scoop of unflavored protein powder.

Serving Tip: Garnish with a sprinkle of crushed nuts or cacao nibs for extra crunch. Pair with a slice of toasted rye bread topped with peanut butter and a sprinkle of dark chocolate chips for a nutritious treat.

Instructions

1. Freeze the banana in advance for a creamier texture.

2. Add ingredients to the blender. Pour the liquid base first, then add frozen berries, banana, peanut butter, and oats. Sprinkle in any optional superfoods.

3. Start blending on low speed and gradually increase to high for 1-2 minutes until creamy. Adjust consistency with more liquid if needed.

4. Pour into glasses and enjoy while fresh.

---

05 Chocolate Banana Power

Total: 5 mins   **Servings:** 2   **Level:** 1/5

Nutritional Info (Per Serving, based on almond milk and no optional additions): 200 kcal; 30g carbs; 6g protein; 7g fat; 5g fiber.

Ingredients

- **Liquid Base (Choose One):** 1 cup unsweetened almond milk, 1 cup coconut water, or 1 cup low-fat dairy milk
- **Main Ingredients:** 1 frozen banana, 1 tablespoon unsweetened cocoa powder, 1 tablespoon almond butter, 1/2 teaspoon vanilla extract
- **Optional Sweetener:** 1 teaspoon honey, maple syrup, or agave syrup
- **Optional Superfood Additions:** 1 tablespoon chia seeds, 1/2 teaspoon ground flaxseeds, 1 teaspoon cacao nibs for added crunch

Optional Variations:
- **Diabetic-Friendly:** Replace banana with 1/4 avocado for lower sugar. Use unsweetened almond milk and avoid additional sweeteners.
- **Vegan:** Avoid low-fat dairy milk and opt for almond or coconut milk.
- **Keto:** Replace banana with 1/4 avocado. Use unsweetened almond milk and avoid sweeteners. Add 1 teaspoon of MCT oil.
- **Pregnancy-Safe:** Ensure all ingredients are fresh and thoroughly washed.
- **Protein-Packed:** Add 1 scoop of unflavored protein powder.

Serving Tip: Garnish with a sprinkle of cocoa powder or a few cacao nibs. Pair with scrambled tofu seasoned with turmeric and a side of whole-wheat crackers for a plant-based breakfast.

Instructions

1. Freeze the banana in advance for a creamier texture.

2. Add ingredients to the blender. Pour the liquid base first, then add frozen banana, cocoa powder, almond butter, and vanilla extract. Sprinkle in any optional superfoods.

3. Start blending on low speed and gradually increase to high for 1-2 minutes until creamy. Adjust consistency with more liquid if needed.

4. Pour into glasses and enjoy while fresh.

06 Sea Buckthorn Oat Delight

🕐 **Total:** 5 mins   🍴 **Servings:** 2   📊 **Level:** 1/5

Nutritional Info *(Per Serving, based on almond milk and no optional additions)*: 180 kcal; 28g carbs; 6g protein; 5g fat; 6g fiber.

Ingredients

- **Liquid Base (Choose One):** 1 cup unsweetened almond milk, 1 cup coconut water, or 1 cup low-fat dairy milk
- **Main Ingredients:** 1/4 cup sea buckthorn berries (fresh or frozen), 1/4 cup rolled oats, 1/2 frozen banana, 1 tablespoon Greek yogurt (or plant-based yogurt), 1/2 teaspoon ground cinnamon
- **Optional Sweetener:** 1 teaspoon honey or maple syrup
- **Optional Superfood Additions:** 1 tablespoon chia seeds, 1/2 teaspoon ground flaxseeds

Optional Variations:
- **Diabetic-Friendly:** Reduce oats to 2 tablespoons. Replace banana with 1/4 avocado. Use unsweetened almond milk and avoid additional sweeteners.
- **Gluten-Free:** Make sure to use certified gluten-free oats or replace oats with 2 tablespoons of cooked quinoa.
- **Vegan:** Replace Greek yogurt with plant-based yogurt. Replace honey with maple syrup.
- **Keto:** Remove oats and replace banana with 1/4 avocado. Use unsweetened almond milk and avoid sweeteners. Add 1 teaspoon of MCT oil.
- **Protein-Packed:** Add 1 scoop of unflavored protein powder.

Serving Tip: Garnish with a sprinkle of rolled oats or a drizzle of honey. Serve with hearty buckwheat waffles topped with Greek yogurt and a generous sea buckthorn drizzle.

Instructions

1. Freeze the banana in advance for a creamier texture.

2. Add ingredients to the blender. Pour the liquid base first, then add sea buckthorn berries, oats, frozen banana, yogurt, and cinnamon. Sprinkle in any optional superfoods.

3. Start blending on low speed and gradually increase to high for 1–2 minutes until creamy. Adjust consistency with more liquid if needed.

4. Pour into glasses and enjoy while fresh.

07 Blackberry Almond Crunch Kickstart

🕐 **Total:** 5 mins   🍴 **Servings:** 2   📊 **Level:** 1/5

Nutritional Info *(Per Serving, based on almond milk and no optional additions)*: 190 kcal; 28g carbs; 7g protein; 6g fat; 6g fiber.

Ingredients

- **Liquid Base (Choose One):** 1 cup unsweetened almond milk, 1 cup coconut water, or 1 cup low-fat dairy milk
- **Main Ingredients:** 1/2 cup fresh or frozen blackberries, 1/2 frozen banana, 1 tablespoon almond butter, 1/4 cup rolled oats
- **Optional Sweetener:** 1 teaspoon honey or maple syrup
- **Optional Superfood Additions:** 1 tablespoon chia seeds, 1/2 teaspoon ground flaxseeds, 1 teaspoon cacao nibs for crunch

Optional Variations:
- **Diabetic-Friendly:** Reduce oats to 2 tablespoons. Replace banana with 1/4 avocado. Use unsweetened almond milk and avoid additional sweeteners.
- **Gluten-Free:** Make sure to use certified gluten-free oats or replace oats with 2 tablespoons of cooked quinoa.
- **Vegan:** Avoid low-fat dairy milk and opt for almond milk or coconut water. Replace honey with maple syrup.
- **Keto:** Remove oats and replace banana with 1/4 avocado. Use unsweetened almond milk and avoid sweeteners. Add 1 teaspoon of MCT oil.
- **Protein-Packed:** Add 1 scoop of unflavored protein powder.

Serving Tip: Garnish with a sprinkle of cacao nibs or crushed almonds for added crunch. Pair with a bowl of cottage cheese topped with juicy blackberries and a sprinkle of flaxseeds for protein and fiber.

Instructions

1. Freeze banana in advance for a creamier texture.

2. Add ingredients to the blender. Pour the liquid base first, then add blackberries, frozen banana, almond butter, and oats. Sprinkle in any optional superfoods.

3. Start blending on low speed and gradually increase to high for 1–2 minutes until creamy. Adjust consistency with more liquid if needed.

4. Pour into glasses and enjoy while fresh.

08 Pineapple Avocado Cream

Total: 5 mins   **Servings:** 2   **Level:** 1/5

Nutritional Info *(Per Serving, based on coconut water and no optional additions)*: 190 kcal; 30g carbs; 4g protein; 8g fat; 5g fiber.

Ingredients

- **Liquid Base (Choose One):** 1 cup coconut water, 1 cup unsweetened almond milk, or 1 cup low-fat dairy milk
- **Main Ingredients:** 1/2 cup fresh or frozen pineapple chunks, 1/4 ripe avocado, 1/2 frozen banana, 1 teaspoon lime juice
- **Optional Sweetener:** 1 teaspoon honey, maple syrup, or agave syrup
- **Optional Superfood Additions:** 1 tablespoon chia seeds, 1/2 teaspoon ground flaxseeds, 1/2 teaspoon grated fresh ginger

Optional Variations:
- **Diabetic-Friendly:** Replace banana with 1/4 cup frozen zucchini. Use unsweetened almond milk and avoid additional sweeteners.
- **Vegan:** Avoid low-fat dairy milk and opt for almond milk or coconut water. Avoid honey and opt for maple syrup or agave.
- **Keto:** Replace banana with 1/2 avocado. Use unsweetened almond milk and avoid sweeteners. Add 1 teaspoon of MCT oil.
- **Pregnancy-Safe:** Ensure all ingredients are fresh and thoroughly washed.
- **Protein-Packed:** Add 1 scoop of unflavored protein powder.

Serving Tip: Garnish with a slice of lime or a sprinkle of shredded coconut. Pair with a handful of cashews or a slice of whole-grain toast for a balanced breakfast.

Instructions

1. Freeze pineapple and banana for a creamier texture.

2. Add ingredients to the blender. Pour the liquid base first, then add pineapple, avocado, frozen banana, and lime juice. Sprinkle in any optional superfoods.

3. Start blending on low speed and gradually increase to high for 1–2 minutes until creamy. Adjust consistency with more liquid if needed.

4. Pour into glasses and enjoy while fresh.

---

09 Black Sesame Papaya Bliss

Total: 5 mins   **Servings:** 2   **Level:** 1/5

Nutritional Info *(Per Serving, based on almond milk and no optional additions)*: 210 kcal; 28g carbs; 6g protein; 8g fat; 5g fiber.

Ingredients

- **Liquid Base (Choose One):** 1 cup unsweetened almond milk, 1 cup coconut water, or 1 cup low-fat dairy milk
- **Main Ingredients:** 1/2 cup fresh or frozen papaya chunks, 1/2 frozen banana, 1 tablespoon black sesame seeds (toasted for extra flavor), 1/2 teaspoon vanilla extract
- **Optional Sweetener:** 1 teaspoon honey, maple syrup, or agave syrup
- **Optional Superfood Additions:** 1 tablespoon chia seeds, 1/2 teaspoon ground flaxseeds, 1/2 teaspoon grated fresh ginger

Optional Variations:
- **Diabetic-Friendly:** Replace banana with 1/4 avocado for lower sugar. Use unsweetened almond milk and avoid additional sweeteners.
- **Vegan:** Avoid low-fat dairy milk and opt for almond milk or coconut water. Avoid honey as a sweetener.
- **Keto:** Replace banana with 1/4 avocado. Use unsweetened almond milk and avoid sweeteners. Add 1 teaspoon of MCT oil.
- **Pregnancy-Safe:** Ensure all ingredients are fresh and thoroughly washed.
- **Protein-Packed:** Add 1 scoop of unflavored protein powder for an extra boost.

Serving Tip: Garnish with a sprinkle of toasted black sesame seeds or a few papaya cubes. Pair with a homemade almond flour muffin and a side of coconut yogurt for a low-carb breakfast option.

Instructions

1. Toast black sesame seeds in a dry pan for 1–2 minutes to enhance their nutty flavor (optional). Freeze banana for a creamier texture.

2. Add ingredients to the blender. Pour the liquid base first, then add papaya, frozen banana, black sesame seeds, and vanilla extract. Sprinkle in any optional superfoods.

3. Start blending on low speed and gradually increase to high for 1–2 minutes until creamy. Adjust consistency with more liquid if needed.

4. Pour into glasses and enjoy while fresh.

10 Butternut Squash Awakening

Total: 5 mins   **Servings:** 2   **Level:** 1/5

Nutritional Info *(Per Serving, based on coconut milk and no optional additions)*: 180 kcal; 22g carbs; 5g protein; 8g fat; 5g fiber.

Ingredients

- **Liquid Base (Choose One):** 1 cup coconut milk, 1 cup unsweetened almond milk, or 1 cup water
- **Main Ingredients:** 1/2 cup cooked and chilled butternut squash, 1/2 cup steamed and chilled cauliflower, 1/2 teaspoon grated fresh ginger, 1/4 teaspoon ground cardamom
- **Optional Sweetener:** 1 teaspoon honey, maple syrup, or agave syrup
- **Optional Superfood Additions:** 1 tablespoon chia seeds, 1/2 teaspoon ground flaxseeds, 1/2 teaspoon cinnamon for extra warmth

Optional Variations:
- **Diabetic-Friendly:** Use unsweetened almond milk and avoid additional sweeteners.
- **Vegan:** Avoid honey and opt for maple syrup or agave.
- **Keto:** Replace butternut squash with 1/4 avocado for fewer carbs. Use unsweetened almond milk and avoid sweeteners. Add 1 teaspoon of MCT oil.
- **Pregnancy-Safe:** Ensure all ingredients are fresh and thoroughly washed.
- **Protein-Packed:** Add 1 scoop of unflavored protein powder for an extra boost.

Serving Tip: Garnish with a sprinkle of cinnamon or toasted coconut flakes. Pair with whole-wheat pancakes drizzled with honey and a few chopped walnuts for extra crunch.

Instructions

1. Steam and chill butternut squash and cauliflower in advance for a creamy texture.

2. Add ingredients to the blender. Pour the liquid base first, then add butternut squash, cauliflower, ginger, and cardamom. Sprinkle in any optional superfoods.

3. Start blending on low speed and gradually increase to high for 1-2 minutes until creamy. Adjust consistency with more liquid if needed.

4. Pour into glasses and enjoy while fresh.

---

11 Tahini Fig Fusion

Total: 5 mins   **Servings:** 2   **Level:** 1/5

Nutritional Info *(Per Serving, based on almond milk and no optional additions)*: 220 kcal; 30g carbs; 6g protein; 9g fat; 6g fiber.

Ingredients

- **Liquid Base (Choose One):** 1 cup unsweetened almond milk, 1 cup coconut milk, or 1 cup low-fat dairy milk
- **Main Ingredients:** 3 dried figs (stems removed, soaked in warm water for 5 minutes), 1 tablespoon tahini, 1/2 frozen banana, 1/2 teaspoon ground cinnamon
- **Optional Sweetener:** 1 teaspoon honey, maple syrup, or agave syrup
- **Optional Superfood Additions:** 1 tablespoon chia seeds, 1/2 teaspoon ground flaxseeds, 1/2 teaspoon vanilla extract

Optional Variations:
- **Diabetic-Friendly:** Replace banana with 1/4 avocado for lower sugar. Use unsweetened almond milk and avoid additional sweeteners.
- **Vegan:** Avoid low-fat dairy milk and opt for almond milk or coconut milk. Avoid honey as a sweetener.
- **Keto:** Replace figs with 1/4 avocado for fewer carbs. Use unsweetened almond milk and avoid sweeteners. Add 1 teaspoon of MCT oil.
- **Pregnancy-Safe:** Ensure all ingredients are fresh and thoroughly washed.
- **Protein-Packed:** Add 1 scoop of unflavored protein powder.

Serving Tip: Garnish with a sprinkle of sesame seeds or crushed walnuts. Pair with a handful of almonds or a slice of whole-grain toast for a balanced breakfast.

Instructions

1. Soak figs in warm water for 5 minutes to soften. Freeze banana in advance for a creamier texture.

2. Add ingredients to the blender. Pour the liquid base first, then add figs, tahini, frozen banana, and cinnamon. Sprinkle in any optional superfoods.

3. Start blending on low speed and gradually increase to high for 1-2 minutes until creamy. Adjust consistency with more liquid if needed.

4. Pour into glasses and enjoy while fresh.

12 Sweet Corn and Mango Hug

Total: 5 mins · **Servings:** 2 · **Level:** 1/5

Nutritional Info *(Per Serving, based on coconut milk and no optional additions)*: 200 kcal; 35g carbs; 5g protein; 6g fat; 4g fiber.

Ingredients

- **Liquid Base (Choose One):** 1 cup coconut milk, 1 cup unsweetened almond milk, or 1 cup low-fat dairy milk
- **Main Ingredients:** 1/2 cup cooked sweet corn (cooled), 1/2 cup fresh or frozen mango chunks, 1/2 frozen banana, 1/2 teaspoon grated fresh ginger
- **Optional Sweetener:** 1 teaspoon honey, maple syrup, or agave syrup
- **Optional Superfood Additions:** 1 tablespoon chia seeds, 1/2 teaspoon ground flaxseeds, 1 teaspoon lime juice for a refreshing twist

Optional Variations:
- **Diabetic-Friendly:** Replace banana with 1/4 avocado. Use unsweetened almond milk and avoid additional sweeteners.
- **Vegan:** Avoid low-fat dairy milk and opt for almond milk or coconut milk. Avoid honey as a sweetener.
- **Keto:** Replace banana with 1/4 avocado for fewer carbs. Use unsweetened almond milk and avoid sweeteners. Add 1 teaspoon of MCT oil.
- **Pregnancy-Safe:** Ensure all ingredients are fresh and thoroughly washed.
- **Protein-Packed:** Add 1 scoop of unflavored protein powder.

Serving Tip: Garnish with a sprinkle of toasted coconut flakes or a drizzle of honey. Pair with a handful of almonds or a slice of whole-grain toast for a balanced breakfast.

Instructions

1. Cook and cool sweet corn in advance. Freeze the banana for a creamier texture.

2. Add ingredients to the blender. Pour the liquid base first, then add sweet corn, mango, frozen banana, and ginger. Sprinkle in any optional superfoods.

3. Start blending on low speed and gradually increase to high for 1–2 minutes until creamy. Adjust consistency with more liquid if needed.

4. Pour into glasses and enjoy while fresh.

---

13 Matcha and Oat Power Shake

Total: 5 mins · **Servings:** 2 · **Level:** 1/5

Nutritional Info *(Per Serving, based on almond milk and no optional additions)*: 190 kcal; 28g carbs; 6g protein; 5g fat; 6g fiber.

Ingredients

- **Liquid Base (Choose One):** 1 cup unsweetened almond milk, 1 cup oat milk, or 1 cup low-fat dairy milk
- **Main Ingredients:** 1/4 cup rolled oats, 1/2 frozen banana, 1 teaspoon matcha green tea powder, 1/2 teaspoon vanilla extract
- **Optional Sweetener:** 1 teaspoon honey, maple syrup, or agave syrup
- **Optional Superfood Additions:** 1 tablespoon chia seeds, 1/2 teaspoon ground flaxseeds, 1 teaspoon cacao nibs for a crunchy texture

Optional Variations:
- **Diabetic-Friendly:** Reduce oats to 2 tablespoons. Replace banana with 1/4 avocado. Use unsweetened almond milk and avoid additional sweeteners.
- **Gluten-Free:** Make sure to use certified gluten-free oats or replace oats with 2 tablespoons of cooked quinoa.
- **Vegan:** Avoid low-fat dairy milk and opt for oat milk or almond milk. Avoid honey as a sweetener.
- **Keto:** Remove oats and replace banana with 1/4 avocado. Use unsweetened almond milk and avoid sweeteners. Add 1 teaspoon of MCT oil.
- **Protein-Packed:** Add 1 scoop of unflavored protein powder.

Serving Tip: Garnish with a sprinkle of matcha powder or a few rolled oats. Pair with a handful of almonds or a slice of whole-grain toast for a balanced breakfast.

Instructions

1. Freeze banana in advance for a creamier texture.

2. Add ingredients to the blender. Pour the liquid base first, then add oats, frozen banana, matcha powder, and vanilla extract. Sprinkle in any optional superfoods.

3. Start blending on low speed and gradually increase to high for 1–2 minutes until creamy. Adjust consistency with more liquid if needed.

4. Pour into glasses and enjoy while fresh.

14 Apple Fennel Boost

🕐 **Total:** 5 mins   🍴 **Servings:** 2   📶 **Level:** 1/5

Nutritional Info (Per Serving, based on almond milk and no optional additions): 160 kcal; 28g carbs; 4g protein; 3g fat; 5g fiber.

Ingredients

- **Liquid Base (Choose One):** 1 cup unsweetened almond milk, 1 cup coconut water, or 1 cup low-fat dairy milk
- **Main Ingredients:** 1 small green apple (cored and chopped), 1/4 cup chopped fennel bulb, 1/2 frozen banana, 1/2 teaspoon grated fresh ginger
- **Optional Sweetener:** 1 teaspoon honey, maple syrup, or agave syrup
- **Optional Superfood Additions:** 1 tablespoon chia seeds, 1/2 teaspoon ground flaxseeds, 1/2 teaspoon ground cinnamon

Optional Variations:
- **Diabetic-Friendly:** Replace banana with 1/4 avocado. Use unsweetened almond milk and avoid additional sweeteners.
- **Vegan:** Avoid low-fat dairy milk and opt for almond milk or coconut water. Avoid honey as a sweetener.
- **Keto:** Remove banana and replace with 1/4 avocado. Use unsweetened almond milk and avoid sweeteners. Add 1 teaspoon of MCT oil.
- **Pregnancy-Safe:** Ensure all ingredients are fresh and thoroughly washed.
- **Protein-Packed:** Add 1 scoop of unflavored protein powder for an extra boost.

Serving Tip: Garnish with a few fennel fronds or a sprinkle of cinnamon. Pair with a handful of nuts or a slice of whole-grain toast for a balanced breakfast.

Instructions

1. Chop apple and fennel. Freeze the banana in advance for a creamier texture.

2. Add ingredients to the blender. Pour the liquid base first, then add apple, fennel, frozen banana, and ginger. Sprinkle in any optional superfoods.

3. Start blending on low speed and gradually increase to high for 1-2 minutes until creamy. Adjust consistency with more liquid if needed.

4. Pour into glasses and enjoy while fresh.

---

15 Persimmon and Ginger Elixir

🕐 **Total:** 5 mins   🍴 **Servings:** 2   📶 **Level:** 1/5

Nutritional Info (Per Serving, based on almond milk and no optional additions): 180 kcal; 32g carbs; 4g protein; 4g fat; 6g fiber.

Ingredients

- **Liquid Base (Choose One):** 1 cup unsweetened almond milk, 1 cup coconut water, or 1 cup low-fat dairy milk
- **Main Ingredients:** 1 ripe persimmon (peeled and chopped), 1/2 frozen banana, 1/2 teaspoon grated fresh ginger, 1/2 teaspoon vanilla extract
- **Optional Sweetener:** 1 teaspoon honey, maple syrup, or agave syrup
- **Optional Superfood Additions:** 1 tablespoon chia seeds, 1/2 teaspoon ground flaxseeds, 1/2 teaspoon cinnamon for warmth

Optional Variations:
- **Diabetic-Friendly:** Replace banana with 1/4 avocado. Use unsweetened almond milk and avoid additional sweeteners.
- **Vegan:** Avoid low-fat dairy milk and opt for almond milk or coconut water. Avoid honey as a sweetener.
- **Keto:** Remove banana and replace with 1/4 avocado. Use unsweetened almond milk and avoid sweeteners. Add 1 teaspoon of MCT oil.
- **Pregnancy-Safe:** Ensure all ingredients are fresh and thoroughly washed.
- **Protein-Packed:** Add 1 scoop of unflavored protein powder.

Serving Tip: Garnish with a sprinkle of cinnamon or a few chia seeds. Pair with a handful of walnuts or a slice of whole-grain toast for a balanced breakfast.

Instructions

1. Peel and chop the persimmon. Freeze the banana in advance for a creamier texture.

2. Add ingredients to the blender. Pour the liquid base first, then add persimmon, frozen banana, ginger, and vanilla extract. Sprinkle in any optional superfoods.

3. Start blending on low speed and gradually increase to high for 1-2 minutes until creamy. Adjust consistency with more liquid if needed.

4. Pour into glasses and enjoy while fresh.

WHY THESE SMOOTHIES ARE EFFECTIVE

Breakfast is the foundation of the day, and the right smoothie can provide the perfect balance of energy, satiety, and essential nutrients to keep you feeling strong, focused, and satisfied. The smoothies in this chapter are designed to fuel your morning with high-quality proteins, fiber-rich ingredients, and metabolism-boosting nutrients that support digestion, brain function, and overall well-being. Each blend contains carefully selected superfoods to stabilize blood sugar, enhance mental clarity, and keep cravings at bay until your next meal.

Let's explore why these breakfast smoothies are an excellent way to start your day:

1. Pumpkin Spice Dream
Pumpkin is rich in beta-carotene, a precursor to vitamin A that supports eye health, skin renewal, and immune function. Rolled oats provide slow-digesting fiber to keep you full, while cinnamon and nutmeg enhance insulin sensitivity and balance blood sugar levels. The combination of Greek yogurt and chia seeds adds protein and probiotics, making this smoothie a gut-friendly, satisfying morning treat.

2. Sweet Potato Vanilla Shake
Sweet potatoes are a powerhouse of complex carbohydrates, fiber, and vitamin C, which supports collagen production and immune health. Paired with banana for natural sweetness and vanilla for a warming flavor, this smoothie is a comforting, nutrient-dense way to fuel your morning. Cinnamon helps regulate blood sugar, while the optional addition of protein powder makes it a great pre- or post-workout meal.

3. Celery Apple Breakfast Blend
Celery is packed with electrolytes that help with hydration and digestion, while green apple provides fiber and a refreshing tartness. Rolled oats ensure long-lasting satiety, and banana contributes potassium for muscle function and energy production. The blend of cinnamon and optional flaxseeds makes this smoothie excellent for heart health and gut support.

4. Peanut Butter Berry Crunch
A perfect blend of protein, healthy fats, and antioxidants, this smoothie combines the nutty richness of peanut butter with the vibrant tartness of mixed berries. Peanut butter provides sustained energy and satiety, while berries offer a boost of vitamin C and fiber. The addition of oats makes it a complete breakfast that keeps you feeling full for hours.

5. Chocolate Banana Power
This smoothie is a delicious way to enjoy the classic combination of chocolate and banana while nourishing your body. Cocoa powder is rich in flavonoids that support brain function and mood, while banana offers a quick energy boost. Almond butter provides healthy fats, and vanilla extract rounds out the flavor, making this a decadent yet nutritious morning treat.

6. Sea Buckthorn Oat Delight
Sea buckthorn berries are packed with vitamin C, supporting skin health and immune function. Oats provide complex carbohydrates for sustained energy, while Greek yogurt contributes probiotics for gut health. This smoothie is a perfect blend of tart, creamy, and slightly nutty flavors that support digestion and cardiovascular health.

7. Blackberry Almond Crunch Kickstart
Blackberries deliver a potent dose of antioxidants and fiber, helping to reduce inflammation and support brain health. Almond butter adds protein and healthy fats for sustained energy, while rolled oats provide slow-digesting carbohydrates to keep blood sugar stable. The optional cacao nibs create

a crunchy texture while offering additional polyphenols for heart health.

8. Pineapple Avocado Cream
Pineapple's bromelain enzymes aid digestion and reduce inflammation, while avocado supplies healthy monounsaturated fats that support brain function and satiety. This smoothie is a creamy, tropical blend that provides hydration, vitamins, and essential nutrients to start your day on a refreshing note.

9. Black Sesame Papaya Bliss
Black sesame seeds are rich in calcium and healthy fats that promote strong bones and cardiovascular health. Papaya contributes digestive enzymes that support gut function, while banana adds natural sweetness and potassium for muscle recovery. This smoothie is a nutrient-dense option for those looking to improve digestion and boost overall wellness.

10. Butternut Squash Awakening
A unique blend of plant-based fiber and antioxidants, this smoothie harnesses the benefits of butternut squash and cauliflower for a naturally creamy, nutrient-packed breakfast. Butternut squash is a great source of vitamin A and potassium, while cauliflower supports liver detoxification and gut health. Ginger adds a touch of warmth and digestive support.

11. Tahini Fig Fusion
Tahini, made from sesame seeds, is rich in magnesium and healthy fats, supporting heart health and metabolism. Figs provide natural sweetness, fiber, and polyphenols that promote gut balance and antioxidant protection. The combination of banana, cinnamon, and tahini makes this smoothie an indulgent yet nutrient-packed option.

12. Sweet Corn and Mango Hug
Sweet corn contains lutein and zeaxanthin, which protect eye health, while mango supplies vitamin A and digestive enzymes. This smoothie is an unusual but highly nutritious breakfast option that delivers hydration, fiber, and energy-boosting vitamins in a naturally sweet package.

13. Matcha and Oat Power Shake
Matcha provides a slow-releasing caffeine boost with L-theanine, which enhances focus and reduces stress. Oats ensure long-lasting satiety, while banana and vanilla add natural sweetness and depth of flavor. This smoothie is perfect for those looking for a clean, sustained energy source without a sugar crash.

14. Apple Fennel Boost
Fennel is known for its digestion-enhancing properties and ability to reduce bloating, while apples provide pectin fiber to support gut health. Banana adds creaminess and potassium, while ginger brings an anti-inflammatory kick. This smoothie is an excellent choice for a light yet revitalizing breakfast.

15. Persimmon and Ginger Elixir
Persimmons are rich in antioxidants and vitamin C, supporting immunity and skin health. Ginger adds digestive support and an anti-inflammatory boost, while banana balances the tartness with natural sweetness. This smoothie is a great seasonal option for those looking to boost their body's defenses.

The Science Behind the Benefits
These breakfast smoothies are formulated to support sustained energy, digestion, and overall wellness by targeting key nutritional needs:
- **Steady Energy Levels:** Whole grains like oats, healthy fats from nuts and seeds, and fiber-rich fruits slow digestion and prevent energy crashes.
- **Metabolism Support:** Spices like cinnamon and ginger, along with green tea and protein-rich ingredients, support metabolic health and fat oxidation.

- **Brain Function & Focus:** Omega-3s from seeds, healthy fats from avocado, and polyphenols from cocoa and berries improve cognitive performance.
- **Gut Health & Digestion:** Probiotic-rich Greek yogurt, fiber-packed fruits, and digestion-friendly ingredients like fennel and ginger promote a balanced microbiome.

A Nourishing Start to Your Day

These smoothies are more than just a quick meal—they are designed to work with your body to optimize energy, digestion, and overall well-being. By incorporating them into your morning routine, you can enjoy delicious flavors while giving your body the nutrients it needs to thrive. Whether you're looking for a creamy, protein-packed shake or a refreshing, fiber-rich blend, these recipes offer a simple yet effective way to kick-start your day with purpose and nutrition.

ENERGY

SMOOTHIES

---

01 Mango Mint Refresh

🕐 **Total:** 5 mins   🍴 **Servings:** 2   📊 **Level:** 1/5

Nutritional Info *(Per Serving, based on coconut water and no optional additions)*: 170 kcal; 35g carbs; 3g protein; 2g fat; 5g fiber.

Ingredients

- **Liquid Base (Choose One):** 1 cup coconut water, 1 cup unsweetened almond milk, or 1 cup low-fat dairy milk
- **Main Ingredients:** 1/2 cup frozen mango chunks, 1/2 frozen banana, 5–6 fresh mint leaves, 1 teaspoon fresh lime juice
- **Optional Sweetener:** 1 teaspoon honey, maple syrup, or agave syrup
- **Optional Superfood Additions:** 1 tablespoon chia seeds, 1/2 teaspoon ground flaxseeds, 1 teaspoon spirulina for an energy boost

Optional Variations:
- **Diabetic-Friendly:** Replace banana with 1/4 avocado. Use unsweetened almond milk and avoid additional sweeteners.
- **Vegan:** Avoid low-fat dairy milk and opt for almond milk or coconut water. Avoid honey as a sweetener.
- **Keto:** Remove banana and replace with 1/4 avocado. Use unsweetened almond milk and avoid sweeteners. Add 1 teaspoon of MCT oil.
- **Pregnancy-Safe:** Ensure all ingredients are fresh and thoroughly washed.
- **Protein-Packed:** Add 1 scoop of unflavored protein powder.

👨‍🍳 **Serving Tip:** Garnish with a fresh mint sprig or a lime wedge for extra freshness. Pair with dark chocolate-covered almonds for a satisfying and antioxidant-rich energy boost.

Instructions

1. Freeze mango and banana in advance for a creamier texture.

2. Add ingredients to the blender. Pour the liquid base first, then add frozen mango, frozen banana, mint leaves, and lime juice. Sprinkle in any optional superfoods.

3. Start blending on low speed and gradually increase to high for 1–2 minutes until creamy. Adjust consistency with more liquid if needed.

4. Pour into glasses and enjoy while fresh.

02 Tropical Turmeric Charger

Total: 5 mins **Servings:** 2 **Level:** 1/5

Nutritional Info *(Per Serving, based on coconut milk and no optional additions)*: 190 kcal; 35g carbs; 4g protein; 6g fat; 5g fiber.

Ingredients

- **Liquid Base (Choose One):** 1 cup coconut milk, 1 cup unsweetened almond milk, or 1 cup low-fat dairy milk
- **Main Ingredients:** 1/2 cup frozen pineapple chunks, 1/2 frozen banana, 1/2 teaspoon ground turmeric or 1/2 inch fresh turmeric root (grated), 1/2 teaspoon grated fresh ginger, a pinch of black pepper (enhances turmeric absorption)
- **Optional Sweetener:** 1 teaspoon honey, maple syrup, or agave syrup
- **Optional Superfood Additions:** 1 tablespoon chia seeds, 1/2 teaspoon ground flaxseeds, 1/2 teaspoon cinnamon for extra warmth

Optional Variations:
- **Diabetic-Friendly:** Replace banana with 1/4 avocado. Use unsweetened almond milk and avoid additional sweeteners.
- **Vegan:** Avoid low-fat dairy milk and opt for almond milk or coconut milk. Avoid honey as a sweetener.
- **Keto:** Replace banana with 1/4 avocado. Use unsweetened almond milk and avoid sweeteners. Add 1 teaspoon of MCT oil.
- **Pregnancy-Safe:** Ensure all ingredients are fresh and thoroughly washed.
- **Protein-Packed:** Add 1 scoop of unflavored protein powder.

Serving Tip: Garnish with a sprinkle of cinnamon or a drizzle of honey. Snack on a mix of cashews, sunflower seeds, dried mango, and coconut flakes for a tropical-inspired energy boost.

Instructions

1. Peel and grate fresh turmeric and ginger if using. Freeze pineapple and banana in advance for a creamier texture.

2. Add ingredients to the blender. Pour the liquid base first, then add frozen pineapple, frozen banana, turmeric, ginger, and black pepper. Sprinkle in any optional superfoods.

3. Start blending on low speed and gradually increase to high for 1–2 minutes until creamy. Adjust consistency with more liquid if needed.

4. Pour into glasses and enjoy while fresh.

03 Apple Cinnamon Energy

Total: 5 mins **Servings:** 2 **Level:** 1/5

Nutritional Info *(Per Serving, based on almond milk and no optional additions)*: 180 kcal; 32g carbs; 5g protein; 4g fat; 6g fiber.

Ingredients

- **Liquid Base (Choose One):** 1 cup unsweetened almond milk, 1 cup oat milk, or 1 cup low-fat dairy milk
- **Main Ingredients:** 1 small apple (cored and chopped), 1/2 frozen banana, 1/4 cup rolled oats, 1/2 teaspoon ground cinnamon
- **Optional Sweetener:** 1 teaspoon honey, maple syrup, or agave syrup
- **Optional Superfood Additions:** 1 tablespoon chia seeds, 1/2 teaspoon ground flaxseeds, 1/2 teaspoon vanilla extract

Optional Variations:
- **Diabetic-Friendly:** Replace banana with 1/4 avocado for lower sugar. Use unsweetened almond milk and avoid additional sweeteners.
- **Vegan:** Avoid low-fat dairy milk and opt for almond or oat milk. Avoid honey as a sweetener.
- **Keto:** Remove oats and replace banana with 1/4 avocado. Use unsweetened almond milk and avoid sweeteners. Add 1 teaspoon of MCT oil.
- **Pregnancy-Safe:** Ensure all ingredients are fresh and thoroughly washed.
- **Protein-Packed:** Add 1 scoop of unflavored protein powder for an extra boost.

Serving Tip: Garnish with a sprinkle of cinnamon or a few rolled oats on top. Pair with a handful of walnuts or a slice of whole-grain toast for a balanced energy boost.

Instructions

1. Core and chop the apple. Freeze the banana in advance for a creamier texture.

2. Add ingredients to the blender. Pour the liquid base first, then add apple, frozen banana, oats, and cinnamon. Sprinkle in any optional superfoods.

3. Start blending on low speed and gradually increase to high for 1–2 minutes until creamy. Adjust consistency with more liquid if needed.

4. Pour into glasses and enjoy while fresh.

04 Beetroot and Cacao Lift

Total: 5 mins   **Servings:** 2   **Level:** 1/5

Nutritional Info (Per Serving, based on almond milk and no optional additions): 180 kcal; 30g carbs; 5g protein; 4g fat; 6g fiber.

Ingredients

- **Liquid Base (Choose One):** 1 cup unsweetened almond milk, 1 cup oat milk, or 1 cup low-fat dairy milk
- **Main Ingredients:** 1/2 cup cooked or raw beetroot (peeled and chopped), 1/2 frozen banana, 1 teaspoon raw cacao powder, 1/2 teaspoon ground cinnamon
- **Optional Sweetener:** 1 teaspoon honey, maple syrup, or agave syrup
- **Optional Superfood Additions:** 1 tablespoon chia seeds, 1/2 teaspoon ground flaxseeds, 1 teaspoon cacao nibs for a crunchy texture

Optional Variations:
- **Diabetic-Friendly:** Replace banana with 1/4 avocado. Use unsweetened almond milk and avoid additional sweeteners.
- **Vegan:** Avoid low-fat dairy milk and opt for oat milk or almond milk. Avoid honey and use maple syrup or agave.
- **Keto:** Replace banana with 1/4 avocado. Use unsweetened almond milk and avoid sweeteners. Add 1 teaspoon of MCT oil.
- **Pregnancy-Safe:** Ensure all ingredients are fresh and thoroughly washed.
- **Protein-Packed:** Add 1 scoop of unflavored protein powder.

> **Serving Tip:** Garnish with a sprinkle of cacao nibs or a dusting of cinnamon. Pair with a handful of almonds or a slice of whole-grain toast for a balanced energy boost.

Instructions

1. Cook and cool the beetroot if using cooked. Freeze the banana in advance for a creamier texture.

2. Add ingredients to the blender. Pour the liquid base first, then add beetroot, frozen banana, cacao powder, and cinnamon. Sprinkle in any optional superfoods.

3. Start blending on low speed and gradually increase to high for 1-2 minutes until creamy. Adjust consistency with more liquid if needed.

4. Pour into glasses and enjoy while fresh.

---

05 Kiwi Berry Flax Blast

Total: 5 mins   **Servings:** 2   **Level:** 1/5

Nutritional Info (Per Serving, based on almond milk and no optional additions): 170 kcal; 30g carbs; 4g protein; 3g fat; 7g fiber.

Ingredients

- **Liquid Base (Choose One):** 1 cup unsweetened almond milk, 1 cup coconut water, or 1 cup low-fat dairy milk
- **Main Ingredients:** 1 ripe kiwi (peeled and chopped), 1/2 cup mixed berries (strawberries, blueberries, or raspberries), 1/2 frozen banana, 1 tablespoon ground flaxseeds
- **Optional Sweetener:** 1 teaspoon honey, maple syrup, or agave syrup
- **Optional Superfood Additions:** 1 tablespoon chia seeds, 1/2 teaspoon spirulina for an extra energy boost

Optional Variations:
- **Diabetic-Friendly:** Replace banana with 1/4 avocado. Use unsweetened almond milk and avoid additional sweeteners.
- **Vegan:** Avoid low-fat dairy milk and opt for almond milk or coconut water. Use maple syrup or agave instead of honey.
- **Keto:** Replace banana with 1/4 avocado. Use unsweetened almond milk and avoid sweeteners. Add 1 teaspoon of MCT oil.
- **Pregnancy-Safe:** Ensure all ingredients are fresh and thoroughly washed.
- **Protein-Packed:** Add 1 scoop of unflavored protein powder.

> **Serving Tip:** Garnish with a slice of kiwi or a few whole berries on top. Serve with roasted sweet potato slices drizzled with tahini and a sprinkle of cinnamon for slow-burning energy.

Instructions

1. Peel and chop the kiwi. Freeze the banana in advance for a creamier texture.

2. Add ingredients to the blender. Pour the liquid base first, then add kiwi, mixed berries, frozen banana, and flaxseeds. Sprinkle in any optional superfoods.

3. Start blending on low speed and gradually increase to high for 1-2 minutes until creamy. If needed, adjust the consistency with more liquid.

4. Pour into glasses and enjoy while fresh.

06 Carrot Date Energy Blend

Total: 5 mins **Servings:** 2 **Level:** 1/5

Nutritional Info (Per Serving, based on almond milk and no optional additions): 190 kcal; 34g carbs; 4g protein; 5g fat; 5g fiber.

Ingredients

- **Liquid Base (Choose One):** 1 cup unsweetened almond milk, 1 cup coconut milk, or 1 cup low-fat dairy milk
- **Main Ingredients:** 1/2 cup grated or steamed carrots, 2 pitted Medjool dates, 1/2 frozen banana, 1/2 teaspoon ground cinnamon
- **Optional Sweetener:** 1 teaspoon honey, maple syrup, or agave syrup
- **Optional Superfood Additions:** 1 tablespoon chia seeds, 1/2 teaspoon ground flaxseeds, 1 teaspoon MCT oil

Optional Variations:
- **Diabetic-Friendly:** Replace banana with 1/4 avocado for lower sugar. Use unsweetened almond milk and avoid additional sweeteners.
- **Vegan:** Avoid low-fat dairy milk and opt for almond or coconut milk. Use maple syrup or agave instead of honey.
- **Keto:** Replace banana with 1/4 avocado. Use unsweetened almond milk and avoid sweeteners.
- **Pregnancy-Safe:** Ensure all ingredients are fresh and thoroughly washed.
- **Protein-Packed:** Add 1 scoop of unflavored protein powder.

Serving Tip: Garnish with a sprinkle of cinnamon or a few chopped nuts for extra crunch. Pair with a handful of almonds or homemade energy bites made from pumpkin seeds, oats, and dates for a quick fuel boost.

Instructions

1. Grate or steam the carrots until soft (if desired for easier blending). Pit and chop the dates. Freeze the banana in advance for a creamier texture.

2. Add ingredients to the blender. Pour the liquid base first, then add carrots, pitted dates, frozen banana, and cinnamon. Sprinkle in any optional superfoods.

3. Start blending on low speed and gradually increase to high for 1-2 minutes until creamy. Adjust consistency with more liquid if needed.

4. Pour into glasses and enjoy while fresh.

07 Dragon Fruit & Spinach Power Shake

Total: 5 mins **Servings:** 2 **Level:** 1/5

Nutritional Info (Per Serving, based on almond milk and no optional additions): 175 kcal; 28g carbs; 6g protein; 4g fat; 7g fiber.

Ingredients

- **Liquid Base (Choose One):** 1 cup unsweetened almond milk, 1 cup coconut water, or 1 cup low-fat dairy milk
- **Main Ingredients:** 1/2 cup dragon fruit (fresh or frozen), 1/2 frozen banana, 1/2 cup fresh spinach, 1 tablespoon ground flaxseeds
- **Optional Sweetener:** 1 teaspoon honey, maple syrup, or agave syrup
- **Optional Superfood Additions:** 1 tablespoon chia seeds, 1 teaspoon spirulina, 1 teaspoon MCT oil

Optional Variations:
- **Diabetic-Friendly:** Replace banana with 1/4 avocado for lower sugar. Use unsweetened almond milk and avoid additional sweeteners.
- **Vegan:** Avoid low-fat dairy milk and opt for almond or coconut milk. Use maple syrup or agave instead of honey.
- **Keto:** Replace banana with 1/4 avocado. Use unsweetened almond milk and avoid sweeteners.
- **Pregnancy-Safe:** Ensure all ingredients are fresh and thoroughly washed.
- **Protein-Packed:** Add 1 scoop of unflavored protein powder for an extra boost.

Serving Tip: Garnish with a few dragon fruit cubes or a sprinkle of chia seeds. Pair with a handful of almonds or a whole-grain avocado toast.

Instructions

1. Peel and chop the dragon fruit. Freeze the banana in advance for a creamier texture.

2. Add ingredients to the blender. Pour the liquid base first, then add dragon fruit, frozen banana, spinach, and flaxseeds. Sprinkle in any optional superfoods.

3. Start blending on low speed and gradually increase to high for 1-2 minutes until creamy. Adjust consistency with more liquid if needed.

4. Pour into glasses and enjoy while fresh.

08 Celery and Blueberry Glow

Total: 5 mins **Servings:** 2 **Level:** 1/5

Nutritional Info *(Per Serving, based on kombucha and no optional additions)*: 150 kcal; 28g carbs; 4g protein; 2g fat; 5g fiber.

Ingredients

- **Liquid Base (Choose One):** 1 cup unsweetened kombucha (preferably ginger, lemon, or berry-flavored), 1 cup coconut water, or 1 cup unsweetened almond milk
- **Main Ingredients:** 1/2 cup fresh or frozen blueberries, 1/2 cup chopped celery, 1/2 frozen banana, 1 tablespoon ground flaxseeds
- **Optional Sweetener:** 1 teaspoon honey or maple syrup
- **Optional Superfood Additions:** 1 tablespoon chia seeds, 1/2 teaspoon spirulina

Optional Variations:
- **Diabetic-Friendly:** Replace banana with 1/4 avocado. Use unsweetened almond milk and avoid additional sweeteners.
- **Vegan:** Avoid low-fat dairy milk and opt for almond or coconut milk. Use maple syrup instead of honey.
- **Keto:** Replace banana with 1/4 avocado. Use unsweetened almond milk instead of kombucha. Add 1 teaspoon of MCT oil.
- **Pregnancy-Safe:** Ensure all ingredients are fresh and thoroughly washed. Opt for pasteurized kombucha or replace it with coconut water.
- **Protein-Packed:** Add 1 scoop of unflavored protein powder.

> **Serving Tip:** Garnish with a few whole blueberries or a sprinkle of flaxseeds. Pair with a handful of almonds or a slice of whole-grain toast for a balanced energy boost.

Instructions

1. Wash and chop the celery. Freeze the banana in advance for a creamier texture.

2. Add ingredients to the blender. Pour the liquid base first, then add celery, blueberries, frozen banana, and flaxseeds. Sprinkle in any optional superfoods.

3. Start blending on low speed and gradually increase to high for 1–2 minutes until creamy. Adjust consistency with more liquid if needed.

4. Pour into glasses and enjoy while fresh.

09 Matcha Tahini Super Smoothie

Total: 5 mins **Servings:** 2 **Level:** 1/5

Nutritional Info *(Per Serving, based on almond milk and no optional additions)*: 190 kcal; 25g carbs; 6g protein; 7g fat; 5g fiber.

Ingredients

- **Liquid Base (Choose One):** 1 cup unsweetened almond milk, 1 cup oat milk, or 1 cup low-fat dairy milk
- **Main Ingredients:** 1 teaspoon matcha green tea powder, 1/2 frozen banana, 1 tablespoon tahini (sesame seed paste), 1/2 teaspoon vanilla extract
- **Optional Sweetener:** 1 teaspoon honey, maple syrup, or agave syrup
- **Optional Superfood Additions:** 1 tablespoon chia seeds, 1/2 teaspoon ground flaxseeds, 1 teaspoon cacao nibs, 1 teaspoon MCT oil

Optional Variations:
- **Diabetic-Friendly:** Replace banana with 1/4 avocado for lower sugar. Use unsweetened almond milk and avoid additional sweeteners.
- **Vegan:** Avoid low-fat dairy milk and opt for oat milk or almond milk. Use maple syrup or agave instead of honey.
- **Keto:** Replace banana with 1/4 avocado. Use unsweetened almond milk and avoid sweeteners.
- **Pregnancy-Safe:** Ensure all ingredients are fresh and thoroughly washed.
- **Protein-Packed:** Add 1 scoop of unflavored protein powder.

> **Serving Tip:** Garnish with a sprinkle of matcha powder or sesame seeds. Serve with apple slices and spiced almond butter for a satisfying crunch and energy boost.

Instructions

1. Freeze the banana in advance for a creamier texture.

2. Add ingredients to the blender. Pour the liquid base first, then add frozen banana, tahini, matcha powder, and vanilla extract. Sprinkle in any optional superfoods.

3. Start blending on low speed and gradually increase to high for 1–2 minutes until creamy. Adjust consistency with more liquid if needed.

4. Pour into glasses and enjoy while fresh.

10 Pear and Cardamom Energizer

Total: 5 mins   **Servings:** 2   **Level:** 1/5

Nutritional Info *(Per Serving, based on almond milk and no optional additions)*: 170 kcal; 30g carbs; 4g protein; 5g fat; 6g fiber.

Ingredients

- **Liquid Base (Choose One):** 1 cup unsweetened almond milk, 1 cup oat milk, or 1 cup low-fat dairy milk
- **Main Ingredients:** 1 ripe pear (cored and chopped), 1/2 frozen banana, 1/2 teaspoon ground cardamom, 1/2 teaspoon vanilla extract
- **Optional Sweetener:** 1 teaspoon honey, maple syrup, or agave syrup
- **Optional Superfood Additions:** 1 tablespoon chia seeds, 1/2 teaspoon ground flaxseeds, 1 teaspoon MCT oil for an energy boost

Optional Variations:
- **Diabetic-Friendly:** Replace banana with 1/4 avocado. Use unsweetened almond milk and avoid additional sweeteners.
- **Vegan:** Avoid low-fat dairy milk and opt for oat milk or almond milk. Use maple syrup or agave instead of honey.
- **Keto:** Replace banana with 1/4 avocado. Use unsweetened almond milk and avoid sweeteners.
- **Pregnancy-Safe:** Ensure all ingredients are fresh and thoroughly washed.
- **Protein-Packed:** Add 1 scoop of unflavored protein powder.

Serving Tip: Add a spoonful of hemp seeds for plant-based protein and essential fatty acids to fuel endurance. Serve with a small serving of cooked quinoa for added plant-based protein and fiber.

Instructions

1. Freeze the banana in advance for a creamier texture.

2. Add ingredients to the blender. Pour the liquid base first, then add pear, frozen banana, cardamom, and vanilla extract. Sprinkle in any optional superfoods.

3. Start blending on low speed and gradually increase to high for 1–2 minutes until creamy. Adjust consistency with more liquid if needed.

4. Pour into glasses and enjoy while fresh.

11 Zucchini Pineapple Twist

Total: 5 mins   **Servings:** 2   **Level:** 1/5

Nutritional Info *(Per Serving, based on coconut water and no optional additions)*: 160 kcal; 35g carbs; 3g protein; 2g fat; 5g fiber.

Ingredients

- **Liquid Base (Choose One):** 1 cup coconut water, 1 cup unsweetened almond milk, or 1 cup low-fat dairy milk
- **Main Ingredients:** 1/2 cup chopped zucchini (peeled if preferred), 1/2 cup frozen pineapple chunks, 1/2 frozen banana, 1/2 teaspoon fresh lime juice
- **Optional Sweetener:** 1 teaspoon honey, maple syrup, or agave syrup
- **Optional Superfood Additions:** 1 tablespoon chia seeds, 1 teaspoon grated fresh ginger, 1/2 teaspoon turmeric

Optional Variations:
- **Diabetic-Friendly:** Replace banana with 1/4 avocado for lower sugar. Use unsweetened almond milk and avoid additional sweeteners.
- **Vegan:** Avoid low-fat dairy milk and opt for coconut water or almond milk. Use maple syrup or agave instead of honey.
- **Keto:** Replace pineapple and banana with 1/4 avocado and 1/4 cup frozen zucchini. Use unsweetened almond milk and avoid sweeteners. Add 1 teaspoon of MCT oil.
- **Pregnancy-Safe:** Ensure all ingredients are fresh and thoroughly washed.
- **Protein-Packed:** Add 1 scoop of unflavored protein powder.

Serving Tip: Garnish with a slice of lime or a few chia seeds. Pair with a handful of almonds or a whole-grain cracker for a light, refreshing snack.

Instructions

1. Slice and freeze the banana for a creamier texture.

2. Add ingredients to the blender. Pour the liquid base first, then add zucchini, frozen pineapple, frozen banana, and lime juice. Sprinkle in any optional superfoods.

3. Start blending on low speed and gradually increase to high for 1–2 minutes until creamy. Adjust consistency with more liquid if needed.

4. Pour into glasses and enjoy while fresh.

12 Energy Blackberry Lavender Bliss

Total: 5 mins **Servings:** 2 **Level:** 1/5

Nutritional Info (Per Serving, based on almond milk and no optional additions): 160 kcal; 32g carbs; 4g protein; 3g fat; 7g fiber.

Ingredients

- **Liquid Base (Choose One):** 1 cup unsweetened almond milk, 1 cup oat milk, or 1 cup coconut water
- **Main Ingredients:** 3/4 cup fresh or frozen blackberries, 1/2 frozen banana, 1/2 teaspoon dried culinary lavender or 1/4 teaspoon lavender extract, 1/2 teaspoon vanilla extract
- **Optional Sweetener:** 1 teaspoon honey, maple syrup, or agave syrup
- **Optional Superfood Additions:** 1 tablespoon chia seeds, 1/2 teaspoon ground flaxseeds, 1 teaspoon MCT oil

Optional Variations:
- **Diabetic-Friendly:** Replace banana with 1/4 avocado for lower sugar. Use unsweetened almond milk and avoid additional sweeteners.
- **Vegan:** Avoid honey and use maple syrup or agave.
- **Keto:** Replace banana with 1/4 avocado. Use unsweetened almond milk and avoid additional sweeteners.
- **Pregnancy-Safe:** Ensure all ingredients are fresh and thoroughly washed.
- **Protein-Packed:** Add 1 scoop of unflavored protein powder for an extra boost.

Serving Tip: Add a spoonful of hemp seeds for plant-based protein and essential fatty acids to fuel endurance. Serve with a small bowl of overnight oats for a fiber-rich, slow-releasing energy boost.

Instructions

1. Freeze the banana in advance for a creamier texture.

2. Add ingredients to the blender. Pour the liquid base first, then add blackberries, frozen banana, lavender, and vanilla extract. Sprinkle in any optional superfoods.

3. Start blending on low speed and gradually increase to high for 1–2 minutes until creamy. Adjust consistency with more liquid if needed.

4. Pour into glasses and enjoy while fresh.

13 Strawberry Ginger Zing

Total: 5 mins **Servings:** 2 **Level:** 1/5

Nutritional Info (Per Serving, based on kombucha and no optional additions): 140 kcal; 30g carbs; 2g protein; 1g fat; 4g fiber.

Ingredients

- **Liquid Base (Choose One):** 1 cup kombucha (ginger or plain works best), 1 cup coconut water, or 1 cup unsweetened almond milk
- **Main Ingredients:** 1 cup fresh or frozen strawberries, 1/2 frozen banana, 1/2 teaspoon freshly grated ginger, 1/2 teaspoon lemon juice
- **Optional Sweetener:** 1 teaspoon honey, maple syrup, or agave syrup
- **Optional Superfood Additions:** 1 tablespoon chia seeds, 1 teaspoon ground flaxseeds, 1/2 teaspoon turmeric

Optional Variations:
- **Diabetic-Friendly:** Replace banana with 1/4 avocado for lower sugar. Use unsweetened almond milk instead of kombucha.
- **Vegan:** Avoid honey and use maple syrup or agave.
- **Keto:** Replace banana with 1/4 avocado. Use unsweetened almond milk instead of kombucha.
- **Pregnancy-Safe:** Ensure kombucha is pasteurized. Reduce ginger to 1/4 teaspoon if sensitive.
- **Protein-Packed:** Add 1 scoop of unflavored protein powder for an extra boost.

Serving Tip: Add pumpkin seeds for a crunchy texture and an extra dose of magnesium, which helps combat fatigue. Serve with a Medjool date for a natural carbohydrate source that supports endurance and recovery.

Instructions

1. Freeze the banana for a creamier texture.

2. Add ingredients to the blender. Pour the liquid base first, then add strawberries, frozen banana, blended ginger, and lemon juice. Sprinkle in any optional superfoods.

3. Start blending on low speed and gradually increase to high for 1–2 minutes until creamy. Adjust consistency with more liquid if needed.

4. Pour into glasses and enjoy while fresh.

14 Grapefruit Coconut Tonic

Total: 5 mins	Servings: 2	Level: 1/5

Nutritional Info *(Per Serving, based on coconut water and no optional additions)*: 130 kcal; 28g carbs; 2g protein; 3g fat; 5g fiber.

Ingredients

- **Liquid Base (Choose One):** 1 cup coconut water, 1 cup unsweetened almond milk, or 1 cup coconut milk
- **Main Ingredients:** 1/2 grapefruit (peeled, seeds removed), 1/2 frozen banana, 1/4 cup shredded coconut (unsweetened), 1/2 teaspoon lime juice
- **Optional Sweetener:** 1 teaspoon honey, maple syrup, or agave syrup
- **Optional Superfood Additions:** 1 tablespoon chia seeds for extra fiber and hydration, 1 teaspoon ground flaxseeds for omega-3s, 1/2 teaspoon turmeric

Optional Variations:
- **Diabetic-Friendly:** Replace banana with 1/4 avocado for lower sugar. Use unsweetened almond milk instead of coconut milk.
- **Vegan:** Avoid honey and use maple syrup or agave.
- **Keto:** Replace banana with 1/4 avocado. Use unsweetened almond milk instead of coconut water.
- **Pregnancy-Safe:** Reduce grapefruit if sensitive to acidity. Ensure all ingredients are fresh and thoroughly washed.
- **Protein-Packed:** Add 1 scoop of unflavored protein powder for an extra boost.

Serving Tip: Garnish with a sprinkle of shredded coconut or a grapefruit slice. Pair with a handful of almonds or a slice of whole-grain toast for a balanced energy boost.

Instructions

1. Peel the grapefruit and remove any seeds. Freeze the banana in advance for a creamier texture.

2. Add ingredients to the blender. Pour the liquid base first, then add grapefruit, frozen banana, shredded coconut, and lime juice. Sprinkle in any optional superfoods.

3. Start blending on low speed and gradually increase to high for 1–2 minutes until creamy. Adjust consistency with more liquid if needed.

4. Pour into glasses and enjoy while fresh.

---

15 Papaya and Turmeric Fuel

Total: 5 mins	Servings: 2	Level: 1/5

Nutritional Info *(Per Serving, based on coconut water and no optional additions)*: 170 kcal; 38g carbs; 3g protein; 3g fat; 5g fiber.

Ingredients

- **Liquid Base (Choose One):** 1 cup coconut water, 1 cup unsweetened almond milk, or 1 cup low-fat dairy milk
- **Main Ingredients:** 1/2 cup fresh or frozen papaya (peeled and deseeded), 1/2 frozen banana, 1/2 teaspoon ground turmeric or 1/2 inch fresh turmeric root (grated), 1/2 teaspoon grated fresh ginger, 1/2 teaspoon fresh lime juice
- **Optional Sweetener:** 1 teaspoon honey, maple syrup, or agave syrup
- **Optional Superfood Additions:** 1 tablespoon chia seeds, 1/2 teaspoon ground cinnamon, 1 tablespoon ground flaxseeds

Optional Variations:
- **Diabetic-Friendly:** Replace banana with 1/4 avocado for lower sugar. Use unsweetened almond milk and avoid additional sweeteners.
- **Vegan:** Avoid low-fat dairy milk and opt for coconut water or almond milk. Use maple syrup or agave instead of honey.
- **Keto:** Replace banana with 1/4 avocado. Use unsweetened almond milk and avoid sweeteners. Add 1 teaspoon of MCT oil.
- **Pregnancy-Safe:** Ensure all ingredients are fresh and thoroughly washed.
- **Protein-Packed:** Add 1 scoop of unflavored protein powder.

Serving Tip: Garnish with a sprinkle of turmeric or chia seeds. Pair with a boiled egg or a serving of Greek yogurt to sustain energy levels longer.

Instructions

1. Slice and freeze the banana for a creamier texture.

2. Add ingredients to the blender. Pour the liquid base first, then add papaya, frozen banana, turmeric, ginger, and lime juice. Sprinkle in any optional superfoods.

3. Start blending on low speed and gradually increase to high for 1–2 minutes until creamy. Adjust consistency with more liquid if needed.

4. Pour into glasses and enjoy while fresh.

WHY THESE SMOOTHIES ARE EFFECTIVE

When you need a quick and powerful boost, energy smoothies provide the perfect balance of carbohydrates, proteins, healthy fats, and superfoods that sustain you throughout the day. Unlike sugary energy drinks that cause crashes, these smoothies use nutrient-dense ingredients to fuel your body naturally, improving stamina, mental clarity, and metabolism. Whether you need a pre-workout charge, a mid-afternoon pick-me-up, or an endurance-friendly meal, these smoothies provide clean energy while supporting overall health.

Let's explore why each of these smoothies is a true energy powerhouse:

1. Mango Mint Refresh
This smoothie combines the tropical sweetness of mango with the refreshing burst of mint, making it both hydrating and energizing. Mango is rich in vitamin C, which enhances iron absorption and reduces fatigue, while banana provides potassium for muscle recovery. Coconut water adds electrolytes, preventing dehydration and keeping you feeling revitalized.

2. Tropical Turmeric Charger
Turmeric and ginger work together to reduce inflammation and boost circulation, increasing energy levels naturally. Pineapple's bromelain enzymes improve digestion and reduce bloating, ensuring your body absorbs nutrients efficiently. A touch of black pepper enhances turmeric absorption, making this smoothie an excellent choice for sustained vitality.

3. Apple Cinnamon Energy
A fiber-rich blend of apple, banana, and rolled oats provides steady energy without blood sugar spikes. Cinnamon helps regulate glucose levels, reducing energy crashes, while the addition of chia seeds or flaxseeds provides healthy fats and protein to sustain energy longer.

4. Beetroot and Cacao Lift
Beets are a natural vasodilator, increasing oxygen delivery to muscles and the brain for improved endurance. Cacao adds flavonoids that enhance mental clarity and mood, making this a great pre-workout or mid-morning energy booster. The banana provides fast-acting carbohydrates for immediate fuel.

5. Kiwi Berry Flax Blast
Kiwi and berries are packed with antioxidants that reduce oxidative stress and improve cellular energy production. Flaxseeds add fiber and omega-3s, supporting heart health and brain function, while coconut water replenishes lost electrolytes after physical exertion.

6. Carrot Date Energy Blend
Carrots provide beta-carotene, which supports cell regeneration and eye health, while dates deliver natural sugars that provide quick yet steady energy. Cinnamon aids in stabilizing blood sugar, and the creamy texture makes this a perfect natural alternative to energy bars.

7. Dragon Fruit and Spinach Power Shake
Dragon fruit contains prebiotics that improve gut health, optimizing nutrient absorption for sustained energy. Spinach provides iron, preventing fatigue, while banana adds natural sweetness and potassium for muscle function.

8. Celery and Blueberry Glow
Celery offers natural electrolytes that prevent dehydration, and blueberries deliver powerful antioxidants that enhance brain function. The combination of kombucha or coconut water makes this a probiotic-rich smoothie that supports digestion and energy metabolism.

9. Matcha Tahini Super Smoothie

Matcha's natural caffeine provides a slow-releasing energy boost without jitters, while tahini delivers healthy fats and magnesium to support muscle function and reduce fatigue. This smoothie is an excellent alternative to coffee, offering long-lasting alertness.

10. Pear and Cardamom Energizer

Pear provides gentle, slow-releasing carbohydrates, making this a great breakfast smoothie to prevent mid-morning slumps. Cardamom aids digestion and enhances circulation, ensuring your body efficiently processes nutrients for sustained energy.

11. Zucchini Pineapple Twist

Zucchini adds fiber and hydration without extra sugar, while pineapple contributes digestive enzymes and vitamin C. Lime juice provides a zesty, refreshing kick, making this a perfect pick-me-up for warm days or post-exercise recovery.

12. Energy Blackberry Lavender Bliss

Lavender promotes relaxation, counteracting stress-induced fatigue, while blackberries offer vitamin C and fiber to maintain steady energy levels. This smoothie is perfect for balancing energy while reducing mental exhaustion.

13. Strawberry Ginger Zing

Ginger provides a stimulating effect on circulation, improving oxygen flow to muscles and the brain. Strawberries deliver vitamin C for immune support, while kombucha or coconut water hydrates and replenishes essential minerals.

14. Grapefruit Coconut Tonic

Grapefruit's citrusy punch wakes up the senses and boosts metabolism, while coconut water prevents dehydration. This smoothie is an excellent fat-burning and energizing option, making it ideal for morning routines.

15. Papaya and Turmeric Fuel

Papaya's digestive enzymes help optimize nutrient absorption, ensuring your body gets the most out of every sip. Turmeric reduces inflammation and supports endurance, while banana and chia seeds provide long-lasting fuel.

The Science Behind the Benefits

These energy-boosting smoothies work by combining key nutrients that enhance physical and mental performance:

- **Electrolytes for Hydration:** Ingredients like coconut water, celery, and kombucha replenish lost minerals, preventing fatigue.
- **Iron and Oxygen Support:** Iron-rich spinach and vitamin C-packed fruits ensure efficient oxygen transport, reducing tiredness.
- **Healthy Carbs for Sustained Energy:** Bananas, oats, and dates provide complex and simple carbohydrates for balanced fuel.
- **Adaptogens and Anti-Inflammatory Agents:** Ginger, turmeric, and matcha reduce inflammation and enhance endurance.

A Natural Way to Stay Energized

These smoothies provide a delicious, nutrient-packed way to fuel your day without relying on artificial stimulants or sugar-laden energy drinks. Whether you're gearing up for a workout, tackling a busy day, or looking for a mid-afternoon refresh, these blends offer sustained energy, improved focus, and overall well-being in every sip.

IMMUNITY-BOOSTING
SMOOTHIES

---

01 Golden Beet Immunity Recharge

🕐 **Total:** 5 mins   🍴 **Servings:** 2   📊 **Level:** 1/5

Nutritional Info *(Per Serving, based on almond milk and no optional additions)*: 170 kcal; 32g carbs; 4g protein; 3g fat; 5g fiber.

Ingredients

- **Liquid Base (Choose One):** 1 cup unsweetened almond milk, 1 cup coconut water, or 1 cup low-fat dairy milk
- **Main Ingredients:** 1/2 cup cooked or raw golden beet (peeled and chopped), 1/2 frozen banana, 1/2 teaspoon fresh grated ginger, 1/2 teaspoon turmeric powder, 1/2 cup pineapple chunks (fresh or frozen), 1 tablespoon lemon juice
- **Optional Sweetener:** 1 teaspoon honey, maple syrup, or agave syrup
- **Optional Superfood Additions:** 1 tablespoon chia seeds, 1/2 teaspoon ground flaxseeds

Optional Variations:
- **Diabetic-Friendly:** Replace banana with 1/4 avocado. Use unsweetened almond milk and avoid additional sweeteners.
- **Vegan:** Avoid low-fat dairy milk and opt for almond milk or coconut water. Avoid honey and use maple syrup or agave.
- **Keto:** Replace banana with 1/4 avocado. Use unsweetened almond milk and avoid sweeteners. Add 1 teaspoon of MCT oil.
- **Pregnancy-Safe:** Ensure all ingredients are fresh and thoroughly washed. Avoid unpasteurized ingredients.
- **Protein-Packed:** Add 1 scoop of unflavored protein powder.

Instructions

1. If using cooked golden beet, allow it to cool before blending. Freeze the banana for a creamier texture.

2. First, pour the liquid base into the blender, followed by golden beet, banana, pineapple, ginger, turmeric, and lemon juice. Sprinkle in any optional superfoods.

3. Start blending on low speed and gradually increase to high for 1-2 minutes until creamy. Adjust consistency with more liquid if needed.

4. Pour into glasses and enjoy immediately.

🧑‍🍳 **Serving Tip:** Garnish with a sprinkle of chia seeds or a few fresh pineapple chunks. Serve with a side of probiotic-rich sauerkraut or kimchi to support gut flora and overall immune function.

02 Coconut Curry Spark

Total: 5 mins   **Servings:** 2   **Level:** 1/5

Nutritional Info *(Per Serving, based on coconut milk and no optional additions)*: 190 kcal; 28g carbs; 4g protein; 8g fat; 5g fiber.

Ingredients

- **Liquid Base (Choose One):** 1 cup unsweetened coconut milk, 1 cup cashew milk, or 1 cup water
- **Main Ingredients:** 1/2 cup frozen mango chunks, 1/2 banana, 1/4 teaspoon turmeric powder, 1/4 teaspoon curry powder, 1/2 teaspoon fresh grated ginger, 1 tablespoon unsweetened shredded coconut, 1 teaspoon lemon juice
- **Optional Sweetener:** 1 teaspoon honey, maple syrup, or agave syrup
- **Optional Superfood Additions:** 1 tablespoon chia seeds, 1/2 teaspoon ground flaxseeds, 1 teaspoon MCT oil

Optional Variations:
- **Diabetic-Friendly:** Replace banana with 1/4 avocado for lower sugar. Use unsweetened coconut milk and avoid additional sweeteners.
- **Vegan:** Avoid low-fat dairy milk and opt for coconut or cashew milk. Avoid honey and use maple syrup or agave.
- **Keto:** Replace banana with 1/4 avocado. Use unsweetened coconut milk and avoid sweeteners.
- **Pregnancy-Safe:** Ensure all ingredients are fresh and thoroughly washed. Avoid unpasteurized ingredients.
- **Protein-Packed:** Add 1 scoop of unflavored protein powder.

Serving Tip: Garnish with a sprinkle of shredded coconut or a dash of turmeric powder. Pair with a handful of almonds or a slice of whole-grain toast for a balanced immunity-boosting meal.

Instructions

1. Freeze mango and banana for a creamier texture.

2. First, pour the liquid base into the blender, followed by frozen mango, banana (or avocado), turmeric, curry powder, ginger, shredded coconut, and lemon juice. Sprinkle in any optional superfoods.

3. Start blending on low speed and gradually increase to high for 1-2 minutes until creamy. Adjust consistency with more liquid if needed.

4. Pour into glasses and enjoy immediately.

---

03 Grapefruit and Ginger Glow

Total: 5 mins   **Servings:** 2   **Level:** 1/5

Nutritional Info *(Per Serving, based on kombucha and no optional additions)*: 120 kcal; 26g carbs; 2g protein; 1g fat; 4g fiber.

Ingredients

- **Liquid Base (Choose One):** 1 cup kombucha (plain or ginger-flavored), 1 cup coconut water, or 1 cup unsweetened almond milk
- **Main Ingredients:** 1/2 cup fresh grapefruit segments (peeled, seeds removed), 1/2 frozen banana, 1/2 teaspoon fresh grated ginger, 1 teaspoon lemon juice
- **Optional Sweetener:** 1/2 teaspoon raw honey or maple syrup
- **Optional Superfood Additions:** 1 tablespoon chia seeds, 1/2 teaspoon ground flaxseeds, 1/2 teaspoon turmeric powder

Optional Variations:
- **Diabetic-Friendly:** Replace banana with 1/4 avocado for lower sugar. Use unsweetened kombucha and avoid additional sweeteners.
- **Vegan:** Avoid honey and opt for maple syrup.
- **Keto:** Replace banana with 1/4 avocado. Use unsweetened kombucha or coconut water. Add 1 teaspoon of MCT oil.
- **Pregnancy-Safe:** Ensure all ingredients are fresh and thoroughly washed. Avoid unpasteurized kombucha.
- **Protein-Packed:** Add 1 scoop of unflavored protein powder for an extra boost.

Serving Tip: Garnish with a slice of grapefruit or a sprinkle of chia seeds. Serve with fresh spinach or kale salad to enhance vitamin C and iron absorption for optimal immunity.

Instructions

1. Freeze the banana for a creamier texture. Peel and remove seeds from grapefruit.

2. First, pour the liquid base into the blender, followed by grapefruit, frozen banana (or avocado), ginger, lemon juice, and honey (if using). Sprinkle in any optional superfoods.

3. Start blending on low speed and gradually increase to high for 1-2 minutes until creamy. Adjust consistency with more liquid if needed.

4. Pour into glasses and enjoy immediately.

04 Carrot & Bell Pepper Defense

Total: 5 mins **Servings:** 2 **Level:** 1/5

Nutritional Info (Per Serving, based on coconut water and no optional additions): 110 kcal; 22g carbs; 3g protein; 1.5g fat; 5g fiber.

Ingredients

- **Liquid Base (Choose One):** 1 cup coconut water, 1 cup unsweetened almond milk, or 1 cup low-fat dairy milk
- **Main Ingredients:** 1/2 cup chopped carrots (steamed and cooled for a smoother texture, or raw for a fiber boost), 1/2 cup red bell pepper (chopped, seeds removed), 1/2 frozen banana, 1 teaspoon lemon juice, 1/2 teaspoon grated fresh ginger
- **Optional Superfood Additions:** 1 tablespoon chia seeds, 1/2 teaspoon turmeric powder, 1/2 teaspoon ground flaxseeds

Optional Variations:
- **Diabetic-Friendly:** Replace banana with 1/4 avocado for lower sugar. Use unsweetened almond milk.
- **Vegan:** Avoid low-fat dairy milk and opt for coconut water or almond milk.
- **Keto:** Replace banana with 1/4 avocado. Use unsweetened almond milk and add 1 teaspoon of MCT oil.
- **Pregnancy-Safe:** Ensure all ingredients are fresh and thoroughly washed.
- **Protein-Packed:** Add 1 scoop of unflavored protein powder for an extra boost.

Serving Tip: Garnish with a sprinkle of turmeric or chia seeds. Pair with a handful of almonds or sunflower seeds, rich in vitamin E and selenium.

Instructions

1. Freeze the banana for a creamier texture if using. Steam carrots and let them cool for a smoother blend (optional).

2. First, pour the liquid base into the blender, followed by carrots, bell pepper, banana or avocado, lemon juice, and ginger. Sprinkle in any optional superfoods.

3. Start blending on low speed and gradually increase to high for 1–2 minutes until creamy. Adjust consistency with more liquid if needed.

4. Pour into glasses and enjoy immediately.

---

05 Pomegranate Berry Shield

Total: 5 mins **Servings:** 2 **Level:** 1/5

Nutritional Info (Per Serving, based on coconut water and no optional additions): 140 kcal; 32g carbs; 3g protein; 1g fat; 6g fiber.

Ingredients

- **Liquid Base (Choose One):** 1 cup coconut water, 1 cup unsweetened almond milk, or 1 cup low-fat dairy milk
- **Main Ingredients:** 1/2 cup pomegranate seeds (fresh or frozen), 1/2 cup mixed berries (strawberries, blueberries, raspberries), 1/2 frozen banana, 1 teaspoon lemon juice
- **Optional Superfood Additions:** 1 tablespoon chia seeds, 1/2 teaspoon ground flaxseeds, 1 teaspoon maca powder

Optional Variations:
- **Diabetic-Friendly:** Replace banana with 1/4 avocado for lower sugar. Use unsweetened almond milk.
- **Vegan:** Avoid low-fat dairy milk and use coconut water or almond milk.
- **Keto:** Replace banana with 1/4 avocado. Use unsweetened almond milk and add 1 teaspoon of MCT oil.
- **Pregnancy-Safe:** Ensure all ingredients are fresh and thoroughly washed.
- **Protein-Packed:** Add 1 scoop of unflavored protein powder for an extra boost.

Serving Tip: Garnish with a sprinkle of chia seeds or a few pomegranate arils. Pair with a handful of almonds or roasted garlic toast for an unexpected yet powerful immunity-boosting combo.

Instructions

1. Freeze the banana for a creamier texture if using.

2. First, pour the liquid base into the blender, followed by pomegranate seeds, berries, banana or avocado, and lemon juice. Sprinkle in any optional superfoods.

3. Start blending on low speed and gradually increase to high for 1–2 minutes until creamy. Adjust consistency with more liquid if needed.

4. Pour into glasses and enjoy immediately.

06 Aloe Vera Citrus Tonic

Total: 5 mins   **Servings:** 2   **Level:** 1/5

Nutritional Info *(Per Serving, based on coconut water and no optional additions)*: 110 kcal; 24g carbs; 2g protein; 1g fat; 3g fiber.

Ingredients

- **Liquid Base (Choose One):** 1 cup coconut water, 1 cup unsweetened almond milk, or 1 cup orange juice (freshly squeezed)
- **Main Ingredients:** 1/4 cup fresh aloe vera gel (gel only, no skin), 1/2 cup fresh orange segments (peeled, seeds removed), 1/2 cup frozen mango chunks, 1 teaspoon fresh lime juice
- **Optional Sweetener:** 1/2 teaspoon raw honey or maple syrup
- **Optional Superfood Additions:** 1 tablespoon chia seeds, 1/2 teaspoon ground turmeric, 1/2 teaspoon spirulina powder

Optional Variations:
- **Diabetic-Friendly:** Replace mango with 1/4 avocado. Use unsweetened coconut water and avoid additional sweeteners.
- **Vegan:** Avoid honey and opt for maple syrup or agave.
- **Keto:** Replace mango with 1/4 avocado. Use unsweetened almond milk or coconut water, and avoid additional sweeteners. Add 1 teaspoon of MCT oil.
- **Pregnancy-Safe:** Avoid aloe vera if pregnant, as it may cause uterine contractions. Instead, replace it with 1/4 cup coconut water or 1/4 cup peeled cucumber for a hydrating alternative. Ensure all ingredients are fresh and thoroughly washed.
- **Protein-Packed:** Add 1 scoop of unflavored protein powder.

Serving Tip: Garnish with a sprinkle of chia seeds or a slice of orange. Pair with a handful of almonds or a whole-grain cracker for a well-rounded immunity boost.

Instructions

1. Scoop fresh aloe vera gel from the leaf (avoiding the green skin) and peel and remove seeds from the orange.

2. First, pour the liquid base into the blender, followed by aloe vera gel, orange segments, frozen mango, and lime juice. Sprinkle in any optional superfoods.

3. Start blending on low speed and gradually increase to high for 1–2 minutes until creamy. Adjust consistency with more liquid if needed.

4. Pour into glasses and enjoy immediately.

---

07 Matcha Mango Booster

Total: 5 mins   **Servings:** 2   **Level:** 1/5

Nutritional Info *(Per Serving, based on almond milk and no optional additions)*: 150 kcal; 28g carbs; 4g protein; 3g fat; 4g fiber.

Ingredients

- **Liquid Base (Choose One):** 1 cup unsweetened almond milk, 1 cup coconut water, or 1 cup oat milk
- **Main Ingredients:** 1/2 cup frozen mango chunks, 1/2 frozen banana, 1 teaspoon matcha green tea powder, 1/2 teaspoon vanilla extract
- **Optional Sweetener:** 1 teaspoon honey, maple syrup, or agave syrup
- **Optional Superfood Additions:** 1 tablespoon chia seeds, 1/2 teaspoon ground flaxseeds, 1 teaspoon MCT oil

Optional Variations:
- **Diabetic-Friendly:** Replace banana with 1/4 avocado for lower sugar. Use unsweetened almond milk and avoid additional sweeteners.
- **Vegan:** Avoid honey and opt for maple syrup or agave.
- **Keto:** Replace banana with 1/4 avocado. Use unsweetened almond milk and avoid sweeteners.
- **Pregnancy-Safe:** Ensure all ingredients are fresh and thoroughly washed.
- **Protein-Packed:** Add 1 scoop of unflavored protein powder for an extra boost.

Serving Tip: Garnish with a sprinkle of matcha powder or chia seeds. Pair with a handful of cashews or a slice of whole-grain toast for a balanced energy boost.

Instructions

1. Freeze banana and mango in advance for a creamier texture.

2. First, pour the liquid base into the blender, then add frozen mango, banana, matcha powder, and vanilla extract. Sprinkle in any optional superfoods.

3. Start blending on low speed and gradually increase to high for 1–2 minutes until creamy. Adjust consistency with more liquid if needed.

4. Pour into glasses and enjoy immediately.

08 Orange Avocado Cream

Total: 5 mins   **Servings:** 2   **Level:** 1/5

Nutritional Info *(Per Serving, based on almond milk and no optional additions)*: 180 kcal; 25g carbs; 4g protein; 8g fat; 5g fiber.

Ingredients

- **Liquid Base (Choose One):** 1 cup unsweetened almond milk, 1 cup coconut water, or 1 cup oat milk
- **Main Ingredients:** 1/2 large orange (peeled and segmented), 1/4 ripe avocado, 1/2 frozen banana, 1/2 teaspoon vanilla extract
- **Optional Sweetener:** 1 teaspoon honey, maple syrup, or agave syrup
- **Optional Superfood Additions:** 1 tablespoon chia seeds, 1/2 teaspoon ground flaxseeds, 1 teaspoon MCT oil

Optional Variations:
- **Diabetic-Friendly:** Replace banana with 1/4 cup frozen zucchini. Use unsweetened almond milk and avoid additional sweeteners.
- **Vegan:** Avoid honey and opt for maple syrup or agave.
- **Keto:** Replace banana with an additional 1/4 avocado. Use unsweetened almond milk and avoid additional sweeteners. Add 1 teaspoon of MCT oil.
- **Pregnancy-Safe:** Ensure all ingredients are fresh and thoroughly washed.
- **Protein-Packed:** Add 1 scoop of unflavored protein powder for an extra boost.

> **Serving Tip:** Garnish with an orange zest sprinkle or a few chia seeds. Pair with a handful of cashews or a hard-boiled egg for a protein boost.

Instructions

1. Freeze the banana ahead of time for a thicker texture.

2.. First, pour the liquid base into the blender, followed by orange, avocado, frozen banana (or zucchini), and vanilla extract. Sprinkle in any optional superfoods.

3. Start blending on low speed and gradually increase to high for 1–2 minutes until creamy. Adjust consistency with more liquid if needed.

4. Pour into glasses and enjoy immediately.

---

09 Golden Kiwi Ginger Zinger

Total: 5 mins   **Servings:** 2   **Level:** 1/5

Nutritional Info *(Per Serving, based on coconut water and no optional additions)*: 160 kcal; 35g carbs; 3g protein; 1g fat; 6g fiber.

Ingredients

- **Liquid Base (Choose One):** 1 cup coconut water, 1 cup unsweetened almond milk, or 1 cup low-fat dairy milk
- **Main Ingredients:** 2 golden kiwis (peeled and chopped), 1/2 frozen banana, 1/2 teaspoon fresh grated ginger, 1 teaspoon lemon juice
- **Optional Sweetener:** 1 teaspoon honey, maple syrup, or agave syrup
- **Optional Superfood Additions:** 1 tablespoon chia seeds, 1/2 teaspoon turmeric powder, 1 teaspoon ground flaxseeds

Optional Variations:
- **Diabetic-Friendly:** Replace banana with 1/4 avocado. Use unsweetened almond milk and avoid additional sweeteners.
- **Vegan:** Avoid honey and use maple syrup or agave instead.
- **Keto:** Replace banana with 1/4 avocado. Use unsweetened almond milk and avoid additional sweeteners. Add 1 teaspoon of MCT oil.
- **Pregnancy-Safe:** Ensure all ingredients are fresh and thoroughly washed. Reduce ginger if experiencing nausea sensitivity.
- **Protein-Packed:** Add 1 scoop of unflavored protein powder.

> **Serving Tip:** Garnish with a kiwi slice or a sprinkle of turmeric. Pair with a handful of almonds or a whole-grain cracker for a vibrant, immunity-boosting refreshment.

Instructions

1. Freeze the banana ahead of time for a thicker texture.

2. First, pour the liquid base into the blender, followed by golden kiwis, frozen banana (or avocado), ginger, and lemon juice. Sprinkle in any optional superfoods.

3. Start blending on low speed and gradually increase to high for 1–2 minutes until creamy. Adjust consistency with more liquid if needed.

4. Pour into glasses and enjoy immediately.

10 Pumpkin and Cranberry Power

Total: 5 mins **Servings:** 2 **Level:** 1/5

Nutritional Info (*Per Serving, based on almond milk and no optional additions*): 180 kcal; 34g carbs; 5g protein; 4g fat; 7g fiber.

Ingredients

- **Liquid Base (Choose One):** 1 cup unsweetened almond milk, 1 cup oat milk, or 1 cup low-fat dairy milk
- **Main Ingredients:** 1/2 cup canned pumpkin puree (unsweetened), 1/2 cup fresh or frozen cranberries, 1/2 frozen banana, 1/2 teaspoon cinnamon, 1/4 teaspoon ground nutmeg
- **Optional Sweetener:** 1 teaspoon maple syrup, honey, or agave syrup
- **Optional Superfood Additions:** 1 tablespoon chia seeds, 1/2 teaspoon ground flaxseeds, 1 teaspoon hemp seeds

Optional Variations:
- **Diabetic-Friendly:** Replace banana with 1/4 avocado. Use unsweetened almond milk and avoid additional sweeteners.
- **Vegan:** Avoid honey and opt for maple syrup or agave instead.
- **Keto:** Remove banana and cranberries, replace with 1/4 avocado, and add 1 teaspoon of MCT oil.
- **Pregnancy-Safe:** Ensure all ingredients are fresh and high quality. Cranberries should be unsweetened.
- **Protein-Packed:** Add 1 scoop of unflavored protein powder for an extra boost.

Serving Tip: Garnish with a sprinkle of cinnamon or a few dried cranberries. Pair with a side of hard-boiled eggs or a handful of walnuts for a balanced meal.

Instructions

1. Freeze the banana ahead of time for a thicker texture.

2. Pour the liquid base into the blender first, followed by pumpkin puree, cranberries, frozen banana (or avocado), cinnamon, and nutmeg. Sprinkle in any optional superfoods.

3. Start blending on low speed and gradually increase to high for 1–2 minutes until creamy. Adjust consistency with more liquid if needed.

4. Pour into glasses and enjoy immediately.

11 Fennel Pear Wellness Boost

Total: 5 mins **Servings:** 2 **Level:** 1/5

Nutritional Info (*Per Serving, based on kombucha and no optional additions*): 140 kcal; 30g carbs; 2g protein; 1g fat; 6g fiber.

Ingredients

- **Liquid Base (Choose One):** 1 cup plain or ginger-flavored kombucha, 1 cup coconut water, or 1 cup unsweetened almond milk
- **Main Ingredients:** 1 small ripe pear (cored and chopped), 1/2 cup thinly sliced fennel bulb, 1/2 frozen banana, 1 teaspoon lemon juice
- **Optional Sweetener:** 1/2 teaspoon raw honey or maple syrup
- **Optional Superfood Additions:** 1 tablespoon chia seeds, 1/2 teaspoon grated fresh ginger, 1/2 teaspoon spirulina

Optional Variations:
- **Diabetic-Friendly:** Replace banana with 1/4 avocado. Use unsweetened kombucha and avoid additional sweeteners.
- **Vegan:** Avoid honey and use maple syrup or agave instead.
- **Keto:** Replace banana with 1/4 avocado. Use unsweetened kombucha or coconut water. Add 1 teaspoon of MCT oil.
- **Pregnancy-Safe:** Ensure all ingredients are fresh and thoroughly washed. Avoid unpasteurized kombucha.
- **Protein-Packed:** Add 1 scoop of unflavored protein powder for an extra boost.

Serving Tip: Garnish with a thin slice of fennel or a sprinkle of chia seeds. Pair with a handful of walnuts or a light whole-grain cracker for a refreshing, digestive-friendly boost.

Instructions

1. Freeze the banana ahead of time for a thicker texture.

2. Pour the liquid base into the blender first, followed by pear, fennel, frozen banana (or avocado), and lemon juice. Sprinkle in any optional superfoods.

3. Start blending on low speed and gradually increase to high for 1–2 minutes until creamy. Adjust consistency with more liquid if needed.

4. Pour into glasses and enjoy immediately.

12 Persimmon and Carrot Delight

Total: 5 mins   **Servings:** 2   **Level:** 1/5

Nutritional Info (Per Serving, based on almond milk and no optional additions): 140 kcal; 32g carbs; 3g protein; 1.5g fat; 5g fiber.

Ingredients

- **Liquid Base (Choose One):** 1 cup coconut water, 1 cup freshly squeezed orange juice, or 1 cup unsweetened almond milk
- **Main Ingredients:** 1 ripe persimmon (peeled and chopped), 1/2 cup shredded carrot, 1/2 frozen banana, 1/2 teaspoon fresh grated ginger
- **Optional Sweetener:** 1 teaspoon raw honey or maple syrup
- **Optional Superfood Additions:** 1 tablespoon chia seeds, 1/2 teaspoon ground turmeric, 1 tablespoon hemp seeds

Optional Variations:
- **Diabetic-Friendly:** Replace banana with 1/4 avocado. Use unsweetened almond milk and avoid additional sweeteners.
- **Vegan:** Avoid honey and opt for maple syrup or agave.
- **Keto:** Replace banana with 1/4 avocado. Use unsweetened almond milk and avoid additional sweeteners. Add 1 teaspoon of MCT oil.
- **Pregnancy-Safe:** Ensure all ingredients are fresh and thoroughly washed. Avoid unpasteurized juices.
- **Protein-Packed:** Add 1 scoop of unflavored protein powder for an extra boost.

Serving Tip: Garnish with a sprinkle of chia seeds or a drizzle of honey. Pair with a handful of almonds or a whole-grain cracker for a balanced immunity-boosting breakfast.

Instructions

1. Freeze the banana in advance for a creamier texture. Peel and chop the persimmon and shred the carrot.

2. First, pour the liquid base into the blender, followed by persimmon, carrot, frozen banana (or avocado), and ginger. Sprinkle in any optional superfoods.

3. Start blending on low speed and gradually increase to high for 1-2 minutes until smooth. Adjust consistency with more liquid if needed.

4. Pour into glasses and enjoy immediately.

---

13 Feijoa and Pineapple Blast

Total: 5 mins   **Servings:** 2   **Level:** 1/5

Nutritional Info (Per Serving, based on coconut water and no optional additions): 150 kcal; 35g carbs; 2g protein; 1g fat; 5g fiber.

Ingredients

- **Liquid Base (Choose One):** 1 cup coconut water, 1 cup freshly squeezed orange juice, or 1 cup unsweetened almond milk
- **Main Ingredients:** 2 ripe feijoas (scooped out), 1/2 cup fresh pineapple chunks, 1/2 frozen banana, 1 teaspoon fresh lime juice
- **Optional Sweetener:** 1 teaspoon raw honey or maple syrup
- **Optional Superfood Additions:** 1 tablespoon chia seeds, 1/2 teaspoon ground turmeric, 1 tablespoon flaxseeds for extra fiber

Optional Variations:
- **Diabetic-Friendly:** Replace banana with 1/4 avocado. Use unsweetened almond milk and avoid additional sweeteners.
- **Vegan:** Avoid honey and opt for maple syrup or agave.
- **Keto:** Replace banana with 1/4 avocado. Use unsweetened almond milk and avoid additional sweeteners. Add 1 teaspoon of MCT oil for an energy boost.
- **Pregnancy-Safe:** Ensure all ingredients are fresh and thoroughly washed.
- **Protein-Packed:** Add 1 scoop of unflavored protein powder for an extra boost.

Serving Tip: Garnish with a sprinkle of chia seeds or a pineapple wedge. Pair with a handful of cashews or pour into a bowl and top with granola, diced kiwi, and a drizzle of honey for a smoothie bowl variation.

Instructions

1. Freeze the banana in advance for a creamier texture. Scoop out the feijoa pulp and chop the pineapple.

2. First, pour the liquid base into the blender, followed by feijoa, pineapple, frozen banana (or avocado), and lime juice. Sprinkle in any optional superfoods.

3. Start blending on low speed and gradually increase to high for 1-2 minutes until smooth. Adjust consistency with more liquid if needed.

4. Pour into glasses and enjoy immediately.

14 Lemon Turmeric Immune Kick

Total: 5 mins   **Servings:** 2   **Level:** 1/5

Nutritional Info *(Per Serving, based on kombucha and no optional additions)*: 110 kcal; 25g carbs; 1g protein; 0.5g fat; 3g fiber.

Ingredients

- **Liquid Base (Choose One):** 1 cup plain or ginger-flavored kombucha, 1 cup coconut water, or 1 cup unsweetened almond milk
- **Main Ingredients:** 1/2 frozen banana, 1/2 teaspoon ground turmeric or 1/2 inch fresh turmeric root (grated), 1 tablespoon freshly squeezed lemon juice, 1/2 teaspoon fresh grated ginger
- **Optional Sweetener:** 1 teaspoon raw honey, maple syrup, or agave syrup
- **Optional Superfood Additions:** 1 tablespoon chia seeds, 1/2 teaspoon black pepper (enhances turmeric absorption), 1/2 teaspoon ground flaxseeds, 1 teaspoon MCT oil

Optional Variations:
- **Diabetic-Friendly:** Replace banana with 1/4 avocado for lower sugar. Use unsweetened kombucha and avoid additional sweeteners.
- **Vegan:** Avoid honey and opt for maple syrup or agave.
- **Keto:** Replace banana with 1/4 avocado. Use unsweetened kombucha or coconut water and avoid additional sweeteners.
- **Pregnancy-Safe:** Ensure all ingredients are fresh and thoroughly washed. Avoid unpasteurized kombucha.
- **Protein-Packed:** Add 1 scoop of unflavored protein powder.

Serving Tip: Garnish with a sprinkle of black pepper or lemon zest. Pair with a handful of almonds or cashews for a balanced, energizing snack.

Instructions

1. Freeze the banana in advance for a creamier texture. Grate fresh turmeric and ginger.

2. Pour the liquid base into the blender first, followed by the banana (or avocado), turmeric, lemon juice, and ginger. Sprinkle in any optional superfoods.

3. Start blending on low speed and gradually increase to high for 1–2 minutes until smooth. Adjust consistency with more liquid if needed.

4. Pour into glasses and enjoy immediately.

---

15 Apple Pomegranate Elixir

Total: 5 mins   **Servings:** 2   **Level:** 1/5

Nutritional Info *(Per Serving, based on kombucha and no optional additions)*: 160 kcal; 38g carbs; 2g protein; 1.5g fat; 5g fiber.

Ingredients

- **Liquid Base (Choose One):** 1 cup unsweetened almond milk, 1 cup coconut water, or 1 cup pomegranate juice
- **Main Ingredients:** 1 small apple (cored and chopped), 1/2 cup fresh or frozen pomegranate seeds, 1/2 frozen banana, 1/2 teaspoon cinnamon
- **Optional Sweetener:** 1 teaspoon raw honey, maple syrup, or agave syrup
- **Optional Superfood Additions:** 1 tablespoon chia seeds, 1/2 teaspoon ground flaxseeds, 1 teaspoon MCT oil

Optional Variations:
- **Diabetic-Friendly:** Replace banana with 1/4 avocado. Use unsweetened almond milk and avoid additional sweeteners.
- **Vegan:** Avoid honey and opt for maple syrup or agave.
- **Keto:** Replace banana with 1/4 avocado. Use unsweetened almond milk and avoid additional sweeteners.
- **Pregnancy-Safe:** Ensure all ingredients are fresh and thoroughly washed. Avoid unpasteurized pomegranate juice.
- **Protein-Packed:** Add 1 scoop of unflavored protein powder for an extra boost.

Serving Tip: Garnish with a few pomegranate seeds or a sprinkle of cinnamon. Pair with a handful of walnuts or a whole-grain cracker for a balanced, antioxidant-rich breakfast.

Instructions

1. Freeze the banana for a creamier texture. Core and chop the apple.

2. Pour the liquid base into the blender first, followed by the apple, pomegranate seeds, frozen banana (or avocado), and cinnamon. Sprinkle in any optional superfoods.

3. Start blending on low speed and gradually increase to high for 1–2 minutes until smooth. Adjust consistency with more liquid if needed.

4. Pour into glasses and enjoy immediately.

WHY THESE SMOOTHIES ARE EFFECTIVE

A strong immune system is your body's first line of defense against illness, and the right nutrition plays a crucial role in keeping it resilient. These smoothies are designed with powerhouse ingredients that fight inflammation, support gut health, and deliver essential vitamins and minerals that strengthen immunity. From vitamin C-rich fruits to anti-inflammatory spices and probiotic-packed bases, each blend works to fortify your body against infections and promote long-term wellness.

Let's explore why each of these smoothies is a potent immunity shield:

1. Golden Beet Immunity Recharge
Golden beets are packed with antioxidants and betalains, which help reduce inflammation and detoxify the liver. Turmeric and ginger work together to enhance immune response and improve circulation, while pineapple adds vitamin C to support white blood cell production. A splash of lemon juice provides an extra vitamin C boost, making this blend a golden elixir for immunity.

2. Coconut Curry Spark
Turmeric and curry powder offer potent anti-inflammatory benefits, helping the body fend off infections. Coconut milk adds lauric acid, a compound known for its antiviral properties. Ginger aids digestion, ensuring your gut—where most of your immune system resides—functions optimally.

3. Grapefruit and Ginger Glow
Grapefruit is loaded with vitamin C and flavonoids, which enhance immune function and combat free radicals. Ginger is known for its antimicrobial properties, and the kombucha base introduces gut-friendly probiotics that strengthen the body's defenses.

4. Carrot and Bell Pepper Defense
Carrots provide beta-carotene, which the body converts into vitamin A, essential for immune cell function. Red bell peppers contain even more vitamin C than oranges, offering a strong boost to your body's ability to fight infections. Together, they create a nutrient-dense smoothie for robust immunity.

5. Pomegranate Berry Shield
Pomegranates are rich in polyphenols that have antimicrobial and antiviral properties. Mixed berries bring a dose of antioxidants that help neutralize free radicals, while chia seeds add fiber to support gut health. This smoothie works to enhance immune function while keeping inflammation in check.

6. Aloe Vera Citrus Tonic
Aloe vera is known for its anti-inflammatory and antimicrobial properties, supporting both gut health and immune resilience. Orange and lime juice provide vitamin C, while mango adds beta-carotene for additional immune support.

7. Matcha Mango Booster
Matcha contains catechins, which help the body fight infections and reduce inflammation. Mango and banana provide a steady release of energy while also supplying essential vitamins for immune function. This blend is ideal for preventing energy crashes while strengthening the body's defenses.

8. Orange Avocado Cream
Avocado delivers healthy fats that aid in the absorption of fat-soluble vitamins, including vitamin E, which supports immune cell function. Orange juice supplies a refreshing boost of vitamin C, while the smoothie's creamy texture makes it a satisfying immune-supporting option.

9. Golden Kiwi Ginger Zinger
Golden kiwis contain even more vitamin C than oranges, making them an excellent choice for

immunity. Combined with ginger's anti-inflammatory properties and a splash of lemon juice, this smoothie is both refreshing and protective.

10. Pumpkin and Cranberry Power
Pumpkin is a rich source of vitamin A and zinc, both of which support immune function and wound healing. Cranberries provide antibacterial benefits, particularly for urinary tract health, while cinnamon adds antimicrobial properties.

11. Fennel Pear Wellness Boost
Fennel contains antimicrobial compounds and is rich in vitamin C, making it an excellent immunity-boosting ingredient. Pears offer hydration and fiber, which aid digestion and ensure that nutrients are effectively absorbed. The combination makes this smoothie a gentle yet powerful immunity enhancer.

12. Persimmon and Carrot Delight
Persimmons are loaded with vitamin A, supporting immune system efficiency, while carrots contribute beta-carotene for added defense. Ginger provides an anti-inflammatory effect, helping the body stay resilient against infections.

13. Feijoa and Pineapple Blast
Feijoa is an often-overlooked superfruit packed with vitamin C and gut-friendly prebiotics, which feed the healthy bacteria that regulate immune function. Pineapple adds bromelain, an enzyme that supports digestion and reduces inflammation, making this smoothie a fantastic choice for overall wellness.

14. Lemon Turmeric Immune Kick
Lemon and turmeric are a dynamic duo when it comes to fighting infections. The vitamin C in lemon enhances white blood cell activity, while turmeric's curcumin content has powerful anti-inflammatory properties. Black pepper enhances curcumin absorption, making this blend a potent immune-booster.

15. Apple Pomegranate Elixir
Apples contain quercetin, a natural antihistamine that can help reduce inflammation and support respiratory health. Pomegranate is known for its high antioxidant content, which helps reduce oxidative stress and protect immune cells. The combination makes this a vibrant and protective smoothie.

The Science Behind the Benefits
These smoothies work because they target the key pillars of immunity:
- **Vitamin C and Antioxidants:** Ingredients like grapefruit, pomegranate, and berries neutralize free radicals and enhance immune cell production.
- **Gut Health:** Probiotic-rich bases (kombucha, coconut water) and fiber-filled ingredients (chia seeds, aloe vera) nourish the gut, where 70% of the immune system is located.
- **Anti-Inflammatory Support:** Turmeric, ginger, and curry powder reduce chronic inflammation that weakens immune defenses.
- **Hydration and Detoxification:** Coconut water, citrus fruits, and aloe vera keep the body hydrated and aid in flushing out toxins.

A Delicious Way to Strengthen Immunity
By incorporating these immunity-boosting smoothies into your daily routine, you're giving your body the nutrients it needs to stay strong, recover faster, and fight off infections naturally. They're not just powerful—they're refreshing, flavorful, and an enjoyable way to invest in your health every day.

PROTEIN POWER
SMOOTHIES

---

01 Peach Coconut Protein Delight

🕐 **Total:** 5 mins   🍴 **Servings:** 2   📶 **Level:** 1/5

Nutritional Info *(Per Serving, based on coconut milk and no optional additions)*: 220 kcal; 30g carbs; 10g protein; 8g fat; 5g fiber.

Ingredients

- **Liquid Base (Choose One):** 1 cup unsweetened coconut milk, 1 cup unsweetened almond milk, or 1 cup low-fat dairy milk
- **Main Ingredients:** 1 cup fresh or frozen peaches (sliced), 1/2 frozen banana, 1/2 cup Greek yogurt, 1 tablespoon shredded coconut, 1 scoop vanilla protein powder
- **Optional Sweetener:** 1 teaspoon honey or maple syrup
- **Optional Superfood Additions:** 1 tablespoon chia seeds, 1 teaspoon ground flaxseeds, 1 teaspoon MCT oil, 1/2 teaspoon cinnamon

Optional Variations:
- **Diabetic-Friendly:** Replace banana with 1/4 avocado. Use unsweetened coconut or almond milk, and avoid additional sweeteners.
- **Vegan:** Use plant-based yogurt and a plant-based protein powder. Avoid honey as a sweetener.
- **Keto:** Replace banana with 1/4 avocado. Use unsweetened almond milk and avoid sweeteners.
- **Pregnancy-Safe:** Ensure all ingredients are fresh and thoroughly washed. Use pasteurized dairy milk.
- **Protein-Packed:** Add 1 tablespoon hemp seeds.

> **Serving Tip:** Add a few chia seeds or hemp seeds on top for a crunchy texture. Serve alongside a handful of raw almonds or cashews for an additional protein boost. Pair with a slice of whole-grain toast spread with almond or peanut butter for a balanced meal.

Instructions

1. Freeze the banana in advance for a creamier texture. Slice the peaches if using fresh ones.

2. Add ingredients to the blender. Pour the liquid base first, then add peaches, frozen banana (or avocado), Greek yogurt, shredded coconut, and protein powder. Sprinkle in any optional superfoods.

3. Start blending on low speed, then gradually increase to high speed for 1–2 minutes until the smoothie is creamy. Adjust consistency with more liquid if needed.

4. Pour into glasses and enjoy while fresh.

02 Kiwi Lime Fresh Kick

Total: 5 mins   **Servings:** 2   **Level:** 1/5

Nutritional Info *(Per Serving, based on almond milk and no optional additions)*: 210 kcal; 25g carbs; 15g protein; 5g fat; 6g fiber.

Ingredients

- **Liquid Base (Choose One):** 1 cup unsweetened almond milk, 1 cup coconut water, or 1 cup low-fat dairy milk
- **Main Ingredients:** 2 ripe kiwis (peeled and sliced), 1/2 frozen banana, 1/2 cup Greek yogurt or plant-based yogurt, juice of 1/2 lime, 1 scoop vanilla or unflavored protein powder
- **Optional Sweetener:** 1 teaspoon honey, maple syrup, or agave syrup
- **Optional Superfood Additions:** 1 tablespoon chia seeds, 1 teaspoon ground flaxseeds, 1 teaspoon MCT oil, 1/2 teaspoon spirulina

Optional Variations:
- **Diabetic-Friendly:** Replace banana with 1/4 avocado. Use unsweetened almond milk and avoid additional sweeteners.
- **Vegan:** Use plant-based yogurt and a plant-based protein powder. Avoid honey.
- **Keto:** Replace banana with 1/4 avocado. Use unsweetened almond milk and avoid sweeteners.
- **Pregnancy-Safe:** Ensure all ingredients are fresh and thoroughly washed. Use pasteurized dairy milk.
- **Protein-Packed:** Add 1 tablespoon hemp seeds for an additional boost.

Serving Tip: Top with hemp seeds and coconut flakes for added crunch and healthy fats. Pair with a high-protein breakfast bowl of Greek yogurt, granola, and sliced almonds for a well-rounded meal.

Instructions

1. Freeze the banana in advance for a creamier texture. Peel and slice the kiwis.

2. Add ingredients to the blender. Pour the liquid base first, then add kiwis, frozen banana (or avocado), Greek yogurt, lime juice, and protein powder. Sprinkle in any optional superfoods.

3. Start blending on low speed, then gradually increase to high speed for 1–2 minutes until the smoothie is creamy. Adjust consistency with more liquid if needed.

4. Pour into glasses and enjoy while fresh.

---

03 Vanilla Cashew Protein Bliss

Total: 5 mins   **Servings:** 2   **Level:** 1/5

Nutritional Info *(Per Serving, based on almond milk and no optional additions)*: 250 kcal; 22g carbs; 15g protein; 10g fat; 4g fiber.

Ingredients

- **Liquid Base (Choose One):** 1 cup unsweetened almond milk, 1 cup oat milk, or 1 cup low-fat dairy milk
- **Main Ingredients:** 1/4 cup raw cashews (soaked for 2+ hours or overnight), 1/2 frozen banana, 1/2 cup Greek yogurt or plant-based yogurt, 1 teaspoon vanilla extract, 1 scoop vanilla or unflavored protein powder
- **Optional Sweetener:** 1 teaspoon honey or maple syrup
- **Optional Superfood Additions:** 1 tablespoon chia seeds, 1 teaspoon ground flaxseeds, 1 teaspoon MCT oil, 1/2 teaspoon cinnamon

Optional Variations:
- **Diabetic-Friendly:** Replace banana with 1/4 avocado. Use unsweetened almond milk and avoid additional sweeteners.
- **Vegan:** Use plant-based yogurt and a plant-based protein powder. Avoid honey.
- **Keto:** Replace banana with 1/4 avocado. Use unsweetened almond milk and avoid sweeteners.
- **Pregnancy-Safe:** Ensure all ingredients are fresh and thoroughly washed. Use pasteurized dairy milk.
- **Protein-Packed:** Add 1 tablespoon hemp seeds.

Serving Tip: Top with cacao nibs and shredded coconut for a dessert-like post-workout recovery drink. Pair with a side of scrambled eggs and spinach for a protein-packed morning meal.

Instructions

1. Soak cashews for at least 2 hours or overnight for a smoother texture. Freeze the banana in advance.

2. Add ingredients to the blender. Pour the liquid base first, then add cashews, frozen banana (or avocado), Greek yogurt, vanilla extract, and protein powder. Sprinkle in any optional superfoods.

3. Start blending on low speed, then gradually increase to high speed for 1–2 minutes until smooth and creamy. Adjust consistency with more liquid if needed.

4. Pour into glasses and enjoy while fresh.

04 Pear and Walnut Super Shake

Total: 5 mins   **Servings:** 2   **Level:** 1/5

Nutritional Info *(Per Serving, based on almond milk and no optional additions)*: 250 kcal; 28g carbs; 12g protein; 10g fat; 6g fiber.

Ingredients

- **Liquid Base (Choose One):** 1 cup unsweetened almond milk, 1 cup oat milk, or 1 cup low-fat dairy milk
- **Main Ingredients:** 1 ripe pear (cored and chopped), 1/4 cup raw walnuts (soaked for 2+ hours or overnight), 1/2 frozen banana, 1/2 cup Greek yogurt or plant-based yogurt, 1 teaspoon vanilla extract, 1 scoop vanilla or unflavored protein powder
- **Optional Sweetener:** 1 teaspoon honey or maple syrup
- **Optional Superfood Additions:** 1 tablespoon chia seeds, 1 teaspoon ground flaxseeds, 1 teaspoon MCT oil, 1/2 teaspoon cinnamon

Optional Variations:
- **Diabetic-Friendly:** Replace banana with 1/4 avocado. Use unsweetened almond milk and avoid additional sweeteners.
- **Vegan:** Use plant-based yogurt and a plant-based protein powder. Avoid honey.
- **Keto:** Replace banana with 1/4 avocado. Use unsweetened almond milk and avoid sweeteners.
- **Pregnancy-Safe:** Ensure all ingredients are fresh and thoroughly washed. Use pasteurized dairy milk.
- **Protein-Packed:** Add 1 tablespoon hemp seeds.

Serving Tip: Top with cacao nibs and shredded coconut for a dessert-like post-workout recovery drink. Pair with whole-grain toast topped with ricotta and a drizzle of honey for a satisfying breakfast.

Instructions

1. Soak walnuts for at least 2 hours or overnight for a smoother texture. Freeze the banana in advance.

2. Add ingredients to the blender. Pour the liquid base first, then add pear, soaked walnuts, frozen banana (or avocado), Greek yogurt, vanilla extract, and protein powder. Sprinkle in any optional superfoods.

3. Start blending on low speed, then gradually increase to high speed for 1–2 minutes until smooth and creamy. Adjust consistency with more liquid if needed.

4. Pour into glasses and enjoy while fresh.

---

05 Orange Creamsicle Protein Perfection

Total: 5 mins   **Servings:** 2   **Level:** 1/5

Nutritional Info *(Per Serving, based on almond milk and no optional additions)*: 240 kcal; 32g carbs; 15g protein; 6g fat; 5g fiber.

Ingredients

- **Liquid Base (Choose One):** 1 cup unsweetened almond milk, 1 cup unsweetened coconut milk, 1 cup low-fat dairy milk
- **Main Ingredients:** 1 cup fresh or frozen orange segments (peeled, seeds removed), 1/2 frozen banana, 1/2 cup Greek yogurt or plant-based yogurt, 1 scoop vanilla protein powder, 1/2 teaspoon vanilla extract, 1/2 teaspoon orange zest
- **Optional Sweetener:** 1 teaspoon raw honey or maple syrup
- **Optional Superfood Additions:** 1 tablespoon chia seeds, 1 teaspoon ground flaxseeds, 1 teaspoon MCT oil, 1/2 teaspoon turmeric powder

Optional Variations:
- **Diabetic-Friendly:** Replace banana with 1/4 avocado. Use unsweetened almond or coconut milk, and avoid additional sweeteners.
- **Vegan:** Use plant-based yogurt and a plant-based protein powder. Avoid honey.
- **Keto:** Replace banana with 1/4 avocado. Use unsweetened almond milk and avoid sweeteners.
- **Pregnancy-Safe:** Ensure all ingredients are fresh and thoroughly washed. Use pasteurized dairy milk.
- **Protein-Packed:** Add 1 tablespoon hemp seeds.

Serving Tip: Top with granola and a few slices of fresh orange for a crunchy texture boost. Pair with a handful of cashews and dried apricots for a nutrient-dense post-workout snack.

Instructions

1. Freeze the banana in advance for a creamier texture. Zest the orange before peeling.

2. Add ingredients to the blender. Pour the liquid base first, then add orange segments, frozen banana (or avocado), Greek yogurt, vanilla protein powder, vanilla extract, and orange zest. Sprinkle in any optional superfoods.

3. Start blending on low speed, then gradually increase to high speed for 1–2 minutes until smooth and creamy. Adjust consistency with more liquid if needed.

4. Pour into glasses and enjoy while fresh.

06 Chocolate Cherry Recovery Smoothie

Total: 5 mins   **Servings:** 2   **Level:** 1/5

Nutritional Info *(Per Serving, based on almond milk and no optional additions)*: 250 kcal; 35g carbs; 15g protein; 7g fat; 6g fiber.

Ingredients

- **Liquid Base (Choose One):** 1 cup unsweetened almond milk, 1 cup unsweetened oat milk, or 1 cup low-fat dairy milk
- **Main Ingredients:** 1 cup frozen dark cherries (pitted), 1/2 frozen banana, 1 scoop chocolate protein powder, 1 tablespoon cacao powder, 1/2 teaspoon vanilla extract, 1/2 teaspoon ground cinnamon
- **Optional Sweetener:** 1 teaspoon raw honey or maple syrup
- **Optional Superfood Additions:** 1 tablespoon chia seeds, 1 teaspoon ground flaxseeds, 1 teaspoon MCT oil, 1/2 teaspoon turmeric powder for anti-inflammatory benefits

Optional Variations:
- **Diabetic-Friendly:** Replace banana with 1/4 avocado. Use unsweetened almond or oat milk and avoid additional sweeteners.
- **Vegan:** Use plant-based protein powder and plant-based milk. Avoid honey.
- **Keto:** Replace banana with 1/4 avocado. Use unsweetened almond milk and avoid sweeteners.
- **Pregnancy-Safe:** Ensure all ingredients are fresh and thoroughly washed. Use pasteurized dairy milk.
- **Protein-Packed:** Add 1 tablespoon hemp seeds.

Serving Tip: Top with cacao nibs or crushed almonds for added crunch and texture. Pair with a handful of walnuts and dried tart cherries for an extra dose of healthy fats and antioxidants.

Instructions

1. Freeze the banana in advance for a creamier texture.

2. Add ingredients to the blender. Pour the liquid base first, then add cherries, frozen banana (or avocado), chocolate protein powder, cacao powder, vanilla extract, and cinnamon. Sprinkle in any optional superfoods.

3. Start blending on low speed, then gradually increase to high speed for 1-2 minutes until smooth and creamy. Adjust consistency with more liquid if needed.

4. Pour into glasses and enjoy while fresh.

---

07 Carrot Cake Muscle Fuel

Total: 5 mins   **Servings:** 2   **Level:** 1/5

Nutritional Info *(Per Serving, based on almond milk and no optional additions)*: 240 kcal; 32g carbs; 12g protein; 7g fat; 6g fiber.

Ingredients

- **Liquid Base (Choose One):** 1 cup unsweetened almond milk, 1 cup unsweetened oat milk, or 1 cup low-fat dairy milk
- **Main Ingredients:** 1/2 cup shredded carrots, 1/2 frozen banana, 1 scoop vanilla protein powder, 1/2 teaspoon cinnamon, 1/4 teaspoon ground nutmeg, 1/4 teaspoon ground ginger, 1 tablespoon chopped walnuts, 1/2 teaspoon vanilla extract
- **Optional Sweetener:** 1 teaspoon raw honey or maple syrup
- **Optional Superfood Additions:** 1 tablespoon chia seeds, 1 teaspoon ground flaxseeds, 1 teaspoon MCT oil, 1 tablespoon unsweetened shredded coconut

Optional Variations:
- **Diabetic-Friendly:** Replace banana with 1/4 avocado. Use unsweetened almond or oat milk and avoid additional sweeteners.
- **Vegan:** Use plant-based protein powder and plant-based milk. Avoid honey.
- **Keto:** Replace banana with 1/4 avocado. Use unsweetened almond milk and avoid sweeteners.
- **Pregnancy-Safe:** Ensure all ingredients are fresh and thoroughly washed. Use pasteurized dairy milk.
- **Protein-Packed:** Add 1 tablespoon hemp seeds.

Serving Tip: Top with crushed walnuts and a sprinkle of cinnamon for a crunchy texture and enhanced flavor. Pair with a warm bowl of spiced oatmeal topped with almonds and dried cranberries for a cozy, energy-packed breakfast.

Instructions

1. Shred fresh carrots or use pre-shredded ones.

2. Add ingredients to the blender. Pour the liquid base first, then add shredded carrots, frozen banana (or avocado), vanilla protein powder, cinnamon, nutmeg, ginger, walnuts, and vanilla extract. Sprinkle in any optional superfoods.

3. Start blending on low speed, then gradually increase to high speed for 1-2 minutes until smooth and creamy. Adjust consistency with more liquid if needed.

4. Pour into glasses and enjoy immediately.

08 Peanut Butter & Apple Pie Power

Total: 5 mins   **Servings:** 2   **Level:** 1/5

Nutritional Info *(Per Serving, based on almond milk and no optional additions)*: 250 kcal; 32g carbs; 14g protein; 9g fat; 6g fiber.

Ingredients

- **Liquid Base (Choose One):** 1 cup unsweetened almond milk, 1 cup unsweetened oat milk, or 1 cup low-fat dairy milk
- **Main Ingredients:** 1 small apple (cored and chopped), 1/2 frozen banana, 1 scoop vanilla protein powder, 1 tablespoon peanut butter (or almond butter), 1/2 teaspoon cinnamon, 1/4 teaspoon nutmeg, 1/2 teaspoon vanilla extract
- **Optional Sweetener:** 1 teaspoon honey or maple syrup
- **Optional Superfood Additions:** 1 tablespoon chia seeds, 1 teaspoon ground flaxseeds, 1 teaspoon MCT oil, 1 tablespoon rolled oats

Optional Variations:
- **Diabetic-Friendly:** Replace banana with 1/4 avocado. Use unsweetened almond or oat milk and avoid additional sweeteners.
- **Vegan:** Use plant-based protein powder and plant-based milk. Avoid honey.
- **Keto:** Replace banana with 1/4 avocado. Use unsweetened almond milk and avoid sweeteners.
- **Pregnancy-Safe:** Ensure all ingredients are fresh and thoroughly washed. Use pasteurized dairy milk.
- **Protein-Packed:** Add 1 tablespoon hemp seeds.

Serving Tip: Top with crushed walnuts and a sprinkle of cinnamon. Pair with Greek yogurt and a sprinkle of granola for a high-protein, satisfying breakfast.

Instructions

1. Core and chop the apple into small pieces.

2. Pour the liquid base first, then add the apple, frozen banana (or avocado), protein powder, peanut butter, cinnamon, nutmeg, and vanilla extract. Sprinkle in any optional superfoods.

3. Start blending on low speed, then gradually increase to high speed for 1–2 minutes until smooth and creamy. Adjust consistency with more liquid if needed.

4. Pour into glasses and enjoy immediately.

---

09 Powerhouse Blueberry Chia

Total: 5 mins   **Servings:** 2   **Level:** 1/5

Nutritional Info *(Per Serving, based on almond milk and no optional additions)*: 230 kcal; 28g carbs; 15g protein; 7g fat; 8g fiber.

Ingredients

- **Liquid Base (Choose One):** 1 cup unsweetened almond milk, 1 cup unsweetened oat milk, 1 cup low-fat dairy milk
- **Main Ingredients:** 1/2 cup fresh or frozen blueberries, 1/2 frozen banana, 1 scoop vanilla or unflavored protein powder, 1 tablespoon chia seeds, 1/2 teaspoon cinnamon, 1/2 teaspoon vanilla extract
- **Optional Sweetener:** 1 teaspoon honey or maple syrup
- **Optional Superfood Additions:** 1 tablespoon ground flaxseeds, 1 teaspoon MCT oil, 1 tablespoon almond butter, 1 tablespoon hemp seeds

Optional Variations:
- **Diabetic-Friendly:** Replace banana with 1/4 avocado. Use unsweetened almond or oat milk and avoid additional sweeteners.
- **Vegan:** Use plant-based protein powder and plant-based milk. Avoid honey.
- **Keto:** Replace banana with 1/4 avocado. Use unsweetened almond milk and avoid sweeteners.
- **Pregnancy-Safe:** Ensure all ingredients are fresh and thoroughly washed. Use pasteurized dairy milk.
- **Protein-Packed:** Add 1 tablespoon hemp seeds.

Serving Tip: Top with additional chia seeds and crushed walnuts for an extra fiber and omega-3 boost. Pair with a handful of raw almonds and dark chocolate pieces for a satisfying snack.

Instructions

1. Freeze the banana for a creamier texture.

2. Add ingredients to the blender. Pour the liquid base first, then add blueberries, frozen banana (or avocado), protein powder, chia seeds, cinnamon, and vanilla extract. Sprinkle in any optional superfoods.

3. Start blending on low speed, then gradually increase to high speed for 1–2 minutes until smooth and creamy. Adjust consistency with more liquid if needed.

4. Pour into glasses and enjoy immediately.

10 Chocolate Mint Muscle Blend

Total: 5 mins   **Servings:** 2   **Level:** 1/5

Nutritional Info *(Per Serving, based on almond milk and no optional additions)*: 250 kcal; 22g carbs; 18g protein; 9g fat; 6g fiber.

Ingredients

- **Liquid Base (Choose One):** 1 cup unsweetened almond milk, 1 cup unsweetened coconut milk, or 1 cup low-fat dairy milk
- **Main Ingredients:** 1/2 frozen banana, 1 scoop chocolate protein powder, 1 tablespoon unsweetened cocoa powder, 1/2 teaspoon peppermint extract, 1/2 teaspoon vanilla extract, 1/2 teaspoon cinnamon (optional)
- **Optional Sweetener:** 1 teaspoon honey or maple syrup
- **Optional Superfood Additions:** 1 tablespoon chia seeds or ground flaxseeds, 1 teaspoon MCT oil, 1 tablespoon almond butter, 1 teaspoon cacao nibs

Optional Variations:
- **Diabetic-Friendly:** Replace banana with 1/4 avocado. Use unsweetened almond or coconut milk and avoid sweeteners.
- **Vegan:** Use plant-based protein powder and plant-based milk. Avoid honey.
- **Keto:** Replace banana with 1/4 avocado. Use unsweetened almond milk and avoid sweeteners.
- **Pregnancy-Safe:** Ensure all ingredients are fresh and thoroughly washed. Use pasteurized dairy milk.
- **Protein-Packed:** Add 1 tablespoon hemp seeds.

Serving Tip: Top with extra cacao nibs or crushed peppermint leaves for a festive touch. Pair with a warm bowl of oatmeal topped with cacao nibs, crushed walnuts, and a drizzle of almond butter for a balanced breakfast.

Instructions

1. Freeze the banana for a creamier texture.

2. Add ingredients to the blender. Pour the liquid base first, then add frozen banana (or avocado), chocolate protein powder, cocoa powder, peppermint extract, and vanilla extract. Sprinkle in any optional superfoods.

3. Start blending on low speed, then gradually increase to high speed for 1–2 minutes until smooth and creamy. Adjust consistency with more liquid if needed.

4. Pour into glasses and enjoy immediately.

---

11 Almond Butter Date Power Surge

Total: 5 mins   **Servings:** 2   **Level:** 1/5

Nutritional Info *(Per Serving, based on almond milk and no optional additions)*: 280 kcal; 32g carbs; 14g protein; 11g fat; 6g fiber.

Ingredients

- **Liquid Base (Choose One):** 1 cup unsweetened almond milk, 1 cup oat milk, or 1 cup low-fat dairy milk
- **Main Ingredients:** 2 pitted Medjool dates, 1 scoop vanilla or unflavored protein powder, 1 tablespoon almond butter, 1/2 frozen banana, 1/2 teaspoon cinnamon, 1/2 teaspoon vanilla extract
- **Optional Sweetener:** 1 teaspoon honey or maple syrup
- **Optional Superfood Additions:** 1 tablespoon chia seeds or ground flaxseeds, 1 teaspoon MCT oil, 1 tablespoon cacao nibs, 1/2 teaspoon ground turmeric

Optional Variations:
- **Diabetic-Friendly:** Reduce dates to 1 or replace with 1/4 avocado. Use unsweetened almond or oat milk and avoid additional sweeteners.
- **Vegan:** Use plant-based protein powder and a dairy-free milk option. Avoid honey.
- **Keto:** Replace dates and banana with 1/4 avocado. Use unsweetened almond milk.
- **Pregnancy-Safe:** Ensure all ingredients are fresh and thoroughly washed. Use pasteurized dairy milk.
- **Protein-Packed:** Add 1 tablespoon hemp seeds.

Serving Tip: Top with cacao nibs or a sprinkle of cinnamon for extra texture and flavor. Pair with a handful of raw almonds and walnuts for sustained energy throughout the morning.

Instructions

1. Freeze the banana for a creamier texture. Soak the dates in warm water for 5 minutes if they are firm.

2. Add ingredients to the blender. Pour the liquid base first, then add dates, protein powder, almond butter, frozen banana (or avocado), cinnamon, and vanilla extract. Sprinkle in any optional superfoods.

3. Start blending on low speed, then gradually increase to high speed for 1–2 minutes until smooth and creamy. Adjust consistency with more liquid if needed.

4. Pour into glasses and enjoy immediately.

12 Banana Matcha Protein Boost

Total: 5 mins **Servings:** 2 **Level:** 1/5

Nutritional Info (*Per Serving, based on almond milk and no optional additions*): 230 kcal; 28g carbs; 12g protein; 7g fat; 5g fiber.

Ingredients

- **Liquid Base (Choose One):** 1 cup unsweetened almond milk, 1 cup oat milk, or 1 cup low-fat dairy milk
- **Main Ingredients:** 1 frozen banana, 1 scoop vanilla or unflavored protein powder, 1 teaspoon matcha green tea powder, 1/2 cup Greek yogurt (or plant-based alternative), 1/2 teaspoon vanilla extract
- **Optional Sweetener:** 1 teaspoon honey or maple syrup
- **Optional Superfood Additions:** 1 tablespoon chia seeds or ground flaxseeds, 1 teaspoon MCT oil, 1/2 teaspoon ground cinnamon

Optional Variations:
- **Diabetic-Friendly:** Replace banana with 1/4 avocado. Use unsweetened almond or oat milk, and avoid additional sweeteners.
- **Vegan:** Use plant-based yogurt and a plant-based protein powder. Avoid honey.
- **Keto:** Replace banana with 1/4 avocado. Use unsweetened almond milk and avoid sweeteners.
- **Pregnancy-Safe:** Ensure all ingredients are fresh and thoroughly washed. Use pasteurized dairy milk.
- **Protein-Packed:** Add 1 tablespoon hemp seeds.

Serving Tip: Top with shredded coconut or cacao nibs. Pair with a hard-boiled egg and a slice of whole-wheat toast for a well-rounded breakfast.

Instructions

1. Freeze the banana in advance for a creamier texture.

2. Add ingredients to the blender. Pour the liquid base first, then add frozen banana (or avocado), protein powder, matcha powder, Greek yogurt, and vanilla extract. Sprinkle in any optional superfoods.

3. Start blending on low speed, then gradually increase to high speed for 1–2 minutes until smooth and creamy. Adjust consistency with more liquid if needed.

4. Pour into glasses and enjoy immediately.

---

13 Sweet Potato Chai Smooth Strength

Total: 5 mins **Servings:** 2 **Level:** 1/5

Nutritional Info (*Per Serving, based on almond milk and no optional additions*): 250 kcal; 35g carbs; 15g protein; 7g fat; 6g fiber.

Ingredients

- **Liquid Base (Choose One):** 1 cup unsweetened almond milk, 1 cup oat milk, or 1 cup low-fat dairy milk
- **Main Ingredients:** 1/2 cup cooked and cooled sweet potato (mashed), 1 scoop vanilla or chai-flavored protein powder, 1/2 frozen banana, 1/2 teaspoon ground cinnamon, 1/4 teaspoon ground ginger, 1/4 teaspoon ground nutmeg, 1/4 teaspoon ground cardamom, 1/2 teaspoon vanilla extract
- **Optional Sweetener:** 1 teaspoon honey or maple syrup
- **Optional Superfood Additions:** 1 tablespoon chia seeds or ground flaxseeds, 1 teaspoon MCT oil, 1/2 teaspoon turmeric

Optional Variations:
- **Diabetic-Friendly:** Replace banana with 1/4 avocado. Use unsweetened almond or oat milk and avoid additional sweeteners.
- **Vegan:** Use plant-based yogurt and a plant-based protein powder. Avoid honey.
- **Keto:** Replace banana with 1/4 avocado. Use unsweetened almond milk and avoid sweeteners.
- **Pregnancy-Safe:** Ensure all ingredients are fresh and thoroughly washed. Use pasteurized dairy milk.
- **Protein-Packed:** Add 1 tablespoon hemp seeds.

Serving Tip: Top with shredded coconut or cacao nibs for added texture and a hint of crunch. Pair with a soft-boiled egg and a whole-wheat English muffin for a well-rounded meal.

Instructions

1. Cook and cool the sweet potato in advance. Freeze the banana for a creamier texture.

2. Add ingredients to the blender. Pour the liquid base first, then add sweet potato, frozen banana (or avocado), protein powder, spices, and vanilla extract. Sprinkle in any optional superfoods.

3. Start blending on low speed, then gradually increase to high speed for 1–2 minutes until smooth and creamy. Adjust consistency with more liquid if needed.

4. Pour into glasses and enjoy immediately.

14 Green Pea & Berry Endurance Smoothie

Total: 5 mins   **Servings:** 2   **Level:** 1/5

Nutritional Info *(Per Serving, based on almond milk and no optional additions)*: 210 kcal; 34g carbs; 14g protein; 5g fat; 7g fiber.

Ingredients

- **Liquid Base (Choose One):** 1 cup unsweetened almond milk, 1 cup oat milk, or 1 cup low-fat dairy milk
- **Main Ingredients:** 1/2 cup fresh or frozen green peas (steamed and cooled if fresh), 1/2 cup mixed berries (blueberries, raspberries, or strawberries), 1/2 frozen banana, 1 scoop vanilla or unflavored protein powder, 1/2 teaspoon vanilla extract, 1/4 teaspoon ground cinnamon
- **Optional Sweetener:** 1 teaspoon honey or maple syrup
- **Optional Superfood Additions:** 1 tablespoon chia seeds or ground flaxseeds, 1 teaspoon MCT oil, 1 teaspoon spirulina

Optional Variations:
- **Diabetic-Friendly:** Replace banana with 1/4 avocado. Use unsweetened almond or oat milk and avoid additional sweeteners.
- **Vegan:** Use plant-based yogurt and a plant-based protein powder. Avoid honey.
- **Keto:** Replace banana with 1/4 avocado. Use unsweetened almond milk and avoid sweeteners.
- **Pregnancy-Safe:** Ensure all ingredients are fresh and thoroughly washed. Use pasteurized dairy milk.
- **Protein-Packed:** Add 1 tablespoon hemp seeds.

Serving Tip: Top with granola and a drizzle of honey for a crunchy texture and natural sweetness.Pair with a slice of whole-grain toast spread with almond or peanut butter for a satisfying and protein-rich breakfast.

Instructions

1. If using fresh green peas, lightly steam and cool them before blending. Freeze the banana for a creamier texture.

2. Add ingredients to the blender. Pour the liquid base first, then add green peas, mixed berries, frozen banana (or avocado), protein powder, vanilla extract, and cinnamon. Sprinkle in any optional superfoods.

3. Start blending on low speed, then gradually increase to high speed for 1–2 minutes until smooth and creamy. Adjust consistency with more liquid if needed.

4. Pour into glasses and enjoy immediately.

---

15 Tropical Tofu Guava Performance Drink

Total: 5 mins   **Servings:** 2   **Level:** 1/5

Nutritional Info *(Per Serving, based on coconut milk and no optional additions)*: 250 kcal; 32g carbs; 15g protein; 8g fat; 6g fiber.

Ingredients

- **Liquid Base (Choose One):** 1 cup unsweetened coconut milk, 1 cup unsweetened almond milk, 1 cup low-fat dairy milk
- **Main Ingredients:** 1/2 cup fresh or frozen guava (seeds removed), 1/2 frozen banana, 1/2 cup silken tofu, 1 scoop vanilla protein powder, 1/2 teaspoon vanilla extract, 1/4 teaspoon ground nutmeg
- **Optional Sweetener:** 1 teaspoon honey or maple syrup
- **Optional Superfood Additions:** 1 tablespoon chia seeds or ground flaxseeds, 1 teaspoon MCT oil, 1 tablespoon hemp seeds for added protein, 1/2 teaspoon turmeric for an anti-inflammatory boost

Optional Variations:
- **Diabetic-Friendly:** Replace banana with 1/4 avocado. Use unsweetened almond or coconut milk and avoid additional sweeteners.
- **Vegan:** Use plant-based protein powder and avoid honey.
- **Keto:** Replace banana with 1/4 avocado. Use unsweetened almond milk and avoid sweeteners.
- **Pregnancy-Safe:** Ensure all ingredients are fresh and thoroughly washed. Use pasteurized coconut milk or dairy milk if applicable.
- **Protein-Packed:** Add 1 tablespoon hemp seeds.

Serving Tip: Top with granola and a drizzle of honey. Pair with a light tofu scramble and a few slices of avocado for a complete, plant-based protein meal.

Instructions

1. If using fresh guava, remove seeds and chop into smaller pieces. Freeze the banana for a creamier texture.

2. Add ingredients to the blender. Pour the liquid base first, then add guava, banana (or avocado), silken tofu, vanilla extract, protein powder, and nutmeg. Sprinkle in any optional superfoods.

3. Start blending on low speed, then gradually increase to high speed for 1–2 minutes until smooth and creamy. Adjust consistency with more liquid if needed.

4. Pour into glasses and enjoy immediately.

WHY THESE SMOOTHIES ARE EFFECTIVE

Protein is the cornerstone of muscle repair, sustained energy, and overall metabolic function. Whether you're looking to build lean muscle, recover from a workout, or simply stay fuller for longer, these protein-rich smoothies deliver the perfect balance of macronutrients and essential micronutrients. Each blend is carefully crafted to provide complete proteins, slow-digesting fiber, and healthy fats—ensuring that your body stays fueled, strong, and energized throughout the day.

Let's explore why each of these smoothies is a nutritional powerhouse:

1. Peach Coconut Protein Delight
This tropical blend is packed with Greek yogurt and protein powder, providing a hefty dose of muscle-repairing protein. Peaches add vitamin C for collagen synthesis, while shredded coconut delivers healthy fats for sustained energy. This smoothie is an ideal post-workout refreshment.

2. Kiwi Lime Fresh Kick
With a tangy citrus boost, this smoothie combines vitamin C-rich kiwis with Greek yogurt and protein powder for optimal muscle recovery. Chia seeds add a fiber boost, keeping digestion steady and energy levels stable. It's a zesty, immune-supporting protein fix.

3. Vanilla Cashew Protein Bliss
Soaked cashews provide plant-based protein and healthy fats, while Greek yogurt adds gut-friendly probiotics. Vanilla extract enhances flavor naturally, and protein powder ensures a strong muscle-building boost. This blend is a creamy, nutrient-dense indulgence.

4. Pear and Walnut Super Shake
Walnuts are an excellent source of Omega-3s, supporting brain function and reducing inflammation. Paired with ripe pear and protein powder, this smoothie offers the perfect mix of healthy fats, fiber, and protein—ideal for a long-lasting energy boost.

5. Orange Creamsicle Protein Perfection
Reminiscent of a classic creamsicle, this smoothie combines fresh oranges with protein powder and vanilla extract for a naturally sweet, recovery-friendly drink. It's rich in vitamin C, supporting collagen production and immune function.

6. Chocolate Cherry Recovery Smoothie
Dark cherries are packed with antioxidants that reduce post-workout muscle soreness. Combined with chocolate protein powder and cacao, this smoothie is a delicious and functional choice for muscle repair and recovery.

7. Carrot Cake Muscle Fuel
A blend of shredded carrots, cinnamon, and walnuts makes this smoothie taste like dessert while fueling muscle repair. Protein powder and Greek yogurt provide ample protein, while warming spices enhance digestion and reduce inflammation.

8. Peanut Butter and Apple Pie Power
Peanut butter adds plant-based protein and heart-healthy fats, while apple provides fiber for digestion. With cinnamon, nutmeg, and vanilla, this smoothie has all the flavors of apple pie in a high-protein package.

9. Powerhouse Blueberry Chia
Blueberries bring a rich dose of antioxidants, while chia seeds add fiber, Omega-3s, and plant-based

protein. The addition of protein powder makes this a well-rounded smoothie for muscle maintenance and sustained energy.

10. Chocolate Mint Muscle Blend
This refreshing smoothie blends chocolate protein powder with peppermint extract for a dessert-like recovery shake. Cacao powder offers natural mood-enhancing benefits, while plant-based fats and protein powder ensure a satiating and muscle-building drink.

11. Almond Butter Date Power Surge
Dates provide natural energy and potassium for muscle recovery, while almond butter delivers plant-based protein and healthy fats. Protein powder ensures a well-balanced macro profile for sustained strength and endurance.

12. Banana Matcha Protein Boost
Matcha is a natural source of L-theanine and caffeine, promoting focus and energy without the crash. Blended with protein powder, banana, and Greek yogurt, this smoothie is perfect for sustained mental and physical performance.

13. Sweet Potato Chai Smooth Strength
Sweet potatoes provide slow-releasing carbohydrates for steady energy, while chai spices add anti-inflammatory benefits. This smoothie is a warm, comforting blend that also delivers a protein-packed boost.

14. Green Pea and Berry Endurance Smoothie
Green peas are an unexpected but excellent source of plant-based protein, combined with antioxidant-rich berries for a naturally sweet and protein-packed smoothie. This blend is ideal for endurance training and sustained energy.

15. Tropical Tofu Guava Performance Drink
Silken tofu provides a complete protein source, while guava adds immune-boosting vitamin C. This smoothie is ideal for those looking for a plant-based, high-protein drink that supports muscle recovery and overall health.

The Science Behind the Benefits
These smoothies work because they provide:
- **Complete Proteins:** Ingredients like Greek yogurt, tofu, nuts, and protein powder deliver essential amino acids needed for muscle repair and growth.
- **Slow-Digesting Carbohydrates:** Sweet potatoes, bananas, and oats provide lasting energy without blood sugar spikes.
- **Healthy Fats:** Nuts, seeds, and coconut enhance nutrient absorption and keep you feeling full longer.
- **Anti-Inflammatory Ingredients:** Turmeric, ginger, cinnamon, and matcha reduce oxidative stress and aid post-workout recovery.

A Delicious Way to Stay Strong and Energized
With these protein-rich smoothies, you can fuel your workouts, recover faster, and keep your metabolism running efficiently. Whether you're an athlete, a busy professional, or just someone who wants to stay full and energized, these blends are a simple and delicious way to meet your daily protein needs.

WEIGHT MANAGEMENT
SMOOTHIES

---

01 Guava Mint Weight Loss Elixir

Total: 5 mins **Servings:** 2 **Level:** 1/5

Nutritional Info *(Per Serving, based on almond milk and no optional additions)*: 170 kcal; 28g carbs; 6g protein; 4g fat; 7g fiber.

Ingredients

- **Liquid Base (Choose One):** 1 cup unsweetened almond milk, 1 cup coconut water, or 1 cup plain water
- **Main Ingredients:** 1 cup ripe guava (seeds removed, chopped), 1/2 cup cucumber (chopped), 1/2 frozen banana, 5 fresh mint leaves, 1/2 teaspoon lime juice, 1/2 teaspoon grated fresh ginger
- **Optional Sweetener:** 1 teaspoon raw honey or maple syrup
- **Optional Superfood Additions:** 1 tablespoon chia seeds, 1 teaspoon flaxseeds, 1/2 teaspoon spirulina powder

Optional Variations:
- **Diabetic-Friendly:** Replace banana with 1/4 avocado. Use unsweetened almond milk and avoid additional sweeteners.
- **Vegan:** Avoid honey and opt for maple syrup.
- **Keto:** Replace banana with 1/4 avocado. Use unsweetened almond milk and add 1 teaspoon of MCT oil.
- **Pregnancy-Safe:** Ensure all ingredients are fresh and thoroughly washed. Avoid unpasteurized coconut water.
- **Protein-Packed:** Add 1 scoop of unflavored protein powder or 1 tablespoon hemp seeds.

Serving Tip: Garnish with a sprig of fresh mint or a few chia seeds for extra fiber. Pair with a slice of whole-grain toast topped with mashed avocado and a pinch of sea salt for a metabolism-boosting breakfast.

Instructions

1. Freeze the banana beforehand for a creamier texture.

2. Add ingredients to the blender. Pour the liquid base first, followed by guava, cucumber, frozen banana (or avocado), mint leaves, lime juice, and ginger. Sprinkle in any optional superfoods.

3. Blend on low speed, then gradually increase to high for 1–2 minutes until the smoothie is creamy and smooth. Adjust consistency with more liquid if needed.

4. Pour into glasses and enjoy immediately.

02 Fat-Burning Apple Broccoli Shake

Total: 5 mins   **Servings:** 2   **Level:** 1/5

Nutritional Info (Per Serving, based on kombucha and no optional additions): 140 kcal; 26g carbs; 5g protein; 2g fat; 6g fiber.

Ingredients

- **Liquid Base (Choose One):** 1 cup plain or ginger-flavored kombucha, 1 cup unsweetened almond milk, or 1 cup coconut water
- **Main Ingredients:** 1/2 cup fresh or frozen broccoli florets, 1 small green apple (cored and chopped), 1/2 frozen banana, 1/2 teaspoon ground cinnamon, 1/4 teaspoon ground turmeric, 1/2 teaspoon grated fresh ginger, 1 teaspoon lemon juice
- **Optional Sweetener:** 1 teaspoon raw honey or maple syrup
- **Optional Superfood Additions:** 1 tablespoon chia seeds, 1 teaspoon flaxseeds, 1/2 teaspoon spirulina powder, 1 teaspoon MCT oil

Optional Variations:
- **Diabetic-Friendly:** Replace banana with 1/4 avocado. Use unsweetened almond milk instead of kombucha, and avoid additional sweeteners.
- **Vegan:** Avoid honey and opt for maple syrup.
- **Keto:** Replace banana with 1/4 avocado. Use unsweetened almond milk. Avoid additional sweeteners.
- **Pregnancy-Safe:** Avoid unpasteurized kombucha.
- **Protein-Packed:** Add 1 scoop of unflavored protein powder or 1 tablespoon hemp seeds.

Serving Tip: Garnish with a sprinkle of cinnamon or a few chia seeds. Pair with a slice of whole-grain toast topped with hummus and arugula for a nutrient-dense, weight-friendly meal.

Instructions

1. Freeze the banana beforehand for a creamier texture.

2. Add ingredients to the blender. Pour the liquid base first, followed by broccoli, apple, frozen banana (or avocado), cinnamon, turmeric, ginger, and lemon juice. Sprinkle in any optional superfoods.

3. Blend on low speed, then gradually increase to high for 1–2 minutes until the smoothie is creamy and smooth. Adjust consistency with more liquid if needed.

4. Pour into glasses and enjoy immediately.

---

03 Tropical Metabolism Booster

Total: 5 mins   **Servings:** 2   **Level:** 1/5

Nutritional Info (Per Serving, based on coconut water and no optional additions): 250 kcal; 32g carbs; 15g protein; 8g fat; 6g fiber.

Ingredients

- **Liquid Base (Choose One):** 1 cup coconut water, 1 cup unsweetened almond milk, or 1 cup filtered water
- **Main Ingredients:** 1 cup fresh or frozen pineapple chunks, 1/2 cup fresh orange juice, 1/2 cup celery (chopped), 1/2 green apple (cored and chopped), 1/2 teaspoon fresh grated ginger
- **Optional Sweetener:** 1 teaspoon raw honey or maple syrup
- **Optional Superfood Additions:** 1 tablespoon chia seeds, 1/2 teaspoon spirulina powder, 1 teaspoon MCT oil

Optional Variations:
- **Diabetic-Friendly:** Replace orange juice with 1/4 avocado for lower sugar. Use unsweetened coconut water and avoid additional sweeteners.
- **Vegan:** Avoid honey and opt for maple syrup if sweetness is needed.
- **Keto:** Remove pineapple and replace with 1/4 avocado. Use unsweetened almond milk and avoid additional sweeteners.
- **Pregnancy-Safe:** Ensure all ingredients are fresh and thoroughly washed. Avoid unpasteurized orange juice.
- **Protein-Packed:** Add 1 scoop of unflavored protein powder or 1 tablespoon hemp seeds.

Serving Tip: For a refreshing touch, garnish with a slice of pineapple or a sprig of fresh mint. For a metabolism-boosting meal, serve with a handful of raw almonds or protein-rich chia pudding.

Instructions

1. Chop the celery and green apple. If using fresh pineapple, cut it into chunks.

2. Add ingredients to the blender. Pour the liquid base first, then add pineapple, orange juice, celery, green apple, and ginger. Sprinkle in any optional superfoods.

3. Start blending on low speed, gradually increasing to high for 1–2 minutes until smooth and creamy. Adjust consistency with more liquid if needed.

5. Pour into glasses and enjoy fresh.

04 Flat Belly Purple Blend

Total: 5 mins   **Servings:** 2   **Level:** 1/5

Nutritional Info *(Per Serving, based on almond milk and no optional additions)*: 130 kcal; 28g carbs; 3g protein; 2g fat; 6g fiber.

Ingredients

- **Liquid Base (Choose One):** 1 cup unsweetened almond milk, 1 cup coconut water, or 1 cup filtered water
- **Main Ingredients:** 1 cup purple cabbage (chopped), 1/2 cup frozen blueberries, 1/2 cup cucumber (chopped), 1/2 teaspoon fresh grated ginger, 1/4 teaspoon ground cinnamon
- **Optional Sweetener:** 1 teaspoon raw honey or maple syrup
- **Optional Superfood Additions:** 1 tablespoon chia seeds,1/2 teaspoon spirulina powder, 1 teaspoon MCT oil

Optional Variations:
- **Diabetic-Friendly:** Replace blueberries with 1/4 avocado. Use unsweetened almond milk and avoid additional sweeteners.
- **Vegan:** Avoid honey and opt for maple syrup if sweetness is needed.
- **Keto:** Replace blueberries with 1/4 avocado. Use unsweetened almond milk and avoid additional sweeteners.
- **Pregnancy-Safe:** Ensure all ingredients are fresh and thoroughly washed. Avoid unpasteurized coconut water.
- **Protein-Packed:** Add 1 scoop of unflavored protein powder or 1 tablespoon hemp seeds.

Serving Tip: Garnish with a sprinkle of cinnamon or a few whole blueberries for a refreshing touch. Pair with a handful of raw almonds or a protein-packed chia pudding for a balanced, metabolism-boosting meal.

Instructions

1. Chop the purple cabbage and cucumber. If using fresh blueberries, freeze them in advance for a thicker texture.

2. Add ingredients to the blender. Pour the liquid base first, then add purple cabbage, blueberries, cucumber, ginger, and cinnamon. Sprinkle in any optional superfoods.

3. Start blending on low speed, gradually increasing to high for 1–2 minutes until smooth and creamy. Adjust consistency with more liquid if needed.

4. Pour into glasses and enjoy fresh.

---

05 Watermelon Strawberry Cream

Total: 5 mins   **Servings:** 2   **Level:** 1/5

Nutritional Info *(Per Serving, based on almond milk and no optional additions)*: 150 kcal; 30g carbs; 4g protein; 3g fat; 5g fiber.

Ingredients

- **Liquid Base (Choose One):** 1 cup unsweetened almond milk, 1 cup oat milk, or 1 cup low-fat dairy milk
- **Main Ingredients:** 1/2 cup cooked and cooled sweet potato (mashed), 1 scoop vanilla or chai-flavored protein powder, 1/2 frozen banana, 1/2 teaspoon ground cinnamon, 1/4 teaspoon ground ginger, 1/4 teaspoon ground nutmeg, 1/4 teaspoon ground cardamom, 1/2 teaspoon vanilla extract
- **Optional Sweetener:** 1 teaspoon honey or maple syrup
- **Optional Superfood Additions:** 1 tablespoon chia seeds or ground flaxseeds, 1 teaspoon MCT oil, 1/2 teaspoon turmeric

Optional Variations:
- **Diabetic-Friendly:** Replace banana with 1/4 avocado. Use unsweetened almond milk and avoid additional sweeteners.
- **Vegan:** Avoid honey and opt for maple syrup if sweetness is needed.
- **Keto:** Replace watermelon with 1/4 avocado. Use unsweetened almond milk and avoid additional sweeteners.
- **Pregnancy-Safe:** Ensure all ingredients are fresh and thoroughly washed. Avoid unpasteurized coconut water.
- **Protein-Packed:** Add 1 scoop of unflavored protein powder or 1 tablespoon of hemp seeds.

Serving Tip: Garnish with a slice of lime or a few fresh strawberry slices. Serve alongside a whole-grain rice cake with almond butter and a sprinkle of cinnamon for a balanced, weight-friendly snack.

Instructions

1. Cube the watermelon and remove the seeds. If using fresh strawberries, hull them. Freeze the banana beforehand for a creamier texture.

2. Add ingredients to the blender. Pour the liquid base first, then add watermelon, strawberries, frozen banana (or avocado), lime zest, and lime juice. Sprinkle in any optional superfoods.

3. Start blending on low speed, gradually increasing to high for 1–2 minutes until smooth and creamy. Adjust consistency with more liquid if needed.

4. Pour into glasses and enjoy fresh.

06 Passion Spinach Slimmer

Total: 5 mins   **Servings:** 2   **Level:** 1/5

Nutritional Info *(Per Serving, based on kombucha and no optional additions)*: 150 kcal; 30g carbs; 4g protein; 2g fat; 6g fiber.

Ingredients

- **Liquid Base (Choose One):** 1 cup coconut water, 1 cup unsweetened almond milk, or 1 cup plain water
- **Main Ingredients:** 1 cup passion fruit pulp (seeds removed), 1 cup fresh spinach (packed), 1/2 green apple (cored and chopped), 1/2 frozen banana
- **Optional Sweetener:** 1 teaspoon raw honey or maple syrup
- **Optional Superfood Additions:** 1 tablespoon chia seeds, 1 teaspoon flaxseeds, 1 teaspoon MCT oil

Optional Variations:
- **Diabetic-Friendly:** Replace banana with 1/4 avocado. Use unsweetened coconut water and avoid additional sweeteners.
- **Vegan:** Avoid honey and opt for maple syrup if sweetness is needed.
- **Keto:** Replace banana with 1/4 avocado. Use unsweetened almond milk and avoid additional sweeteners.
- **Pregnancy-Safe:** Ensure all ingredients are fresh and thoroughly washed. Avoid unpasteurized passion fruit juice.
- **Protein-Packed:** Add 1 scoop of unflavored protein powder or 1 tablespoon of hemp seeds.

Serving Tip: Garnish with a slice of lime or a few passion fruit seeds for an extra refreshing touch. Pair with a handful of raw almonds or a protein-packed chia pudding for a metabolism-boosting meal.

Instructions

1. Scoop out passion fruit pulp and remove seeds. Core and chop the green apple. Freeze the banana beforehand for a creamier texture.

2. Add ingredients to the blender. Pour the liquid base first, then add passion fruit pulp, spinach, green apple, and frozen banana (or avocado). Sprinkle in any optional superfoods.

3. Start blending on low speed, gradually increasing to high for 1–2 minutes until smooth and creamy. Adjust consistency with more liquid if needed.

4. Pour into glasses and enjoy fresh.

---

07 Parsley Ginger Zing

Total: 5 mins   **Servings:** 2   **Level:** 1/5

Nutritional Info *(Per Serving, based on kombucha and no optional additions)*: 90 kcal; 20g carbs; 2g protein; 1g fat; 4g fiber.

Ingredients

- **Liquid Base (Choose One):** 1 cup ginger or plain kombucha, 1 cup coconut water, or 1 cup filtered water
- **Main Ingredients:** 1/2 cup fresh parsley (packed), 1/2 green apple (cored and chopped), 1/2 cup cucumber (chopped), 1/2 teaspoon fresh grated ginger, 1/2 frozen banana
- **Optional Sweetener:** 1 teaspoon raw honey or maple syrup
- **Optional Superfood Additions:** 1 tablespoon chia seeds, 1 teaspoon flaxseeds, 1 teaspoon MCT oil

Optional Variations:
- **Diabetic-Friendly:** Replace banana with 1/4 avocado for lower sugar. Use unsweetened coconut water and avoid additional sweeteners.
- **Vegan:** Avoid honey and opt for maple syrup if sweetness is needed.
- **Keto:** Replace banana with 1/4 avocado. Use unsweetened almond milk and avoid additional sweeteners.
- **Pregnancy-Safe:** Ensure all ingredients are fresh and thoroughly washed. Avoid unpasteurized kombucha.
- **Protein-Packed:** Add 1 scoop of unflavored protein powder or 1 tablespoon of hemp seeds for an additional boost.

Serving Tip: Garnish with a few parsley leaves or a slice of green apple for a vibrant touch. Pair with a handful of raw almonds or a flaxseed cracker for a digestion-friendly snack.

Instructions

1. Core and chop the green apple, chop the cucumber, and freeze the banana beforehand for a creamier texture.

2. Add ingredients to the blender. Pour the liquid base first, then add parsley, green apple, cucumber, grated ginger, and frozen banana (or avocado). Sprinkle in any optional superfoods.

3. Start blending on low speed, gradually increasing to high for 1–2 minutes until smooth and creamy. Adjust consistency with more liquid if needed.

4. Pour into glasses and enjoy fresh.

08 Spirulina Light & Fit

Total: 5 mins **Servings:** 2 **Level:** 1/5

Nutritional Info *(Per Serving, based on almond milk and no optional additions):* 160 kcal; 18g carbs; 12g protein; 5g fat; 6g fiber.

Ingredients

- **Liquid Base (Choose One):** 1 cup unsweetened almond milk, 1 cup coconut water, or 1 cup plain water
- **Main Ingredients:** 1 teaspoon spirulina powder, 1 tablespoon chia seeds, 1 scoop vanilla protein powder (plant-based or whey), 1/2 cup frozen blueberries
- **Optional Sweetener:** 1 teaspoon raw honey or maple syrup
- **Optional Superfood Additions:** 1 tablespoon ground flaxseeds, 1 teaspoon MCT oil, 1/2 teaspoon cinnamon

Optional Variations:
- **Diabetic-Friendly:** Reduce blueberries to 1/4 cup and replace with 1/4 avocado for lower sugar. Use unsweetened almond milk and avoid additional sweeteners.
- **Vegan:** Ensure you use a plant-based protein powder and avoid honey.
- **Keto:** Reduce blueberries to 1/4 cup. Avoid additional sweeteners.
- **Pregnancy-Safe:** Ensure all ingredients are fresh and thoroughly washed. Avoid unpasteurized almond milk.
- **Protein-Packed:** Add 1 tablespoon of hemp seeds.

Serving Tip: Garnish with a sprinkle of chia seeds or hemp seeds for added texture and fiber. Serve alongside a slice of whole-grain toast with mashed avocado for a metabolism-boosting breakfast.

Instructions

1. Freeze blueberries in advance for a thicker texture.

2. Add ingredients to the blender. Pour the liquid base first, followed by spirulina, chia seeds, protein powder, and frozen blueberries. Sprinkle in any optional superfoods.

3. Start blending on low speed, gradually increasing to high for 1–2 minutes until smooth and creamy. Adjust consistency with more liquid if needed.

4. Pour into glasses and enjoy fresh.

---

09 Acai Weight Loss Drink

Total: 5 mins **Servings:** 2 **Level:** 1/5

Nutritional Info *(Per Serving, based on kombucha and no optional additions):* 160 kcal; 34g carbs; 4g protein; 2g fat; 6g fiber.

Ingredients

- **Liquid Base (Choose One):** 1 cup kombucha (plain, lemon, or ginger-flavored), 1 cup coconut water, 1 cup unsweetened almond milk
- **Main Ingredients:** 1/2 cup frozen acai purée or 1 tablespoon acai powder, 1/2 frozen banana, 1/2 cup fresh or frozen blueberries, 1/2 teaspoon fresh grated ginger, 1/2 teaspoon fresh lime zest, 1 teaspoon lemon juice
- **Optional Sweetener:** 1 teaspoon raw honey or maple syrup
- **Optional Superfood Additions:** 1 tablespoon chia seeds, 1 teaspoon ground flaxseeds, 1/2 teaspoon spirulina powder, 1 teaspoon MCT oil

Optional Variations:
- **Diabetic-Friendly:** Replace banana with 1/4 avocado. Use unsweetened almond milk and avoid additional sweeteners.
- **Vegan:** Avoid honey and opt for maple syrup.
- **Keto:** Replace banana with 1/4 avocado. Use unsweetened almond milk and avoid additional sweeteners.
- **Pregnancy-Safe:** Ensure all ingredients are fresh and thoroughly washed. Avoid unpasteurized kombucha.
- **Protein-Packed:** Add 1 scoop of unflavored protein powder or 1 tablespoon hemp seeds.

Serving Tip: Garnish with a few fresh blueberries or a sprinkle of chia seeds for added texture. Pair with a handful of raw almonds or a whole-grain cracker for a satisfying, metabolism-boosting snack.

Instructions

1. Freeze the banana in advance for a creamier texture.

2. Add ingredients to the blender. Pour the liquid base first. Add acai, frozen banana (or avocado), blueberries, ginger, lime zest, and lemon juice. Sprinkle in any optional superfoods.

3. Blend on low speed, gradually increasing to high for 1–2 minutes until smooth and creamy. Adjust consistency with more liquid if needed.

4. Pour into glasses and enjoy immediately.

10 Spiced Kale and Pear Mix

Total: 5 mins   **Servings:** 2   **Level:** 1/5

Nutritional Info (Per Serving, based on almond milk and no optional additions): 160 kcal; 32g carbs; 5g protein; 3g fat; 8g fiber.

Ingredients

- **Liquid Base (Choose One):** 1 cup unsweetened almond milk, 1 cup coconut water, or 1 cup plain water
- **Main Ingredients:** 1 cup fresh kale (stems removed, chopped), 1 ripe pear (cored and chopped), 1/2 frozen banana, 1/2 teaspoon ground cinnamon, 1/4 teaspoon ground nutmeg, 1/2 teaspoon grated fresh ginger
- **Optional Sweetener:** 1 teaspoon raw honey or maple syrup
- **Optional Superfood Additions:** 1 tablespoon chia seeds, 1 teaspoon ground flaxseeds, 1 teaspoon MCT oil

Optional Variations:
- **Diabetic-Friendly:** Replace banana with 1/4 avocado for lower sugar. Use unsweetened almond milk and avoid sweeteners.
- **Vegan:** Avoid honey and opt for maple syrup.
- **Keto:** Replace pear and banana with 1/4 avocado. Avoid additional sweeteners.
- **Pregnancy-Safe:** Ensure all ingredients are fresh and thoroughly washed. Use pasteurized almond milk if opting for a plant-based liquid.
- **Protein-Packed:** Add 1 scoop of unflavored protein powder or 1 tablespoon of hemp seeds.

Serving Tip: Garnish with a sprinkle of cinnamon or a few chia seeds for extra fiber. Pair with a handful of walnuts for healthy fats or a slice of whole-grain toast topped with almond butter for a filling, metabolism-boosting breakfast.

Instructions

1. Remove stems from kale, core and chop the pear, and freeze the banana in advance for a creamier texture.

2. Add ingredients to the blender. Pour the liquid base first, then add kale, pear, frozen banana (or avocado), cinnamon, nutmeg, and ginger. Sprinkle in any optional superfoods.

3. Start blending on low speed, then gradually increase to high for 1–2 minutes until the smoothie is creamy and smooth. Adjust consistency with more liquid if needed.

4. Pour into glasses and enjoy immediately.

---

11 Goji Spinach Fit Fuel

Total: 5 mins   **Servings:** 2   **Level:** 1/5

Nutritional Info (Per Serving, based on almond milk and no optional additions): 180 kcal; 30g carbs; 5g protein; 3g fat; 6g fiber.

Ingredients

- **Liquid Base (Choose One):** 1 cup unsweetened almond milk, 1 cup coconut water, or 1 cup plain water
- **Main Ingredients:** 1/4 cup goji berries (soaked in warm water for 10 minutes, then drained), 1 cup fresh spinach (packed), 1/2 green apple (cored and chopped), 1/2 teaspoon grated fresh ginger
- **Optional Sweetener:** 1 teaspoon raw honey or maple syrup
- **Optional Superfood Additions:** 1 tablespoon chia seeds, 1 teaspoon ground flaxseeds, 1/2 teaspoon spirulina powder, 1 teaspoon MCT oil

Optional Variations:
- **Diabetic-Friendly:** Replace apple with 1/4 avocado. Use unsweetened almond milk and avoid additional sweeteners.
- **Vegan:** Avoid honey and opt for maple syrup.
- **Keto:** Replace apple with 1/4 avocado. Use unsweetened almond milk and avoid additional sweeteners.
- **Pregnancy-Safe:** Ensure all ingredients are fresh and thoroughly washed. Avoid unpasteurized coconut water.
- **Protein-Packed:** Add 1 scoop of unflavored protein powder or 1 tablespoon hemp seeds.

Serving Tip: Garnish with a few whole goji berries or a sprinkle of chia seeds for extra fiber. Pair with a handful of raw almonds or a slice of whole-grain toast with almond butter for a metabolism-boosting, energy-sustaining meal.

Instructions

1. Soak the goji berries in warm water for 10 minutes, then drain.

2. Add ingredients to the blender. Pour the liquid base first, followed by goji berries, spinach, green apple, and ginger. Sprinkle in any optional superfoods.

3. Start blending on low speed, then gradually increase to high for 1–2 minutes until smooth. Adjust consistency with more liquid if needed.

4. Pour into glasses and enjoy immediately.

12 Chocolate Chickpea Weight Cut

Total: 5 mins **Servings:** 2 **Level:** 1/5

Nutritional Info (*Per Serving, based on almond milk and no optional additions*): 210 kcal; 32g carbs; 9g protein; 5g fat; 7g fiber.

Ingredients

- **Liquid Base (Choose One):** 1 cup unsweetened almond milk, 1 cup coconut water, or 1 cup low-fat dairy milk
- **Main Ingredients:** 1/2 cup cooked and drained chickpeas, 1 frozen banana, 1 tablespoon unsweetened cocoa powder, 1/2 teaspoon ground cinnamon
- **Optional Sweetener:** 1 teaspoon raw honey or maple syrup
- **Optional Superfood Additions:** 1 tablespoon chia seeds, 1 teaspoon MCT oil, 1 scoop unflavored or chocolate protein powder, 1 teaspoon ground flaxseeds

Optional Variations:
- **Diabetic-Friendly:** Replace banana with 1/4 avocado. Use unsweetened almond milk and avoid sweeteners.
- **Vegan:** Use plant-based milk and avoid honey; opt for maple syrup. Choose plant-based protein powder.
- **Keto:** Replace banana with 1/4 avocado. Use unsweetened almond milk and avoid sweeteners.
- **Pregnancy-Safe:** Ensure all ingredients are fresh and thoroughly washed. Use pasteurized dairy if using milk.

Serving Tip: Garnish with a sprinkle of cacao nibs or a dusting of cinnamon for extra flavor. Pair with a handful of walnuts or a slice of whole-grain toast with almond butter for a balanced, metabolism-boosting breakfast.

Instructions

1. Prepare the chickpeas. If using canned, rinse and drain thoroughly.

2. Add ingredients to the blender. Pour the liquid base first, followed by chickpeas, banana (or avocado), cocoa powder, cinnamon, and any optional superfoods.

3. Start blending on low speed, gradually increasing to high for 1–2 minutes until creamy. Adjust consistency with more liquid if needed.

4. Serve immediately.

---

13 Metabo Chai Cauliflower

Total: 5 mins **Servings:** 2 **Level:** 1/5

Nutritional Info (*Per Serving, based on kombucha and no optional additions*): 180 kcal; 24g carbs; 7g protein; 6g fat; 6g fiber.

Ingredients

- **Liquid Base (Choose One):** 1 cup unsweetened almond milk, 1 cup unsweetened coconut milk, or 1 cup low-fat dairy milk
- **Main Ingredients:** 1/2 cup frozen cauliflower florets, 1/2 frozen banana, 1/2 teaspoon ground cinnamon, 1/4 teaspoon ground ginger, 1/4 teaspoon ground nutmeg, 1/8 teaspoon ground cardamom
- **Optional Sweetener:** 1 teaspoon raw honey or maple syrup
- **Optional Superfood Additions:** 1 tablespoon chia seeds, 1 teaspoon flaxseeds, 1/2 teaspoon MCT oil, 1 scoop unflavored or vanilla protein powder

Optional Variations:
- **Diabetic-Friendly:** Replace banana with 1/4 avocado. Use unsweetened almond milk and avoid sweeteners.
- **Vegan:** Use plant-based milk and avoid honey; opt for maple syrup. Choose plant-based protein powder.
- **Keto:** Replace banana with 1/4 avocado. Use unsweetened almond milk and avoid sweeteners.
- **Pregnancy-Safe:** Ensure all ingredients are fresh and thoroughly washed. Use pasteurized dairy if using milk.
- **Protein-Packed:** Add 1 scoop of plant-based or whey protein powder.

Serving Tip: Garnish with a sprinkle of cinnamon or a few crushed walnuts for added texture. Pair with a small bowl of Greek yogurt topped with chia seeds for an extra metabolism-boosting breakfast.

Instructions

1. Prepare the cauliflower. If using fresh, blanch and freeze in advance for a smoother texture.

2. Add ingredients to the blender. Pour the liquid base first, followed by cauliflower, banana (or avocado), spices, and any optional superfoods.

3. Start blending on low speed, gradually increasing to high for 1–2 minutes until creamy. Adjust consistency with more liquid if needed.

4. Serve immediately.

14 Mushroom and Carrot Slimmer

Total: 5 mins **Servings:** 2 **Level:** 1/5

Nutritional Info (Per Serving, based on almond milk and no optional additions): 160 kcal; 22g carbs; 7g protein; 4g fat; 5g fiber.

Ingredients

- **Liquid Base (Choose One):** 1 cup unsweetened almond milk, 1 cup coconut water, or 1 cup plain water
- **Main Ingredients:** 1/2 cup cooked and cooled mushrooms (shiitake, reishi, or cremini for best results), 1/2 cup fresh or frozen carrots (chopped), 1/2 frozen banana (for creaminess, optional), 1 teaspoon fresh grated ginger, 1/2 teaspoon cinnamon
- **Optional Superfood Additions:** 1 tablespoon chia seeds, 1 teaspoon ground flaxseeds, 1 scoop plant-based or whey protein powder, 1 teaspoon MCT oil, 1/2 teaspoon turmeric powder

Optional Variations:
- **Diabetic-Friendly:** Replace banana with 1/4 avocado. Use unsweetened almond milk.
- **Vegan:** Use plant-based milk and plant-based protein powder if adding protein.
- **Keto:** Replace banana with 1/4 avocado. Use unsweetened almond milk.
- **Pregnancy-Safe:** Use pasteurized plant-based milk or dairy if preferred.
- **Protein-Packed:** Add 1 tablespoon hemp seeds.

Serving Tip: Garnish with a sprinkle of ground cinnamon or a few chia seeds. Pair with a handful of walnuts or a slice of whole-grain toast topped with nut butter for a balanced, weight-friendly breakfast.

Instructions

1. Cook and cool the mushrooms beforehand for better digestion and smoother texture.

2. Chop the carrots into small pieces for easier blending.

3. Add ingredients to the blender. Pour the liquid base first, followed by cooked mushrooms, chopped carrots, frozen banana (or avocado), ginger, and cinnamon. Sprinkle in any optional superfoods.

4. Start blending on low speed, then gradually increase to high for 1–2 minutes until smooth. Adjust consistency with more liquid if needed.

5. Pour into glasses and enjoy immediately.

---

15 SlimBerry Blend

Total: 5 mins **Servings:** 2 **Level:** 1/5

Nutritional Info (Per Serving, based on almond milk and no optional additions): 150 kcal; 28g carbs; 5g protein; 3g fat; 7g fiber.

Ingredients

- **Liquid Base (Choose One):** 1 cup unsweetened almond milk, 1 cup coconut water, or 1 cup plain water
- **Main Ingredients:** 1/2 cup fresh or frozen cranberries, 1/2 cup pomegranate seeds, 1/2 frozen banana, 1 teaspoon lemon juice, 1/2 teaspoon grated fresh ginger
- **Optional Superfood Additions:** 1 tablespoon chia seeds, 1 teaspoon flaxseeds, 1 scoop plant-based or whey protein powder, 1 teaspoon MCT oil, 1/2 teaspoon turmeric powder

Optional Variations:
- **Diabetic-Friendly:** Replace banana with 1/4 avocado. Use unsweetened almond milk.
- **Vegan:** Use plant-based milk and plant-based protein powder if adding protein.
- **Keto:** Replace banana with 1/4 avocado. Use unsweetened almond milk.
- **Pregnancy-Safe:** Ensure all ingredients are fresh and thoroughly washed. Use pasteurized plant-based milk or dairy if preferred.
- **Protein-Packed:** Add 1 tablespoon hemp seeds.

Serving Tip: Garnish with a sprinkle of chia seeds or a few extra pomegranate seeds. Pair with a handful of raw almonds or a small bowl of Greek yogurt with cinnamon for a metabolism-boosting breakfast.

Instructions

1. Freeze the banana beforehand for a creamier texture.

2. Add ingredients to the blender. Pour the liquid base first, followed by cranberries, pomegranate seeds, frozen banana (or avocado), lemon juice, and ginger. Sprinkle in any optional superfoods.

3. Start blending on low speed, then gradually increase to high for 1–2 minutes until smooth. Adjust consistency with more liquid if needed.

4. Pour into glasses and enjoy immediately.

WHY THESE SMOOTHIES ARE EFFECTIVE

Each smoothie in this collection has been carefully crafted to help support sustainable weight management, enhance metabolism, and promote overall well-being. By combining fiber-rich ingredients, metabolism-boosting spices, and hydrating elements, these blends work to regulate digestion, curb cravings, and provide essential nutrients without excess calories.

Let's explore why each of these smoothies deserves a place in your weight management routine:

1. Guava Mint Weight Loss Elixir
This refreshing blend pairs guava's high fiber content with the cooling properties of mint, aiding digestion and reducing bloating. Cucumber contributes hydration and a light diuretic effect, while lime juice and ginger help stimulate metabolism. The combination makes this a powerhouse smoothie for weight balance and gut health.

2. Fat-Burning Apple Broccoli Shake
With fiber-rich green apple and cruciferous broccoli, this shake supports digestion and provides antioxidants that combat inflammation. Cinnamon and turmeric help stabilize blood sugar levels and reduce fat storage, while kombucha (if chosen) introduces probiotics for a balanced gut microbiome—essential for weight regulation.

3. Tropical Metabolism Booster
Pineapple and orange juice offer natural enzymes that improve digestion and support fat metabolism. Celery provides hydration and essential minerals, while ginger enhances thermogenesis, the process by which the body burns calories to generate heat. This tropical blend is both energizing and weight-friendly.

4. Flat Belly Purple Blend
Purple cabbage is an unexpected but powerful weight-loss ingredient, packed with fiber and anthocyanins that support a healthy metabolism. Blueberries add antioxidants and natural sweetness, while cucumber and ginger reduce bloating and inflammation, making this blend perfect for achieving a flatter stomach.

5. Watermelon Strawberry Cream
This hydrating smoothie features watermelon's natural amino acids, which may enhance fat metabolism. Strawberries provide vitamin C and fiber, while lime zest and chia seeds add an extra detoxifying boost. It's a light, refreshing drink that satisfies cravings without excess calories.

6. Passion Spinach Slimmer
Passion fruit is rich in dietary fiber, which slows digestion and keeps you feeling full longer. Combined with spinach's metabolism-friendly nutrients and green apple's natural sweetness, this blend offers a perfect mix of energy and satiety, reducing the urge to snack between meals.

7. Parsley Ginger Zing
Parsley helps flush out excess water weight, while ginger supports digestion and thermogenesis. Green apple and cucumber add hydration and fiber, making this an ideal smoothie for reducing bloating and maintaining energy throughout the day.

8. Spirulina Light & Fit
With high-protein spirulina, this smoothie is designed to maintain lean muscle mass while keeping calorie intake in check. Blueberries provide antioxidants, while chia seeds add fiber to enhance satiety. It's a nutrient-dense choice for those looking to balance their diet without compromising on essential nutrients.

9. Acai Weight Loss Drink

Acai berries are loaded with antioxidants that support fat metabolism, while kombucha (if used) improves gut health—an important factor in maintaining a healthy weight. Ginger and lemon juice further enhance digestion, making this smoothie an excellent choice for those aiming for a leaner physique.

10. Spiced Kale and Pear Mix

Kale's fiber content helps control hunger, while pear adds natural sweetness and gut-friendly pectin. Warming spices like cinnamon and nutmeg help stabilize blood sugar levels, reducing cravings for unhealthy snacks.

11. Goji Spinach Fit Fuel

Goji berries have been linked to improved metabolism, while spinach provides iron and fiber to sustain energy levels. Green apple's tartness complements the sweetness of goji berries, creating a well-balanced smoothie that supports both weight management and vitality.

12. Chocolate Chickpea Weight Cut

Chickpeas add plant-based protein and fiber, keeping you full longer while supporting muscle maintenance. Unsweetened cocoa powder offers a chocolatey indulgence without added sugar, and cinnamon further aids in blood sugar regulation. This is an excellent post-workout or meal replacement smoothie.

13. Metabo Chai Cauliflower

Frozen cauliflower might sound unusual in a smoothie, but it adds creaminess without excess sugar or calories. Chai spices like cinnamon, ginger, and cardamom rev up metabolism, while almond milk provides a smooth base for this warming, metabolism-boosting blend.

14. Mushroom and Carrot Slimmer

Mushrooms contain beta-glucans, which support gut health and immune function, while carrots provide fiber and natural sweetness. Ginger and cinnamon enhance digestion and metabolism, making this an earthy, nutrient-dense addition to a weight-conscious diet.

15. SlimBerry Blend

This antioxidant-rich smoothie blends cranberries and pomegranate seeds, both known for supporting metabolism and reducing inflammation. The fiber from the fruit and chia seeds ensures prolonged satiety, making this a great option for those looking to curb cravings naturally.

The Science Behind the Benefits

These smoothies are effective for weight management because they target key factors that influence body composition and metabolism:

- **Fiber-Rich Ingredients:** Fruits, vegetables, and seeds help regulate digestion, slow the release of sugar into the bloodstream, and promote satiety.
- **Metabolism-Boosting Spices:** Ingredients like cinnamon, ginger, and turmeric enhance calorie burning and improve metabolic function.
- **Hydration and Detoxification:** High-water-content ingredients, such as cucumber, celery, and coconut water, help flush out excess water weight and support liver function.
- **Blood Sugar Balance:** Low-glycemic fruits, fiber, and healthy fats help prevent energy crashes and cravings, making it easier to maintain a calorie deficit.

A Delicious Way to Stay in Shape

Unlike restrictive diets, these smoothies provide a delicious and sustainable way to manage weight. They nourish your body with whole, natural ingredients that keep you feeling full, energized, and satisfied. By incorporating them into your daily routine, you can achieve your wellness goals without sacrificing taste or nutrition.

DETOX
SMOOTHIES

Bright Start Cleanse

Total: 5 mins   **Servings:** 2   **Level:** 1/5

Nutritional Info (Per Serving, based on hibiscus tea and no optional additions): 130 kcal; 28g carbs; 2g protein; 1g fat; 6g fiber.

Ingredients

- **Liquid Base (Choose One):** 1 cup brewed and cooled hibiscus tea, 1 cup coconut water, or 1 cup plain filtered water
- **Main Ingredients:** 1/2 cup fresh passion fruit pulp (about 2 passion fruits), 1 cup fresh or frozen pineapple chunks, 1/2 cup cucumber (chopped), 1/2 teaspoon fresh lime juice
- **Optional Sweetener:** 1 teaspoon raw honey or maple syrup
- **Optional Superfood Additions:** 1 tablespoon chia seeds, 1/2 teaspoon spirulina powder, 1 teaspoon ground flaxseeds

Optional Variations:
- **Diabetic-Friendly:** Reduce pineapple to 1/2 cup and replace with 1/4 avocado. Use unsweetened hibiscus tea as the base. Avoid additional sweeteners.
- **Vegan:** Avoid honey and opt for maple syrup.
- **Keto:** Replace pineapple with 1/4 avocado. Use coconut water and avoid additional sweeteners. Add 1 teaspoon of MCT oil.
- **Pregnancy-Safe:** Ensure all ingredients are fresh and thoroughly washed. Use pasteurized coconut water if choosing this option.
- **Protein-Packed:** Add 1 scoop of unflavored plant-based protein powder or 1 tablespoon hemp seeds.

Serving Tip: Garnish with a slice of lime or a sprinkle of chia seeds for extra fiber. Pair with a handful of raw almonds or a side of coconut yogurt with granola for a hydrating and cleansing start to your day.

Instructions

1. Brew hibiscus tea in advance and allow it to cool completely.

2. Add ingredients to the blender. Pour the liquid base first, followed by passion fruit pulp, pineapple, cucumber, and lime juice. Sprinkle in any optional superfoods.

3. Start blending on low speed, then gradually increase to high for 1–2 minutes until the smoothie is smooth and creamy. Adjust consistency with more liquid if needed.

4. Pour into glasses and enjoy immediately.

02 Cleansing Citrus Fire

Total: 5 mins **Servings:** 2 **Level:** 1/5

Nutritional Info *(Per Serving, based on water and no optional additions):* 120 kcal; 24g carbs; 3g protein; 2g fat; 5g fiber.

Ingredients

- **Liquid Base (Choose One):** 1 cup plain filtered water, 1 cup coconut water, or 1 cup unsweetened almond milk
- **Main Ingredients:** 1/2 medium red bell pepper (chopped), 3/4 cup fresh grapefruit juice (from about 1 grapefruit), 1 tablespoon ground flax seeds, 1 tablespoon fresh lemon juice, 5 fresh mint leaves
- **Optional Sweetener:** 1 teaspoon raw honey, maple syrup, or agave syrup
- **Optional Superfood Additions:** 1/2 teaspoon spirulina powder, 1 teaspoon chia seeds, 1/2 teaspoon turmeric powder

Optional Variations:
- **Diabetic-Friendly:** Reduce grapefruit juice to 1/2 cup and add 1/4 avocado. Use plain filtered water as the base. Avoid additional sweeteners.
- **Vegan:** Avoid honey and opt for maple syrup or agave.
- **Keto:** Remove grapefruit juice and replace with 1/4 avocado. Use unsweetened almond milk as the base and avoid additional sweeteners. Add 1 teaspoon of MCT oil.
- **Pregnancy-Safe:** Ensure all ingredients are fresh and thoroughly washed. Avoid unpasteurized grapefruit juice.
- **Protein-Packed:** Add 1 scoop of unflavored plant-based protein powder or 1 tablespoon hemp seeds.

Serving Tip: Garnish with a few extra mint leaves or a sprinkle of chia seeds. Pair with a small handful of walnuts or a bowl of coconut yogurt topped with granola.

Instructions

1. Chop the red bell pepper and juice the grapefruit and lemon.

2. Add ingredients to the blender. Pour the liquid base first, then add red bell pepper, grapefruit juice, lemon juice, mint leaves, and flax seeds. Sprinkle in any optional superfoods.

3. Start blending on low speed, then gradually increase to high for 1–2 minutes until smooth. Adjust consistency with more liquid if needed.

4. Pour into glasses and enjoy immediately.

03 Zingy Dandelion Detox

Total: 5 mins **Servings:** 2 **Level:** 1/5

Nutritional Info *(Per Serving, based on kombucha and no optional additions):* 120 kcal; 24g carbs; 3g protein; 1.5g fat; 5g fiber.

Ingredients

- **Liquid Base (Choose One):** 1 cup unsweetened kombucha (plain or citrus-flavored), 1 cup coconut water, or 1 cup filtered water
- **Main Ingredients:** 1/2 cup fresh dandelion greens (washed, packed), 1/2 medium orange (peeled and segmented), 1/2 grapefruit (peeled and segmented), 1/2 small cucumber (chopped), 1 teaspoon fresh lemon juice
- **Optional Sweetener:** 1 teaspoon raw honey or maple syrup
- **Optional Superfood Additions:** 1 tablespoon chia seeds, 1 teaspoon ground flaxseeds, 1/2 teaspoon spirulina powder, 1 teaspoon grated fresh ginger

Optional Variations:
- **Diabetic-Friendly:** Reduce orange and grapefruit to 1/4 each and replace with 1/4 avocado. Use unsweetened kombucha or water. Avoid additional sweeteners.
- **Vegan:** Avoid honey and opt for maple syrup.
- **Keto:** Remove orange and grapefruit and replace with 1/4 avocado. Use coconut water. Avoid additional sweeteners. Add 1 teaspoon of MCT oil.
- **Pregnancy-Safe:** Avoid unpasteurized kombucha.
- **Protein-Packed:** Add 1 scoop of unflavored plant-based protein powder or 1 tablespoon hemp seeds.

Serving Tip: Garnish with a few extra chia seeds or a lemon slice. Pair with a handful of soaked almonds or a bowl of unsweetened coconut yogurt topped with flaxseeds.

Instructions

1. Wash the dandelion greens, peel and segment the citrus fruits, and chop the cucumber.

2. Add ingredients to the blender. Pour the liquid base first, followed by dandelion greens, orange, grapefruit, cucumber, and lemon juice. Sprinkle in any optional superfoods.

3. Start blending on low speed, then gradually increase to high for 1–2 minutes until smooth. Adjust consistency with more liquid if needed.

4. Pour into glasses and enjoy immediately.

04 Cilantro Lime Detox Tonic

Total: 5 mins   **Servings:** 2   **Level:** 1/5

Nutritional Info *(Per Serving, based on coconut water and no optional additions)*: 110 kcal; 24g carbs; 2g protein; 0.5g fat; 5g fiber.

Ingredients

- **Liquid Base (Choose One):** 1 cup coconut water, 1 cup unsweetened aloe vera juice, or 1 cup filtered water
- **Main Ingredients:** 1/2 cup celery (chopped), 1/4 cup fresh cilantro leaves (packed), 1/2 medium orange (peeled and segmented), 1/2 lemon (juiced), 1/2 green apple (cored and chopped), 1/2 teaspoon fresh grated ginger
- **Optional Sweetener:** 1 teaspoon raw honey or maple syrup
- **Optional Superfood Additions:** 1 tablespoon chia seeds, 1 teaspoon ground flaxseeds, 1/2 teaspoon spirulina powder, 1/2 teaspoon turmeric powder

Optional Variations:
- **Diabetic-Friendly:** Reduce orange to 1/4 and replace with 1/4 avocado. Use unsweetened aloe vera juice as the base. Avoid additional sweeteners.
- **Vegan:** Avoid honey and opt for maple syrup.
- **Keto:** Remove orange and green apple, replace with 1/4 avocado. Use coconut water and avoid additional sweeteners. Add 1 teaspoon of MCT oil.
- **Pregnancy-Safe:** Avoid unpasteurized aloe vera juice.
- **Protein-Packed:** Add 1 scoop of unflavored plant-based protein powder or 1 tablespoon hemp seeds.

Serving Tip: Garnish with a sprig of cilantro or a few chia seeds. Pair with a handful of soaked almonds or a side of plain coconut yogurt topped with flaxseeds.

Instructions

1. Wash and chop the celery, cilantro, and green apple. Peel and segment the orange. Juice the lemon.

2. Add ingredients to the blender. Pour the liquid base first, followed by celery, cilantro, orange, lemon juice, green apple, and ginger. Sprinkle in any optional superfoods.

3. Start blending on low speed, then gradually increase to high for 1–2 minutes until smooth. Adjust consistency with more liquid if needed.

4. Pour into glasses and enjoy immediately.

---

05 Green Tea Spinach Detox Drink

Total: 5 mins   **Servings:** 2   **Level:** 1/5

Nutritional Info *(Per Serving, based on green tea and no optional additions)*: 95 kcal; 22g carbs; 3g protein; 0.5g fat; 4g fiber.

Ingredients

- **Liquid Base (Choose One):** 1 cup brewed and cooled green tea, 1 cup coconut water, or 1 cup unsweetened almond milk
- **Main Ingredients:** 1 cup fresh spinach (packed), 1/2 cup cucumber (chopped), 1/2 green apple (cored and chopped), 1 teaspoon fresh lemon juice, 1/2 teaspoon grated fresh ginger
- **Optional Sweetener:** 1 teaspoon raw honey or maple syrup
- **Optional Superfood Additions:** 1 tablespoon chia seeds, 1 teaspoon ground flaxseeds, 1/2 teaspoon spirulina powder, 1/4 teaspoon matcha powder

Optional Variations:
- **Diabetic-Friendly:** Use unsweetened green tea as the base and reduce apple to 1/4. Avoid additional sweeteners.
- **Vegan:** Avoid honey and opt for maple syrup.
- **Keto:** Remove green apple and replace with 1/4 avocado. Use unsweetened almond milk and avoid additional sweeteners. Add 1 teaspoon of MCT oil.
- **Pregnancy-Safe:** Ensure all ingredients are fresh and thoroughly washed. Avoid unpasteurized coconut water.
- **Protein-Packed:** Add 1 scoop of unflavored plant-based protein powder or 1 tablespoon hemp seeds.

Serving Tip: Garnish with a slice of lemon or a sprinkle of chia seeds for extra fiber. Pair with a handful of raw walnuts or a spoonful of unsweetened coconut yogurt for a light, detoxifying meal.

Instructions

1. Brew the green tea and allow it to cool. Wash and chop the spinach, cucumber, and green apple.

2. Add ingredients to the blender. Pour the liquid base first, followed by spinach, cucumber, green apple, lemon juice, and ginger. Sprinkle in any optional superfoods.

3. Start blending on low speed, then gradually increase to high for 1–2 minutes until smooth. Adjust consistency with more liquid if needed.

4. Pour into glasses and enjoy immediately.

06 Citrus Spiced Gut Cleanse

Total: 5 mins **Servings:** 2 **Level:** 1/5

Nutritional Info *(Per Serving, based on kombucha and no optional additions)*: 105 kcal; 24g carbs; 2g protein; 0.5g fat; 3g fiber.

Ingredients

- **Liquid Base (Choose One):** 1 cup unflavored kombucha (preferably ginger or turmeric-infused), 1 cup coconut water, or 1 cup brewed and cooled turmeric tea
- **Main Ingredients:** 1/2 cup fresh orange juice (about 1 medium orange), 1/2 cup chopped carrots, 1/2 teaspoon fresh grated turmeric (or 1/4 teaspoon ground turmeric), 1/2 teaspoon fresh grated ginger, 1 teaspoon lemon juice
- **Optional Sweetener:** 1 teaspoon raw honey or maple syrup
- **Optional Superfood Additions:** 1 tablespoon chia seeds, 1/2 teaspoon ground flaxseeds, 1/4 teaspoon cayenne pepper, 1 teaspoon apple cider vinegar

Optional Variations:
- **Diabetic-Friendly:** Reduce orange juice to 1/4 cup and replace with 1/4 avocado. Use unsweetened kombucha. Avoid additional sweeteners.
- **Vegan:** Avoid honey and opt for maple syrup.
- **Keto:** Replace orange juice with 1/4 avocado. Use brewed turmeric tea instead of kombucha. Avoid additional sweeteners. Add 1 teaspoon of MCT oil.
- **Pregnancy-Safe:** Avoid unpasteurized kombucha.
- **Protein-Packed:** Add 1 scoop of unflavored plant-based protein powder or 1 tablespoon hemp seeds.

Serving Tip: Garnish with a slice of orange or a sprinkle of chia seeds. Pair with a handful of raw almonds or a light avocado toast.

Instructions

1. Brew the turmeric tea (if using) and let it cool. Juice the orange and grate the turmeric and ginger.

2. Add ingredients to the blender. Pour the liquid base first, followed by orange juice, chopped carrots, turmeric, ginger, and lemon juice. Sprinkle in any optional superfoods.

3. Start blending on low speed, then gradually increase to high for 1–2 minutes until smooth. Adjust consistency with more liquid if needed.

4. Pour into glasses and enjoy immediately.

---

07 Watermelon Cucumber Blend

Total: 5 mins **Servings:** 2 **Level:** 1/5

Nutritional Info *(Per Serving, based on coconut water and no optional additions)*: 90 kcal; 22g carbs; 1g protein; 0.5g fat; 2g fiber.

Ingredients

- **Liquid Base (Choose One):** 1 cup coconut water, 1 cup filtered water, or 1 cup unsweetened aloe vera juice
- **Main Ingredients:** 1 cup fresh watermelon chunks (seedless), 1/2 cup cucumber (chopped, skin on for extra fiber), 1/2 teaspoon fresh lime juice, 4 fresh mint leaves
- **Optional Sweetener:** 1 teaspoon raw honey or maple syrup
- **Optional Superfood Additions:** 1 tablespoon chia seeds, 1/2 teaspoon grated ginger, 1 teaspoon flaxseeds

Optional Variations:
- **Diabetic-Friendly:** Reduce watermelon to 1/2 cup and replace with 1/4 avocado. Use unsweetened coconut water. Avoid additional sweeteners.
- **Vegan:** Avoid honey and use maple syrup.
- **Keto:** Replace watermelon with 1/2 avocado. Use unsweetened aloe vera juice and avoid additional sweeteners. Add 1 teaspoon of MCT oil.
- **Pregnancy-Safe:** Ensure all ingredients are fresh and thoroughly washed. Use pasteurized coconut water.
- **Protein-Packed:** Add 1 scoop of unflavored protein powder or 1 tablespoon hemp seeds.

Serving Tip: Garnish with a slice of lime or a sprig of mint. Pair with a handful of raw cashews or a light coconut yogurt bowl with granola.

Instructions

1. Chop the watermelon and cucumber into chunks. Juice the lime.

2. Add ingredients to the blender. Pour the liquid base first, followed by watermelon, cucumber, lime juice, and mint leaves. Sprinkle in any optional superfoods.

3. Start blending on low speed, then gradually increase to high for 1–2 minutes until smooth. Adjust consistency with more liquid if needed.

4. Pour into glasses and enjoy immediately.

08 Beet Celery Detox Elixir

Total: 5 mins   **Servings:** 2   **Level:** 1/5

Nutritional Info *(Per Serving, based on coconut water and no optional additions):* 100 kcal; 22g carbs; 3g protein; 0.5g fat; 4g fiber.

Ingredients

- **Liquid Base (Choose One):** 1 cup coconut water, 1 cup unsweetened green tea, or 1 cup filtered water
- **Main Ingredients:** 1/2 medium raw beet (peeled and chopped), 1 small celery stalk (chopped), 1/2 green apple (cored and chopped), 1/2 teaspoon fresh lemon juice, 1/2 teaspoon fresh grated ginger
- **Optional Sweetener:** 1 teaspoon raw honey or maple syrup
- **Optional Superfood Additions:** 1 tablespoon chia seeds, 1/2 teaspoon spirulina powder, 1 teaspoon flaxseeds

Optional Variations:
- **Diabetic-Friendly:** Replace apple with 1/4 avocados. Use unsweetened green tea or water as the base. Avoid additional sweeteners.
- **Vegan:** Avoid honey and use maple syrup.
- **Keto:** Replace apple with 1/4 avocado. Use unsweetened green tea and avoid additional sweeteners. Add 1 teaspoon of MCT oil.
- **Pregnancy-Safe:** Ensure all ingredients are fresh and thoroughly washed. Avoid unpasteurized juices.
- **Protein-Packed:** Add 1 scoop of unflavored protein powder or 1 tablespoon hemp seeds.

Serving Tip: Garnish with a slice of lemon or a few chia seeds for extra fiber. Pair with a handful of almonds or a light avocado toast on whole-grain bread for a balanced detox breakfast.

Instructions

1. Peel and chop the beet, chop the celery and apple, and grate the ginger.

2. Add ingredients to the blender. Pour the liquid base first, followed by beets, celery, apple, lemon juice, and ginger. Sprinkle in any optional superfoods.

3. Start blending on low speed, then gradually increase to high for 1–2 minutes until smooth. Adjust consistency with more liquid if needed.

4. Pour into glasses and enjoy immediately.

---

09 Starfruit Detox Refresher

Total: 5 mins   **Servings:** 2   **Level:** 1/5

Nutritional Info *(Per Serving, based on coconut water and no optional additions):* 90 kcal; 20g carbs; 2g protein; 0.5g fat; 5g fiber.

Ingredients

- **Liquid Base (Choose One):** 1 cup brewed and cooled green tea, 1 cup coconut water, or 1 cup unsweetened almond milk
- **Main Ingredients:** 1 cup fresh spinach (packed), 1/2 cup cucumber (chopped), 1/2 green apple (cored and chopped), 1 teaspoon fresh lemon juice, 1/2 teaspoon grated fresh ginger
- **Optional Sweetener:** 1 teaspoon raw honey or maple syrup
- **Optional Superfood Additions:** 1 tablespoon chia seeds, 1 teaspoon ground flaxseeds, 1/2 teaspoon spirulina powder, 1/4 teaspoon matcha powder

Optional Variations:
- **Diabetic-Friendly:** Replace apple with 1/4 avocado. Use unsweetened green tea or water as the base. Avoid additional sweeteners.
- **Vegan:** Avoid honey and use maple syrup.
- **Keto:** Replace apple with 1/4 avocado. Use unsweetened green tea and avoid additional sweeteners. Add 1 teaspoon of MCT oil.
- **Pregnancy-Safe:** Ensure all ingredients are fresh and thoroughly washed. Avoid unpasteurized juices.
- **Protein-Packed:** Add 1 scoop of unflavored protein powder or 1 tablespoon hemp seeds.

Serving Tip: Garnish with a starfruit slice or a few chia seeds. Serve alongside a bowl of coconut yogurt with granola or a light avocado toast.

Instructions

1. Slice the starfruit, chop the cucumber and apple, and juice the lime.

2. Add ingredients to the blender. Pour the liquid base first, followed by starfruit, cucumber, apple, lime juice, and mint leaves. Sprinkle in any optional superfoods.

3. Start blending on low speed, then gradually increase to high for 1–2 minutes until smooth. Adjust consistency with more liquid if needed.

4. Pour into glasses and enjoy immediately.

10 Watermelon Aloe Mint Cooler

Total: 5 mins **Servings:** 2 **Level:** 1/5

Nutritional Info *(Per Serving, based on peppermint tea and no optional additions)*: 60 kcal; 14g carbs; 1g protein; 0.5g fat; 3g fiber.

Ingredients

- **Liquid Base (Choose One):** 1 cup brewed and cooled peppermint tea, 1 cup coconut water, or 1 cup plain filtered water
- **Main Ingredients:** 1 ½ cups fresh watermelon (cubed), 2 tablespoons fresh aloe vera gel, Juice of 1/2 lime, 4–5 fresh mint leaves
- **Optional Sweetener:** 1 teaspoon raw honey, maple syrup, or agave syrup
- **Optional Superfood Additions:** 1 tablespoon chia seeds, 1/2 teaspoon spirulina powder, 1 teaspoon ground flaxseeds

Optional Variations:
- **Diabetic-Friendly:** Use unsweetened peppermint tea or plain water as the base. Avoid additional sweeteners.
- **Vegan:** Avoid honey and use maple syrup or agave.
- **Keto:** Reduce watermelon to 1 cup and add 1/4 avocado for healthy fats. Use unsweetened peppermint tea as the base. Avoid additional sweeteners.
- **Pregnancy-Safe:** Ensure all ingredients are fresh and thoroughly washed. Avoid unpasteurized aloe vera gel.
- **Protein-Packed:** Add 1 scoop of unflavored plant-based protein powder or 1 tablespoon hemp seeds.

Serving Tip: Garnish with a sprig of mint or a lime wedge for extra freshness. Pair with a handful of raw almonds or a coconut yogurt parfait for a hydrating and cleansing start to your day.

Instructions

1. Cube the watermelon, extract fresh aloe vera gel, and juice the lime. If using peppermint tea, brew and cool it.

2. Add ingredients to the blender. Pour the liquid base first, followed by watermelon, aloe vera gel, lime juice, and mint leaves. Sprinkle in any optional superfoods.

3. Start blending on low speed, then gradually increase to high for 1–2 minutes until smooth. Adjust consistency with more liquid if needed.

4. Pour into glasses and enjoy immediately.

11 Fresh Start Detox Blend

Total: 5 mins **Servings:** 2 **Level:** 1/5

Nutritional Info *(Per Serving, based on water and no optional additions)*: 90 kcal; 22g carbs; 2g protein; 0.5g fat; 5g fiber.

Ingredients

- **Liquid Base (Choose One):** 1 cup filtered water, 1 cup coconut water, or 1 cup cooled green tea
- **Main Ingredients:** 1 medium carrot (peeled and chopped), 1 medium green apple (cored and chopped), juice of 1/2 lemon, 5–6 fresh mint leaves
- **Optional Sweetener:** 1 teaspoon raw honey, maple syrup, or agave syrup
- **Optional Superfood Additions:** 1 tablespoon chia seeds, 1 teaspoon ground flaxseeds, 1/2 teaspoon fresh grated ginger, 1/2 teaspoon turmeric powder

Optional Variations:
- **Diabetic-Friendly:** Use unsweetened green tea or water as the base. Avoid additional sweeteners.
- **Vegan:** Avoid honey and use maple syrup or agave if needed.
- **Keto:** Reduce apple to 1/2 and add 1/4 avocado for healthy fats. Use green tea or water as the base. Avoid additional sweeteners.
- **Pregnancy-Safe:** Ensure all ingredients are fresh and thoroughly washed. Avoid unpasteurized juice.
- **Protein-Packed:** Add 1 scoop of unflavored plant-based protein powder or 1 tablespoon hemp seeds.

Serving Tip: Garnish with a mint leaf or a pinch of cinnamon for extra warmth. Pair with a handful of walnuts or a light quinoa salad for a balanced, cleansing snack.

Instructions

1. Peel and chop the carrot, core and chop the apple, and juice the lemon.

2. Add ingredients to the blender. Pour the liquid base first, followed by carrot, apple, lemon juice, and mint leaves. Sprinkle in any optional superfoods.

3. Start blending on low speed, then gradually increase to high for 1–2 minutes until smooth. Adjust consistency with more liquid if needed.

4. Pour into glasses and enjoy immediately.

12   Floral Detox Infusion

Total: 5 mins   **Servings:** 2   **Level:** 1/5

Nutritional Info *(Per Serving, based on coconut water and no optional additions)*: 110 kcal; 25g carbs; 2g protein; 0.5g fat; 5g fiber.

Ingredients

- **Liquid Base (Choose One):** 1 cup unsweetened coconut water, 1 cup brewed and cooled dandelion tea, or 1 cup filtered water
- **Main Ingredients:** 1 cup fresh or frozen pineapple chunks, 1/2 cup fresh dandelion greens, 1/2 small cucumber (chopped), juice of 1/2 lemon, 4–5 fresh mint leaves, 1/4 teaspoon cayenne pepper
- **Optional Sweetener:** 1 teaspoon raw honey or maple syrup
- **Optional Superfood Additions:** 1 tablespoon chia seeds, 1/2 teaspoon turmeric powder, 1/2 teaspoon fresh grated ginger, 1 teaspoon ground flaxseeds

Optional Variations:
- **Diabetic-Friendly:** Reduce pineapple to 1/2 cup and replace with 1/4 avocado. Use unsweetened dandelion tea. Avoid additional sweeteners.
- **Vegan:** Avoid honey and use maple syrup.
- **Keto:** Replace pineapple with 1/4 avocado. Use coconut water or dandelion tea. Avoid additional sweeteners. Add 1 teaspoon of MCT oil.
- **Pregnancy-Safe:** Avoid unpasteurized coconut water. Reduce cayenne to a pinch.
- **Protein-Packed:** Add 1 scoop of unflavored plant-based protein powder or 1 tablespoon hemp seeds.

Serving Tip: Garnish with a slice of lemon or a few chia seeds. Pair with a handful of raw almonds or a small serving of avocado toast.

Instructions

1. Brew the dandelion tea in advance and allow it to cool completely if using this base.

2. Chop the cucumber and pineapple, and juice the lemon.

3. Add ingredients to the blender. Pour the liquid base first, followed by pineapple, dandelion greens, cucumber, lemon juice, mint leaves, and cayenne pepper. Sprinkle in any optional superfoods.

4. Start blending on low speed, then gradually increase to high for 1–2 minutes until smooth. Adjust consistency with more liquid if needed.

5. Pour into glasses and enjoy immediately.

---

13   Rhubarb Beet Glow

Total: 5 mins   **Servings:** 2   **Level:** 1/5

Nutritional Info *(Per Serving, based on coconut water and no optional additions)*: 120 kcal; 28g carbs; 3g protein; 0.5g fat; 6g fiber.

Ingredients

- **Liquid Base (Choose One):** 1 cup brewed and cooled green tea, 1 cup coconut water, or 1 cup unsweetened almond milk
- **Main Ingredients:** 1 cup fresh spinach (packed), 1/2 cup cucumber (chopped), 1/2 green apple (cored and chopped), 1 teaspoon fresh lemon juice, 1/2 teaspoon grated fresh ginger
- **Optional Sweetener:** 1 teaspoon raw honey or maple syrup
- **Optional Superfood Additions:** 1 tablespoon chia seeds, 1 teaspoon ground flaxseeds, 1/2 teaspoon spirulina powder, 1/4 teaspoon matcha powder

Optional Variations:
- **Diabetic-Friendly:** Replace banana with 1/4 avocado. Use unsweetened hibiscus tea as the base. Avoid additional sweeteners.
- **Vegan:** Avoid honey and opt for maple syrup.
- **Keto:** Replace banana with 1/4 avocado. Use coconut water or hibiscus tea as the base. Avoid additional sweeteners.
- **Pregnancy-Safe:** Ensure all ingredients are fresh and thoroughly washed. Avoid unpasteurized coconut water.
- **Protein-Packed:** Add 1 scoop of unflavored plant-based protein powder or 1 tablespoon hemp seeds.

Serving Tip: Garnish with a sprinkle of chia seeds or a small slice of rhubarb for a decorative touch. Pair with a handful of walnuts or a small serving of coconut yogurt for a nutrient-dense, antioxidant-rich snack.

Instructions

1. Chop the rhubarb, beet, and strawberries. Peel and juice the orange.

2. Add ingredients to the blender. Pour the liquid base first, followed by rhubarb, beet, strawberries, frozen banana (or avocado), and orange juice. Sprinkle in any optional superfoods.

3. Start blending on low speed, then gradually increase to high for 1–2 minutes until smooth. Adjust consistency with more liquid if needed.

4. Pour into glasses and enjoy immediately.

14 Gooseberry and Apple Reset

Total: 5 mins **Servings:** 2 **Level:** 1/5

Nutritional Info *(Per Serving, based on coconut water and no optional additions)*: 110 kcal; 25g carbs; 2g protein; 0.5g fat; 5g fiber.

Ingredients

- **Liquid Base (Choose One):** 1 cup coconut water, 1 cup brewed and cooled green tea, or 1 cup plain filtered water
- **Main Ingredients:** 1/2 cup fresh or frozen gooseberries, 1/2 green apple (cored and chopped), 1/2 cucumber (chopped), juice of 1/2 lemon, 1 teaspoon fresh grated ginger
- **Optional Sweetener:** 1 teaspoon raw honey or maple syrup
- **Optional Superfood Additions:** 1 tablespoon chia seeds, 1/2 teaspoon spirulina powder, 1/2 teaspoon ground flaxseeds, 1/8 teaspoon cayenne pepper

Optional Variations:
- **Diabetic-Friendly:** Replace green apple with 1/4 avocado. Use unsweetened green tea as the base. Avoid additional sweeteners.
- **Vegan:** Avoid honey and opt for maple syrup.
- **Keto:** Replace apple with 1/4 avocado. Use coconut water or green tea as the base. Avoid additional sweeteners.
- **Pregnancy-Safe:** Ensure all ingredients are fresh and thoroughly washed. Avoid unpasteurized coconut water.
- **Protein-Packed:** Add 1 scoop of unflavored plant-based protein powder or 1 tablespoon hemp seeds.

Serving Tip: Garnish with a thin slice of green apple or a few chia seeds for a decorative touch. Pair with a handful of raw almonds or a side of coconut yogurt with granola for a nutrient-dense, refreshing detox meal.

Instructions

1. Wash and chop the gooseberries, green apple, and cucumber. Juice the lemon.

2. Add ingredients to the blender. Pour the liquid base first, followed by gooseberries, green apple, cucumber, lemon juice, and ginger. Sprinkle in any optional superfoods.

3. Start blending on low speed, then gradually increase to high for 1–2 minutes until smooth. Adjust consistency with more liquid if needed.

4. Pour into glasses and enjoy immediately.

15 Zesty Prune Flush

Total: 5 mins **Servings:** 2 **Level:** 1/5

Nutritional Info *(Per Serving, based on coconut water and no optional additions)*: 160 kcal; 40g carbs; 2g protein; 0.5g fat; 6g fiber.

Ingredients

- **Liquid Base (Choose One):** 1 cup coconut water or 1 cup filtered water
- **Main Ingredients:** 1/2 cup prunes, 1/2 cup fresh orange juice, 1/2 cup fresh grapefruit juice, 1/2 teaspoon fresh grated ginger
- **Optional Sweetener:** 1 teaspoon raw honey or maple syrup
- **Optional Superfood Additions:** 1 tablespoon chia seeds, 1/2 teaspoon turmeric powder, 1/2 teaspoon ground flaxseeds, 1/8 teaspoon cayenne pepper

Optional Variations:
- **Diabetic-Friendly:** Reduce prunes to 1/4 cup and replace with 1/4 avocado. Use unsweetened coconut water as the base. Avoid additional sweeteners.
- **Vegan:** Avoid honey and opt for maple syrup.
- **Keto:** Replace prunes with 1/4 avocado. Use unsweetened coconut water and avoid additional sweeteners.
- **Pregnancy-Safe:** Ensure all ingredients are fresh and thoroughly washed. Avoid unpasteurized grapefruit juice.
- **Protein-Packed:** Add 1 scoop of unflavored plant-based protein powder or 1 tablespoon hemp seeds.

Serving Tip: Garnish with a slice of grapefruit or a sprinkle of chia seeds. Pair with a handful of almonds or a small bowl of Greek yogurt for a fiber-packed, digestion-friendly snack.

Instructions

1. Soak prunes in warm water for 5 minutes if they are firm. Juice the orange and grapefruit.

2. Add ingredients to the blender. Pour the liquid base first, followed by prunes, orange juice, grapefruit juice, and ginger. Sprinkle in any optional superfoods.

3. Start blending on low speed, then gradually increase to high for 1–2 minutes until smooth. Adjust consistency with more liquid if needed.

4. Pour into glasses and enjoy immediately.

WHY THESE SMOOTHIES ARE EFFECTIVE

Detoxification isn't about extreme cleansing or starvation—it's about supporting your body's natural ability to eliminate toxins, reduce inflammation, and restore balance. These smoothies use carefully selected ingredients that enhance digestion, flush out excess waste, and replenish essential nutrients, making them ideal for gentle detox and cleansing.

Let's take a closer look at why each blend in this collection contributes to a cleaner, more energized body.

1. Bright Start Cleanse
This blend harnesses the power of hibiscus tea, a natural diuretic that helps eliminate excess water retention and supports liver function. Passion fruit provides gut-friendly fiber, while pineapple's bromelain aids digestion. Cucumber and lime juice hydrate and promote alkalinity, making this an ideal smoothie for resetting your system.

2. Cleansing Citrus Fire
Red bell pepper is a surprising but powerful addition to this blend, as it's loaded with vitamin C and antioxidants that help neutralize free radicals. Grapefruit and lemon juice enhance liver detoxification, while mint soothes digestion. Flaxseeds contribute fiber to promote regularity, ensuring that your cleanse is both effective and gentle.

3. Zingy Dandelion Detox
Dandelion greens are a natural liver cleanser, packed with antioxidants that support bile production and digestion. The combination of orange and grapefruit provides a vitamin C boost, while cucumber and lemon juice hydrate and flush out toxins. This smoothie is a refreshing way to promote liver health and a glowing complexion.

4. Cilantro Lime Detox Tonic
Cilantro is known for its ability to bind to heavy metals and remove them from the body, while celery aids in hydration and mineral replenishment. Green apple and orange add natural sweetness, while ginger provides a thermogenic boost to kickstart metabolism. This blend is a perfect choice for those looking to gently detoxify without feeling deprived.

5. Green Tea Spinach Detox Drink
Green tea is loaded with catechins, which enhance liver function and help break down toxins. Spinach provides chlorophyll, a natural detoxifier, while cucumber and green apple add fiber to support digestion. This smoothie is a powerhouse for cellular repair and renewal.

6. Citrus Spiced Gut Cleanse
This blend combines turmeric and ginger, two of the most potent anti-inflammatory and gut-healing ingredients. Carrots provide beta-carotene for liver support, while orange juice and apple cider vinegar improve digestion and promote alkalinity. A touch of cayenne pepper boosts circulation, making this an energizing, gut-friendly detox drink.

7. Watermelon Cucumber Blend
Watermelon and cucumber are hydration champions, helping to flush toxins while keeping your body replenished with essential electrolytes. Mint adds a cooling effect, and lime juice enhances digestion and alkalinity. This smoothie is perfect for post-indulgence days when your body needs a light yet effective reset.

8. Beet Celery Detox Elixir
Beets contain betaine, a compound that supports liver detoxification and improves bile flow, while

celery provides key minerals to restore balance. Green apple and lemon juice add vitamin C and fiber, ensuring this smoothie is as effective at cleansing as it is delicious.

9. Starfruit Detox Refresher
Starfruit is rich in antioxidants and polyphenols, which help fight oxidative stress and inflammation. Cucumber and green apple aid digestion, while lime juice and mint provide a refreshing, cleansing boost. This smoothie is perfect for those looking to brighten their skin and revitalize their energy.

10. Watermelon Aloe Mint Cooler
Aloe vera is known for its soothing and digestive-supporting properties, while peppermint tea calms the stomach and aids detoxification. Watermelon hydrates and flushes out toxins, and lime juice provides a refreshing, vitamin C-rich twist. This blend is ideal for promoting gut health and overall hydration.

11. Fresh Start Detox Blend
Carrots are rich in fiber and beta-carotene, supporting liver detoxification and skin renewal. Green apple and lemon juice provide a tangy balance, while fresh mint aids digestion. This smoothie is a great way to start the day feeling light and refreshed.

12. Floral Detox Infusion
Dandelion greens help cleanse the liver, while pineapple adds enzymes that improve digestion. Cucumber and lemon juice work together to alkalize and hydrate, and a touch of cayenne pepper supports circulation and metabolism. This blend is a flavorful way to restore balance and energy.

13. Rhubarb Beet Glow
Rhubarb is a natural digestive aid, while beets support liver function and blood circulation. Strawberries provide antioxidants, and orange juice gives a bright, vitamin-rich lift. This smoothie helps cleanse the body while enhancing skin radiance.

14. Gooseberry and Apple Reset
Gooseberries are packed with vitamin C and fiber, promoting gut health and immune function. Cucumber and green apple contribute hydration and digestion-friendly enzymes, while lemon juice and ginger give this blend a zesty kick. It's a simple yet powerful reset for your digestive system.

15. Zesty Prune Flush
Prunes are one of the best natural sources of fiber, promoting regular digestion and gentle cleansing. Orange and grapefruit juices provide antioxidants and support liver function, while ginger reduces bloating and inflammation. This smoothie is a delicious and effective way to promote digestive health.

The Science Behind the Benefits
- **Liver Support:** Ingredients like dandelion greens, beets, and turmeric assist in breaking down toxins and improving liver function.
- **Hydration & Alkalinity:** Coconut water, cucumber, and watermelon restore electrolyte balance and maintain optimal pH levels.
- **Fiber-Packed Cleansing:** Prunes, flaxseeds, and apples promote regularity and eliminate waste buildup.
- **Antioxidant Protection:** Citrus fruits, starfruit, and hibiscus tea help fight free radicals and reduce oxidative stress.
- **Gut Health & Digestion:** Aloe vera, kombucha, and mint support gut bacteria and improve digestion.

A Refreshing Way to Cleanse
Unlike extreme cleanses that leave you feeling drained, these smoothies provide a nourishing

way to support your body's natural detoxification processes. Packed with hydration, fiber, and essential nutrients, they help eliminate toxins, reduce bloating, and restore balance—all while keeping you satisfied and energized. Enjoy them as part of a daily wellness routine, and feel the difference in your digestion, energy, and overall vitality.

GREEN
SMOOTHIES

---

01 Fresh Aloe Breeze

Total: 5 mins **Servings:** 2 **Level:** 1/5

Nutritional Info *(Per Serving, based on coconut water and no optional additions)*: 110 kcal; 20g carbs; 2g protein; 1g fat; 4g fiber.

Ingredients

- **Liquid Base (Choose One):** 1 cup coconut water, 1 cup plain filtered water, or 1 cup unsweetened almond milk
- **Main Ingredients:** 1/2 cup fresh aloe vera gel (from the leaf, thoroughly cleaned), 1 cup cucumber, chopped (peeled for a smoother texture), 1/2 frozen banana, 1 teaspoon fresh lime juice, 5 fresh mint leaves
- **Optional Sweetener:** 1 teaspoon raw honey or maple syrup
- **Optional Superfood Additions:** 1 tablespoon chia seeds, 1 teaspoon spirulina powder, 1 teaspoon ground flaxseeds

Optional Variations:
- **Diabetic-Friendly:** Replace banana with 1/4 avocado. Use unsweetened almond milk or water and avoid additional sweeteners.
- **Vegan:** Avoid honey and opt for maple syrup.
- **Keto:** Replace banana with 1/4 avocado. Use unsweetened almond milk or coconut water, and avoid sweeteners. Add 1 teaspoon of MCT oil.
- **Pregnancy-Safe:** Ensure all ingredients are fresh and thoroughly washed. Use pasteurized coconut water or filtered water.
- **Protein-Packed:** Add 1 scoop of unflavored plant-based protein powder or 1 tablespoon hemp seeds.

Serving Tip: Garnish with a slice of lime or a sprinkle of chia seeds. Pair with a handful of raw almonds or a light avocado toast.

Instructions

1. Scoop fresh aloe vera gel from the leaf, rinse thoroughly to remove the yellow latex (aloin), and pat dry.

2. Add ingredients to the blender. Pour the liquid base first, followed by aloe vera gel, cucumber, frozen banana (or avocado), lime juice, and mint leaves. Sprinkle in any optional superfoods.

3. Start blending on low speed, gradually increasing to high for 1–2 minutes until smooth and creamy. Adjust consistency with more liquid if needed.

4. Pour into glasses and enjoy immediately.

02 Classic Spinach Banana Smoothie

Total: 5 mins **Servings:** 2 **Level:** 1/5

Nutritional Info *(Per Serving, based on almond milk and no optional additions)*: 150 kcal; 30g carbs; 3g protein; 2g fat; 5g fiber.

Ingredients

- **Liquid Base (Choose One):** 1 cup unsweetened almond milk, 1 cup coconut water, or 1 cup plain filtered water
- **Main Ingredients:** 1 ½ cups fresh spinach (lightly packed), 1 frozen banana, 1/2 small apple (cored and chopped), 1 teaspoon fresh lemon juice, 1/2 teaspoon cinnamon
- **Optional Sweetener:** 1 teaspoon raw honey or maple syrup
- **Optional Superfood Additions:** 1 tablespoon chia seeds, 1 teaspoon ground flaxseeds, 1/2 teaspoon spirulina powder

Optional Variations:
- **Diabetic-Friendly:** Replace banana with 1/4 avocado. Use unsweetened almond milk or water and avoid additional sweeteners.
- **Vegan:** Avoid honey and opt for maple syrup.
- **Keto:** Replace banana with 1/4 avocado. Use unsweetened almond milk or coconut water and avoid sweeteners. Add 1 teaspoon of MCT oil.
- **Pregnancy-Safe:** Ensure all ingredients are fresh and thoroughly washed. Use pasteurized coconut water or filtered water.
- **Protein-Packed:** Add 1 scoop of unflavored plant-based protein powder or 1 tablespoon hemp seeds.

Serving Tip: Garnish with a sprinkle of cinnamon or a few chia seeds. Pair with a handful of raw almonds or a light oatmeal bowl.

Instructions

1. Freeze the banana beforehand for a creamier texture. Wash the spinach and chop the apple.

2. Add ingredients to the blender. Pour the liquid base first, followed by spinach, frozen banana (or avocado), apple, lemon juice, and cinnamon. Sprinkle in any optional superfoods.

3. Start blending on low speed, gradually increasing to high for 1–2 minutes until smooth and creamy. Adjust consistency with more liquid if needed.

4. Pour into glasses and enjoy immediately.

---

03 Pineapple Green Fuel

Total: 5 mins **Servings:** 2 **Level:** 1/5

Nutritional Info *(Per Serving, based on coconut water and no optional additions)*: 160 kcal; 35g carbs; 3g protein; 1.5g fat; 5g fiber.

Ingredients

- **Liquid Base (Choose One):** 1 cup coconut water, 1 cup unsweetened almond milk, or 1 cup plain filtered water
- **Main Ingredients:** 1 cup fresh kale (lightly packed, stems removed), 1 cup fresh or frozen pineapple chunks, 1/2 frozen banana, 1/2 teaspoon fresh grated ginger, 1/2 teaspoon lime juice
- **Optional Sweetener:** 1 teaspoon raw honey or maple syrup
- **Optional Superfood Additions:** 1 tablespoon chia seeds, 1 teaspoon ground flaxseeds, 1/2 teaspoon spirulina powder, 1 teaspoon MCT oil, 1/2 teaspoon matcha powder

Optional Variations:
- **Diabetic-Friendly:** Replace banana with 1/4 avocado. Use unsweetened almond milk or water and avoid sweeteners.
- **Vegan:** Avoid honey and opt for maple syrup.
- **Keto:** Replace pineapple and banana with 1/4 avocado. Use unsweetened almond milk and avoid sweeteners.
- **Pregnancy-Safe:** Ensure all ingredients are fresh and thoroughly washed. Use pasteurized coconut water or filtered water.
- **Protein-Packed:** Add 1 scoop of unflavored plant-based protein powder or 1 tablespoon hemp seeds.

Serving Tip: Garnish with a few chia seeds or a sprig of mint. Pair with a handful of raw almonds or a small bowl of Greek yogurt with granola.

Instructions

1. Freeze the banana beforehand for a creamier texture. Wash the kale and remove the tough stems.

2. Add ingredients to the blender. Pour the liquid base first, followed by kale, pineapple, frozen banana (or avocado), ginger, and lime juice. Sprinkle in any optional superfoods.

3. Start blending on low speed, gradually increasing to high for 1–2 minutes until smooth and creamy. Adjust consistency with more liquid if needed.

4. Pour into glasses and enjoy immediately.

04 Swiss Chard Mango Delight

Total: 5 mins   **Servings:** 2   **Level:** 1/5

Nutritional Info (Per Serving, based on coconut water and no optional additions): 180 kcal; 38g carbs; 4g protein; 2g fat; 6g fiber.

Ingredients

- **Liquid Base (Choose One):** 1 cup coconut water, 1 cup unsweetened almond milk, or 1 cup plain filtered water
- **Main Ingredients:** 1 cup Swiss chard (stems removed, chopped), 1 cup fresh or frozen mango chunks, 1/2 frozen banana, 1/2 teaspoon fresh grated ginger, 1/2 teaspoon lime juice
- **Optional Sweetener:** 1 teaspoon raw honey or maple syrup
- **Optional Superfood Additions:** 1 tablespoon chia seeds, 1 teaspoon ground flaxseeds, 1/2 teaspoon spirulina powder, 1 teaspoon hemp seeds

Optional Variations:
- **Diabetic-Friendly:** Replace banana with 1/4 avocado. Use unsweetened almond milk or water and avoid additional sweeteners.
- **Vegan:** Avoid honey and opt for maple syrup.
- **Keto:** Replace mango and banana with 1/4 avocado. Use unsweetened almond milk and avoid sweeteners. Add 1 teaspoon of MCT oil.
- **Pregnancy-Safe:** Ensure all ingredients are fresh and thoroughly washed. Use pasteurized coconut water or filtered water.
- **Protein-Packed:** Add 1 scoop of unflavored plant-based protein powder or 1 tablespoon hemp seeds.

> **Serving Tip:** Garnish with a few hemp seeds or a sprig of mint for extra freshness. Pair with a handful of raw almonds or a bowl of Greek yogurt topped with granola.

Instructions

1. Freeze the banana beforehand for a creamier texture. Wash the Swiss chard and remove the tough stems.

2. Add ingredients to the blender. Pour the liquid base first, followed by Swiss chard, mango, frozen banana (or avocado), ginger, and lime juice. Sprinkle in any optional superfoods.

3. Start blending on low speed, gradually increasing to high for 1–2 minutes until smooth and creamy. Adjust consistency with more liquid if needed.

4. Pour into glasses and enjoy immediately.

---

05 Green Apple Rocket Drink

Total: 5 mins   **Servings:** 2   **Level:** 1/5

Nutritional Info (Per Serving, based on coconut water and no optional additions): 140 kcal; 30g carbs; 3g protein; 1.5g fat; 6g fiber.

Ingredients

- **Liquid Base (Choose One):** 1 cup coconut water, 1 cup filtered water, or 1 cup unsweetened aloe vera juice
- **Main Ingredients:** 1 cup fresh watermelon chunks (seedless), 1/2 cup cucumber (chopped, skin on for extra fiber), 1/2 teaspoon fresh lime juice, 4 fresh mint leaves
- **Optional Sweetener:** 1 teaspoon raw honey or maple syrup
- **Optional Superfood Additions:** 1 tablespoon chia seeds, 1/2 teaspoon grated ginger, 1 teaspoon flaxseeds

Optional Variations:
- **Diabetic-Friendly:** Replace banana with 1/4 avocado. Use unsweetened almond milk or water and avoid additional sweeteners.
- **Vegan:** Avoid honey and opt for maple syrup.
- **Keto:** Replace green apple with 1/4 avocado. Use unsweetened almond milk and avoid sweeteners. Add 1 teaspoon of MCT oil.
- **Pregnancy-Safe:** Ensure all ingredients are fresh and thoroughly washed. Use pasteurized coconut water or filtered water.
- **Protein-Packed:** Add 1 scoop of unflavored plant-based protein powder or 1 tablespoon hemp seeds.

> **Serving Tip:** Garnish with a few chia seeds or a sprinkle of cinnamon for a warming touch. Pair with a handful of raw walnuts or a piece of whole-grain toast with almond butter.

Instructions

1. Freeze the banana beforehand for a creamier texture. Wash the arugula and green apple thoroughly.

2. Add ingredients to the blender. Pour the liquid base first, followed by arugula, green apple, frozen banana (or avocado), ginger, and lemon juice. Sprinkle in any optional superfoods.

3. Start blending on low speed, gradually increasing to high for 1–2 minutes until smooth and creamy. Adjust consistency with more liquid if needed.

4. Pour into glasses and enjoy immediately.

06 Romaine Kiwi Elixir

Total: 5 mins **Servings:** 2 **Level:** 1/5

Nutritional Info *(Per Serving, based on coconut water and no optional additions):* 140 kcal; 30g carbs; 3g protein; 1.5g fat; 6g fiber.

Ingredients

- **Liquid Base (Choose One):** 1 cup coconut water, 1 cup unsweetened almond milk, or 1 cup plain filtered water
- **Main Ingredients:** 2 cups chopped romaine lettuce, 2 ripe kiwis (peeled), 1/2 frozen banana, 1/2 teaspoon fresh lime juice
- **Optional Sweetener:** 1 teaspoon raw honey or maple syrup
- **Optional Superfood Additions:** 1 tablespoon chia seeds, 1 teaspoon flaxseeds, 1/2 teaspoon spirulina powder

Optional Variations:
- **Diabetic-Friendly:** Replace banana with 1/4 avocado. Use unsweetened almond milk and avoid additional sweeteners.
- **Vegan:** Use plant-based milk and avoid honey.
- **Keto:** Remove banana and replace with 1/4 avocado. Use unsweetened almond milk and avoid additional sweeteners. Add MCT oil.
- **Pregnancy-Safe:** Ensure all ingredients are fresh and thoroughly washed. Use pasteurized almond milk or coconut water.

Serving Tip: Garnish with a few chia seeds or a slice of kiwi. Pair with a handful of raw almonds or a light granola bar for an energizing snack.

Instructions

1. Wash and chop the romaine lettuce. Peel the kiwis.

2. Add ingredients to the blender. Pour the liquid base first, followed by romaine, kiwi, banana (or alternative), and lime juice. Sprinkle in any optional superfoods.

3. Start blending on low speed, gradually increasing to high for 1–2 minutes until smooth and creamy. Adjust consistency with more liquid if needed.

4. Pour into glasses and enjoy immediately.

---

07 Kale Avocado Protein Mix

Total: 5 mins **Servings:** 2 **Level:** 1/5

Nutritional Info *(Per Serving, based on almond milk and no optional additions):* 250 kcal; 18g carbs; 12g protein; 14g fat; 6g fiber.

Ingredients

- **Liquid Base (Choose One):** 1 cup unsweetened almond milk, 1 cup coconut water, or 1 cup plain filtered water
- **Main Ingredients:** 1 cup fresh kale (stems removed), 1/2 ripe avocado, 1/2 frozen banana, 1 scoop vanilla or unflavored protein powder, juice of 1/2 lemon, 1/2 teaspoon grated fresh ginger
- **Optional Sweetener:** 1 teaspoon raw honey or maple syrup
- **Optional Superfood Additions:** 1 tablespoon chia seeds, 1 teaspoon MCT oil, 1 tablespoon hemp seeds, 1/2 teaspoon spirulina powder

Optional Variations:
- **Diabetic-Friendly:** Replace banana with 1/4 cup blueberries. Use unsweetened almond milk and avoid sweeteners.
- **Vegan:** Use plant-based protein powder and avoid honey.
- **Keto:** Remove banana and replace with 1/4 cup frozen cauliflower. Use unsweetened almond milk and avoid sweeteners.
- **Pregnancy-Safe:** Ensure all ingredients are fresh and thoroughly washed. Use pasteurized almond milk or coconut water.
- **Protein-Packed:** Add 1 tablespoon ground flaxseeds.

Serving Tip: Top with a few hemp seeds or a sprinkle of cinnamon for a nutritional boost. Pair with a handful of raw almonds or a slice of whole-grain toast with peanut butter for a balanced meal.

Instructions

1. Wash the kale and remove the stems. Peel and chop the avocado.

2. Add ingredients to the blender. Pour the liquid base first, followed by kale, avocado, banana (or alternative), protein powder, lemon juice, and ginger. Sprinkle in any optional superfoods.

3. Start blending on low speed, gradually increasing to high for 1–2 minutes until smooth and creamy. Adjust consistency with more liquid if needed.

4. Pour into glasses and enjoy immediately.

08 Green Peach Infusion

Total: 5 mins   **Servings:** 2   **Level:** 1/5

Nutritional Info (Per Serving, based on almond milk and no optional additions): 280 kcal; 30g carbs; 10g protein; 14g fat; 5g fiber.

Ingredients

- **Liquid Base (Choose One):** 1 cup unsweetened almond milk,1 cup oat mill, or 1 cup low-fat dairy milk
- **Main Ingredients:** 1 cup fresh spinach, 1/2 frozen banana, 2 tablespoons natural peanut butter (unsweetened, unsalted), 1/2 teaspoon cinnamon, 1 teaspoon vanilla extract
- **Optional Superfood Additions:** 1 tablespoon chia seeds, 1 tablespoon ground flaxseeds, 1 scoop vanilla protein powder, 1/2 teaspoon maca powder

Optional Variations:
- **Diabetic-Friendly:** Replace banana with 1/4 avocado for lower sugar. Use unsweetened almond milk.
- **Vegan:** Use plant-based milk and ensure peanut butter is dairy-free. Choose plant-based protein powder.
- **Keto:** Replace banana with 1/4 avocado. Use unsweetened almond milk. Add 1 teaspoon of MCT oil.
- **Pregnancy-Safe:** Ensure all ingredients are fresh and thoroughly washed. Use pasteurized plant-based or dairy milk.

Serving Tip: Top with crushed peanuts, a sprinkle of cinnamon, or a drizzle of honey. Serve with a slice of whole-grain toast or a handful of walnuts for a balanced, satisfying meal.

Instructions

1. Wash the spinach thoroughly. Slice the banana into chunks if using fresh.

2. Add ingredients to the blender. Pour the liquid base first, followed by spinach, frozen banana (or avocado), peanut butter, cinnamon, and vanilla extract. Sprinkle in any optional superfoods.

3. Start blending on low speed, gradually increasing to high for 1–2 minutes until smooth and creamy. Adjust consistency with more liquid if needed.

4. Pour into glasses and enjoy immediately.

---

09 Peanut Butter Spinach Bliss

Total: 5 mins   **Servings:** 2   **Level:** 1/5

Nutritional Info (Per Serving, based on almond milk and no optional additions): 280 kcal; 30g carbs; 10g protein; 14g fat; 5g fiber.

Ingredients

- **Liquid Base (Choose One):** 1 cup unsweetened almond milk,1 cup oat mill, or 1 cup low-fat dairy milk
- **Main Ingredients:** 1 cup fresh spinach, 1/2 frozen banana, 2 tablespoons natural peanut butter (unsweetened, unsalted), 1/2 teaspoon cinnamon, 1 teaspoon vanilla extract
- **Optional Superfood Additions:** 1 tablespoon chia seeds, 1 tablespoon ground flaxseeds, 1 scoop vanilla protein powder, 1/2 teaspoon maca powder

Optional Variations:
- **Diabetic-Friendly:** Replace banana with 1/4 avocado for lower sugar. Use unsweetened almond milk.
- **Vegan:** Use plant-based milk and ensure peanut butter is dairy-free. Choose plant-based protein powder.
- **Keto:** Replace banana with 1/4 avocado. Use unsweetened almond milk. Add 1 teaspoon of MCT oil.
- **Pregnancy-Safe:** Ensure all ingredients are fresh and thoroughly washed. Use pasteurized plant-based or dairy milk.

Serving Tip: Top with crushed peanuts, a sprinkle of cinnamon, or a drizzle of honey. Serve with a slice of whole-grain toast or a handful of walnuts for a balanced, satisfying meal..

Instructions

1. Wash the spinach thoroughly. Slice the banana into chunks if using fresh.

2. Add ingredients to the blender. Pour the liquid base first, followed by spinach, frozen banana (or avocado), peanut butter, cinnamon, and vanilla extract. Sprinkle in any optional superfoods.

3. Start blending on low speed, gradually increasing to high for 1–2 minutes until smooth and creamy. Adjust consistency with more liquid if needed.

4. Pour into glasses and enjoy immediately.

10 Refreshing Green Fire

Total: 5 mins   **Servings:** 2   **Level:** 1/5

Nutritional Info (Per Serving, based on almond milk and no optional additions): 110 kcal; 18g carbs; 4g protein; 3g fat; 5g fiber.

Ingredients

- **Liquid Base (Choose One):** 1 cup unsweetened almond milk, 1 cup coconut water, 1 cup plain filtered water
- **Main Ingredients:** 1 cup fresh arugula, 1/2 medium zucchini (chopped, skin on for fiber), 1/2 frozen banana, 1 teaspoon fresh lemon juice, 1/2 teaspoon grated fresh ginger
- **Optional Superfood Additions:** 1 tablespoon chia seeds, 1 teaspoon ground flaxseeds, 1/2 teaspoon spirulina powder, 1 teaspoon hemp seeds

Optional Variations:
- **Diabetic-Friendly:** Replace banana with 1/4 avocado for lower sugar. Use unsweetened almond milk.
- **Vegan:** Use plant-based milk options.
- **Keto:** Replace banana with 1/4 avocado. Use unsweetened almond milk and add 1 teaspoon of MCT oil.
- **Pregnancy-Safe:** Ensure all ingredients are fresh and thoroughly washed. Use pasteurized almond milk or filtered water.

Serving Tip: Garnish with extra chia seeds or a slice of lemon for a fresh citrus note. Serve with a handful of raw almonds or a piece of whole-grain toast with avocado for a nutrient-dense meal.

Instructions

1. Wash arugula and zucchini thoroughly. Slice zucchini into chunks.

2. Add ingredients to the blender. Pour the liquid base first, followed by arugula, zucchini, frozen banana (or avocado), lemon juice, and ginger. Sprinkle in any optional superfoods.

3. Start blending on low speed, gradually increasing to high for 1–2 minutes until smooth and creamy. Adjust consistency with more liquid if needed.

4. Pour into glasses and enjoy immediately.

---

11 Basil Pear Serenity

Total: 5 mins   **Servings:** 2   **Level:** 1/5

Nutritional Info (Per Serving, based on almond milk and no optional additions): 140 kcal; 28g carbs; 3g protein; 3g fat; 5g fiber.

Ingredients

- **Liquid Base (Choose One):** 1 cup unsweetened almond milk, 1 cup coconut water, or 1 cup plain filtered water
- **Main Ingredients:** 1 medium pear (cored and chopped), 1 cup fresh spinach, 5–6 fresh basil leaves, 1/2 teaspoon ground cardamom
- **Optional Sweetener:** 1 teaspoon raw honey or maple syrup
- **Optional Superfood Additions:** 1 tablespoon chia seeds, 1 teaspoon flaxseeds, 1/2 teaspoon spirulina powder

Optional Variations:
- **Diabetic-Friendly:** Replace pear with 1/4 avocado for lower sugar. Use unsweetened almond milk and omit honey.
- **Vegan:** Use maple syrup instead of honey.
- **Keto:** Replace pear with 1/4 avocado. Use unsweetened almond milk and omit honey. Add MCT oil.
- **Pregnancy-Safe:** Ensure all ingredients are fresh and thoroughly washed. Use pasteurized almond milk or filtered water.

Serving Tip: Garnish with a sprinkle of extra cardamom or a basil leaf for a fresh aroma. Serve with a handful of walnuts or a slice of whole-grain toast topped with almond butter for a balanced, energizing breakfast.

Instructions

1. Wash the basil, spinach, and pear. Core and chop the pear into smaller pieces.

2. Add ingredients to the blender. Pour the liquid base first, followed by pear, spinach, basil leaves, cardamom, and honey. Sprinkle in any optional superfoods.

3. Start blending on low speed, gradually increasing to high for 1–2 minutes until smooth and creamy. Adjust consistency with more liquid if needed.

4. Pour into glasses and enjoy immediately.

12 Bok Choy Herbal Tonic

⏱ **Total:** 5 mins   🍴 **Servings:** 2   📊 **Level:** 2/5

Nutritional Info *(Per Serving, based on coconut water and no optional additions)*: 90 kcal; 15g carbs; 3g protein; 1g fat; 4g fiber.

Ingredients

- **Liquid Base (Choose One):** 1 cup coconut water, 1 cup plain filtered water, 1 cup unsweetened almond milk
- **Main Ingredients:** 1 cup bok choy leaves and stems (chopped), 1/2 cup cucumber (peeled for a smoother texture), 1 tablespoon fresh dill (or 1/2 teaspoon dried dill), 1/2 frozen banana, 1 teaspoon fresh lemon juice
- **Optional Sweetener:** 1 teaspoon raw honey, maple syrup, or agave syrup
- **Optional Superfood Additions:** 1 tablespoon chia seeds, 1 teaspoon flaxseeds, 1/2 teaspoon spirulina powder

Optional Variations:
- **Diabetic-Friendly:** Replace banana with 1/4 avocado for lower sugar. Use unsweetened almond milk and avoid additional sweeteners.
- **Vegan:** Use plant-based milk and avoid honey.
- **Keto:** Remove banana and replace with 1/4 avocado. Use unsweetened almond milk and avoid additional sweeteners. Add MCT oil.
- **Pregnancy-Safe:** Ensure all ingredients are fresh and thoroughly washed. Use pasteurized coconut water or filtered water.

🍳 **Serving Tip:** Garnish with a sprig of fresh dill or a slice of cucumber. Pair with a handful of almonds or a slice of whole-grain toast topped with hummus for a light, refreshing meal.

Instructions

1. Wash and chop the bok choy and cucumber. If using fresh dill, remove stems and chop finely.

2. Add ingredients to the blender. Pour the liquid base first, followed by bok choy, cucumber, dill, banana (or avocado), and lemon juice. Sprinkle in any optional superfoods.

3. Start blending on low speed, gradually increasing to high for 1–2 minutes until smooth and creamy. Adjust consistency with more liquid if needed.

4. Pour into glasses and enjoy immediately.

---

13 Moringa Spiced Shake

⏱ **Total:** 5 mins   🍴 **Servings:** 2   📊 **Level:** 3/5

Nutritional Info *(Per Serving, based on coconut water and no optional additions)*: 140 kcal; 28g carbs; 4g protein; 2g fat; 6g fiber.

Ingredients

- **Liquid Base (Choose One):** 1 cup coconut water, 1 cup plain filtered water, or 1 cup unsweetened almond milk
- **Main Ingredients:** 2 ripe kiwis (peeled and chopped), 1/2 small jalapeño (seeded for milder heat, or leave seeds for extra spice), 1/2 frozen banana, 1 teaspoon moringa powder, 1/2 teaspoon fresh lime juice
- **Optional Sweetener:** 1 teaspoon raw honey, maple syrup, or agave syrup
- **Optional Superfood Additions:** 1 tablespoon chia seeds, 1 teaspoon flaxseeds, 1 scoop plant-based protein powder, 1 teaspoon MCT oil

Optional Variations:
- **Diabetic-Friendly:** Replace banana with 1/4 avocado for lower sugar. Use unsweetened almond milk and avoid additional sweeteners.
- **Vegan:** Use plant-based milk and avoid honey. Choose plant-based protein powder.
- **Keto:** Remove banana and replace with 1/4 avocado. Use unsweetened almond milk and avoid additional sweeteners.
- **Pregnancy-Safe:** Ensure all ingredients are fresh and thoroughly washed. Use pasteurized coconut water or filtered water, and reduce jalapeño if sensitive to spice.

🍳 **Serving Tip:** Garnish with a slice of kiwi or a sprinkle of moringa powder. Pair with a handful of pumpkin seeds or a light avocado toast for a metabolism-boosting snack.

Instructions

1. Peel and chop the kiwis. Remove seeds from the jalapeño for milder heat or leave them for extra spice.

2. Add ingredients to the blender. Pour the liquid base first, followed by kiwis, jalapeño, banana (or alternative), moringa powder, and lime juice. Sprinkle in any optional superfoods.

3. Start blending on low speed, gradually increasing to high for 1–2 minutes until smooth and creamy. Adjust consistency with more liquid if needed.

4. Pour into glasses and enjoy immediately.

14 Fennel Wellness Blend

Total: 5 mins **Servings:** 2 **Level:** 2/5

Nutritional Info *(Per Serving, based on coconut water and no optional additions)*: 120 kcal; 18g carbs; 4g protein; 2g fat; 5g fiber.

Ingredients

- **Liquid Base (Choose One):** 1 cup coconut water, 1 cup plain filtered water, or 1 cup unsweetened almond milk
- **Main Ingredients:** 1/2 cup fresh parsley (stems and leaves), 1/2 cup fresh fennel bulb (chopped), 1/2 green apple (cored and chopped), 1/2 frozen banana, 1/2 teaspoon fresh lemon juice
- **Optional Sweetener:** 1 teaspoon raw honey or maple syrup
- **Optional Superfood Additions:** 1 tablespoon chia seeds, 1 teaspoon flaxseeds, 1 scoop unflavored protein powder, 1 teaspoon MCT oil

Optional Variations:
- **Diabetic-Friendly:** Replace banana with 1/4 avocado for lower sugar. Use unsweetened almond milk and avoid additional sweeteners.
- **Vegan:** Use plant-based milk and avoid honey. Choose plant-based protein powder.
- **Keto:** Remove banana and replace with 1/4 avocado. Use unsweetened almond milk and avoid additional sweeteners.
- **Pregnancy-Safe:** Ensure all ingredients are fresh and thoroughly washed. Use pasteurized almond milk or coconut water.

Serving Tip: Garnish with fennel fronds or a few pumpkin seeds for a crunchy texture. Pair with a handful of almonds or a light whole-grain cracker with hummus for a refreshing and nourishing snack.

Instructions

1. Chop the fennel bulb and core the green apple.

2. Add ingredients to the blender. Pour the liquid base first, followed by parsley, fennel, green apple, frozen banana (or alternative), and lemon juice. Sprinkle in any optional superfoods.

3. Start blending on low speed, gradually increasing to high for 1–2 minutes until smooth and creamy. Adjust consistency with more liquid if needed.

4. Pour into glasses and enjoy immediately.

15 Creamy Green Power

Total: 5 mins **Servings:** 2 **Level:** 1/5

Nutritional Info *(Per Serving, based on almond milk and no optional additions)*: 180 kcal; 18g carbs; 6g protein; 10g fat; 7g fiber.

Ingredients

- **Liquid Base (Choose One):** 1 cup unsweetened almond milk, 1 cup coconut water, or 1 cup plain filtered water
- **Main Ingredients:** 1/2 cup steamed and cooled broccoli florets, 1/2 ripe avocado, 1/2 frozen banana, 1/2 teaspoon fresh lemon juice
- **Optional Sweetener:** 1 teaspoon raw honey, maple syrup, or agave syrup
- **Optional Superfood Additions:** 1 tablespoon chia seeds, 1 teaspoon flaxseeds, 1 scoop unflavored protein powder, 1 teaspoon MCT oil

Optional Variations:
- **Diabetic-Friendly:** Replace banana with 1/4 cup zucchini for a lower glycemic option. Use unsweetened almond milk and avoid sweeteners.
- **Vegan:** Use plant-based milk and avoid honey. Choose plant-based protein powder.
- **Keto:** Remove banana and replace with 1/4 avocado. Use unsweetened almond milk and avoid sweeteners.
- **Pregnancy-Safe:** Ensure all ingredients are fresh and thoroughly washed. Use pasteurized almond milk or coconut water.

Serving Tip: Garnish with a few hemp seeds or a drizzle of almond butter. Pair with a handful of raw walnuts or a slice of whole-grain toast with hummus for a balanced meal.

Instructions

1. Steam broccoli and let it cool. Slice the avocado and banana.

2. Add ingredients to the blender. Pour the liquid base first, followed by broccoli, avocado, banana (or alternative), and lemon juice. Sprinkle in any optional superfoods.

3. Start blending on low speed, gradually increasing to high for 1–2 minutes until smooth and creamy. Adjust consistency with more liquid if needed.

4. Pour into glasses and enjoy immediately.

WHY THESE SMOOTHIES ARE EFFECTIVE

Green smoothies are more than just a vibrant addition to your daily routine—they are a nutritional powerhouse designed to nourish, detoxify, and energize. Packed with leafy greens, hydrating ingredients, and superfoods, these blends provide essential vitamins, minerals, and fiber while being low in calories and high in antioxidants. Whether you're looking to boost digestion, promote glowing skin, or fuel your body with plant-based goodness, each smoothie in this collection is formulated to support your overall well-being.

1. Fresh Aloe Breeze
Aloe vera is rich in antioxidants and enzymes that support digestion and skin health. Combined with cucumber for hydration, mint for digestion, and lime for alkalinity, this smoothie is a cooling, gut-friendly refreshment that also soothes inflammation.

2. Classic Spinach Banana Smoothie
This blend pairs iron-rich spinach with potassium-packed banana for a perfect balance of nutrients. Apple adds fiber, while cinnamon helps regulate blood sugar. It's a simple yet effective way to sneak in greens while enjoying a naturally sweet and creamy smoothie.

3. Pineapple Green Fuel
Pineapple's bromelain enzyme aids digestion and reduces inflammation, while kale delivers fiber and essential minerals. A touch of ginger and lime juice adds metabolism-boosting benefits, making this a great pre-workout or morning smoothie.

4. Swiss Chard Mango Delight
Swiss chard is packed with vitamins A, K, and C, supporting immune function and bone health. Mango provides beta-carotene for skin renewal, while ginger adds digestive support. This smoothie is a vibrant blend of flavor and nutrition.

5. Green Apple Rocket Drink
Arugula's peppery flavor and detoxifying properties make it an excellent addition to this apple-ginger-laced smoothie. Rich in fiber and antioxidants, it supports liver function and provides a natural energy boost.

6. Romaine Kiwi Elixir
Romaine lettuce hydrates and alkalizes the body, while kiwi offers vitamin C for immune defense. The combination of banana and lime creates a deliciously smooth and tropical taste that makes greens easy to enjoy.

7. Kale Avocado Protein Mix
A high-protein green smoothie featuring kale, avocado, and protein powder for sustained energy. Healthy fats from avocado enhance nutrient absorption, while ginger and lemon aid digestion. This is a perfect post-workout recovery drink.

8. Green Peach Infusion
Butter lettuce provides a delicate, mild base, while juicy peaches add vitamin C and fiber. Vanilla extract enhances the natural sweetness, creating a light and refreshing smoothie that's both nutritious and delicious.

9. Peanut Butter Spinach Bliss
This creamy, protein-rich smoothie blends spinach with natural peanut butter for a perfect balance of greens and indulgence. Banana adds potassium, while cinnamon enhances flavor and stabilizes blood sugar levels.

10. Refreshing Green Fire
Arugula and zucchini make a unique, slightly spicy combination, with ginger and lemon amplifying detox benefits. This blend is perfect for reducing inflammation and keeping digestion on track.

11. Basil Pear Serenity
Basil is known for its anti-inflammatory and stress-reducing properties, while pears provide hydration and fiber. Cardamom enhances digestion, making this smoothie a fragrant and calming experience.

12. Bok Choy Herbal Tonic
Bok choy is a cruciferous green that supports detoxification and hormone balance. Dill adds a fresh, cleansing flavor, while banana provides a creamy texture. This is a must-try for those looking for something beyond the usual greens.

13. Moringa Spiced Shake
Moringa is a superfood loaded with protein, iron, and antioxidants, making this smoothie a nutrient-dense powerhouse. Kiwi and lime add a tangy contrast, while a hint of jalapeño gives it a metabolism-boosting kick.

14. Fennel Wellness Blend
Fennel supports digestion and reduces bloating, while parsley provides detoxifying chlorophyll. Paired with apple for sweetness and banana for texture, this smoothie is ideal for gut health and hydration.

15. Creamy Green Power
A satisfying, high-fiber blend that combines broccoli, avocado, and banana for a smooth, creamy texture. This smoothie is loaded with healthy fats, plant-based protein, and fiber to keep you full and energized.

The Science Behind the Benefits
- **Alkalizing and Hydrating:** Greens like romaine, cucumber, and aloe vera help restore pH balance and hydrate the body.
- **Antioxidant-Packed:** Kiwi, mango, and pineapple provide vitamins A and C to boost immunity and fight free radicals.
- **Gut Health & Digestion:** Fennel, ginger, and dill soothe the digestive system and promote a healthy microbiome.
- **Energy & Recovery:** Protein-rich ingredients like peanut butter, avocado, and hemp seeds provide sustained energy and muscle recovery support.
- **Detoxification Support:** Arugula, kale, and bok choy assist liver function and natural detoxification pathways.

Green, Clean, and Delicious
These green smoothies prove that healthy eating doesn't have to be boring. With a balance of leafy greens, fresh fruit, and superfoods, they offer a delicious and refreshing way to nourish your body, whether you're looking for energy, detoxification, or a glowing complexion. Enjoy them daily and experience the benefits of vibrant, plant-based nutrition!

ANTIOXIDANT
SMOOTHIES

---

01 Blueberry Antioxidant Vitality Blend

Total: 5 mins   **Servings:** 2   **Level:** 2/5

Nutritional Info *(Per Serving, based on kombucha and no optional additions):* 160 kcal; 30g carbs; 5g protein; 3g fat; 7g fiber.

Ingredients

- **Liquid Base (Choose One):** 1 cup unflavored kombucha, 1 cup coconut water, or 1 cup unsweetened almond milk
- **Main Ingredients:** 1 cup fresh or frozen blueberries, 1 cup fresh spinach leaves, 1/2 frozen banana, 1/2 teaspoon grated fresh ginger, 1 teaspoon fresh lemon juice
- **Optional Sweetener:** 1 teaspoon raw honey, maple syrup, or agave syrup
- **Optional Superfood Additions:** 1 tablespoon chia seeds, 1 teaspoon ground flaxseeds, 1 teaspoon MCT oil, 1 scoop vanilla protein powder

Optional Variations:
- **Diabetic-Friendly:** Replace banana with 1/4 cup zucchini. Use unsweetened almond milk and avoid sweeteners.
- **Vegan:** Use plant-based protein powder and avoid honey.
- **Keto:** Remove banana and replace with 1/4 avocado. Use unsweetened almond milk and avoid sweeteners.
- **Pregnancy-Safe:** Ensure all ingredients are fresh and thoroughly washed. Use pasteurized kombucha or replace with coconut water.
- **Protein-Packed:** Add 1 tablespoon hemp seeds.

Serving Tip: Garnish with fresh blueberries or a sprinkle of chia seeds. Serve with a handful of raw almonds or a light avocado toast for a balanced meal.

Instructions

1. If using fresh banana, freeze it ahead for a creamier texture. Rinse spinach thoroughly.

2. Add ingredients to the blender. Pour the liquid base first, followed by blueberries, spinach, banana (or substitute), ginger, and lemon juice. Sprinkle in any optional superfoods.

3. Start blending on low speed, then gradually increase to high for 1–2 minutes until smooth and creamy. Adjust consistency with more liquid if needed.

4. Pour into glasses and drink immediately.

02 Raspberry Superfood Glow

Total: 5 mins   **Servings:** 2   **Level:** 2/5

Nutritional Info *(Per Serving, based on almond milk and no optional additions)*: 180 kcal; 28g carbs; 6g protein; 7g fat; 8g fiber.

Ingredients

- **Liquid Base (Choose One):** 1 cup unsweetened almond milk,1 cup coconut water, or 1 unsweetened oat milk
- **Main Ingredients:** 1 cup fresh or frozen raspberries, 1 teaspoon fresh lime juice, 1 tablespoon raw cacao powder, 1/2 frozen banana, 1 tablespoon almond butter
- **Optional Sweetener:** 1 teaspoon raw honey, maple syrup, or agave syrup
- **Optional Superfood Additions:** 1 tablespoon chia seeds, 1 teaspoon ground flaxseeds, 1 teaspoon MCT oil, 1 scoop vanilla or chocolate protein powder

Optional Variations:
- **Diabetic-Friendly:** Replace banana with 1/4 avocado. Use unsweetened almond milk and avoid sweeteners.
- **Vegan:** Use plant-based protein powder and avoid honey.
- **Keto:** Remove banana and replace with 1/4 avocado. Use unsweetened almond milk and avoid sweeteners.
- **Pregnancy-Safe:** Ensure all ingredients are fresh and thoroughly washed. Use pasteurized nut milk.
- **Protein-Packed:** Add 1 tablespoon hemp seeds.

Serving Tip: Garnish with fresh raspberries or a sprinkle of cacao nibs. Pair with a handful of raw almonds or a dark chocolate square for an antioxidant-rich snack.

Instructions

1. If using fresh banana, freeze it ahead for a creamier texture. Rinse raspberries thoroughly.

2. Add ingredients to the blender. Pour the liquid base first, followed by raspberries, lime juice, cacao powder, frozen banana (or substitute), and almond butter. Sprinkle in any optional superfoods.

3. Start blending on low speed, then gradually increase to high for 1-2 minutes until smooth and creamy. Adjust consistency with more liquid if needed.

4. Pour into glasses and drink immediately.

---

03 Acai Turmeric Wellness Boost

Total: 5 mins   **Servings:** 2   **Level:** 1/5

Nutritional Info *(Per Serving, based on coconut water and no optional additions)*: 170 kcal; 35g carbs; 4g protein; 3g fat; 6g fiber.

Ingredients

- **Liquid Base (Choose One):** 1 cup coconut water, 1 cup unsweetened almond milk, or 1 cup plain filtered water
- **Main Ingredients:** 1/2 cup frozen acai purée (or 1 tablespoon acai powder), 3/4 cup fresh or frozen pineapple chunks, 1/2 teaspoon ground turmeric (or 1 teaspoon freshly grated turmeric root), 1/2 frozen banana, 1/2 teaspoon grated fresh ginger, 1 teaspoon fresh lime juice
- **Optional Sweetener:** 1 teaspoon raw honey or maple syrup
- **Optional Superfood Additions:** 1 tablespoon chia seeds, 1 teaspoon ground flaxseeds, 1 teaspoon MCT oil, 1 scoop vanilla protein powder

Optional Variations:
- **Diabetic-Friendly:** Replace banana with 1/4 avocado. Use unsweetened almond milk and avoid sweeteners.
- **Vegan:** Use plant-based protein powder and avoid honey.
- **Keto:** Remove banana and replace with 1/4 avocado. Use unsweetened almond milk and avoid sweeteners.
- **Pregnancy-Safe:** Ensure all ingredients are fresh and thoroughly washed. Use pasteurized coconut water or filtered water.
- **Protein-Packed:** Add 1 tablespoon hemp seeds.

Serving Tip: Garnish with a sprinkle of chia seeds or a few fresh pineapple chunks. Pair with a handful of raw almonds or a side of coconut yogurt with granola for an antioxidant-packed snack.

Instructions

1. If using fresh banana, freeze it ahead for a creamier texture. Rinse all produce thoroughly.

2. Add ingredients to the blender. Pour the liquid base first, followed by acai, pineapple, turmeric, banana (or substitute), ginger, and lime juice. Sprinkle in any optional superfoods.

3. Start blending on low speed, then gradually increase to high for 1-2 minutes until smooth and creamy. Adjust consistency with more liquid if needed.

4. Pour into glasses and enjoy fresh.

04 Pomegranate Kiwi Lime Burst Smoothie

Total: 5 mins **Servings:** 2 **Level:** 1/5

Nutritional Info *(Per Serving, based on coconut water and no optional additions):* 160 kcal; 34g carbs; 3g protein; 2g fat; 7g fiber.

Ingredients

- **Liquid Base (Choose One):** 1 cup coconut water, 1 cup unsweetened almond milk, or 1 cup plain filtered water
- **Main Ingredients:** 3/4 cup fresh pomegranate seeds (or 1/2 cup pomegranate juice), 1 large kiwi, peeled and chopped, 1/2 frozen banana, 1 teaspoon fresh lime juice, 1/2 teaspoon grated fresh ginger
- **Optional Sweetener:** 1 teaspoon raw honey or maple syrup
- **Optional Superfood Additions:** 1 tablespoon chia seeds, 1 teaspoon flaxseeds, 1 teaspoon MCT oil, 1 scoop unflavored or vanilla protein powder

Optional Variations:
- **Diabetic-Friendly:** Replace banana with 1/4 avocado for a lower glycemic option. Use unsweetened almond milk and avoid sweeteners.
- **Vegan:** Use plant-based protein powder and avoid honey.
- **Keto:** Remove banana and replace with 1/4 avocado. Use unsweetened almond milk and avoid sweeteners.
- **Pregnancy-Safe:** Ensure all ingredients are fresh and thoroughly washed. Use pasteurized coconut water or filtered water.
- **Protein-Packed:** Add 1 tablespoon hemp seeds.

Serving Tip: Garnish with a few extra pomegranate seeds or a slice of kiwi. Pair with a handful of raw walnuts or a side of Greek yogurt with granola for a fiber-rich, antioxidant-packed meal.

Instructions

1. If using fresh banana, freeze it ahead for a creamier texture. Rinse all produce thoroughly.

2. Add ingredients to the blender. Pour the liquid base first, followed by pomegranate seeds (or juice), kiwi, banana (or substitute), lime juice, and ginger. Sprinkle in any optional superfoods.

3. Start blending on low speed, then gradually increase to high for 1-2 minutes until smooth and creamy. Adjust consistency with more liquid if needed.

4. Pour into glasses and enjoy fresh.

---

05 Hibiscus Berry Antioxidant Power

Total: 5 mins **Servings:** 2 **Level:** 1/5

Nutritional Info *(Per Serving, based on hibiscus tea and no optional additions):* 145 kcal; 32g carbs; 2g protein; 1.5g fat; 7g fiber.

Ingredients

- **Liquid Base (Choose One):** 1 cup brewed and cooled hibiscus tea, 1 cup coconut water, or 1 cup plain filtered water
- **Main Ingredients:** 1 cup fresh or frozen blackberries, 1/2 frozen banana, 1 teaspoon fresh lime juice, 1/2 teaspoon grated fresh ginger, 1/2 teaspoon cinnamon
- **Optional Sweetener:** 1 teaspoon raw honey or maple syrup
- **Optional Superfood Additions:** 1 tablespoon chia seeds, 1 teaspoon flaxseeds, 1 teaspoon MCT oil, 1 scoop unflavored or vanilla protein powder

Optional Variations:
- **Diabetic-Friendly:** Replace banana with 1/4 avocado for a lower glycemic option. Use unsweetened hibiscus tea as the base and avoid additional sweeteners.
- **Vegan:** Use plant-based protein powder and avoid honey.
- **Keto:** Remove banana and replace with 1/4 avocado. Use unsweetened almond milk instead of hibiscus tea and avoid sweeteners.
- **Pregnancy-Safe:** Ensure all ingredients are fresh and thoroughly washed. Use pasteurized coconut water or filtered water.
- **Protein-Packed:** Add 1 tablespoon hemp seeds.

Serving Tip: Garnish with a few extra blackberries or a sprinkle of chia seeds. Pair with a handful of raw almonds or a small bowl of coconut yogurt for a complete antioxidant-packed meal.

Instructions

1. Brew hibiscus tea in advance and allow it to cool completely.

2. If using fresh banana, freeze it ahead for a creamier texture. Rinse all produce thoroughly.

3. Add ingredients to the blender. Pour the liquid base first, followed by blackberries, banana (or substitute), lime juice, and ginger. Sprinkle in any optional superfoods.

4. Start blending on low speed, then gradually increase to high for 1-2 minutes until smooth and creamy. Adjust consistency with more liquid if needed.

5. Pour into glasses and enjoy fresh.

06 Cherry Matcha Antioxidant Shield

Total: 5 mins   **Servings:** 2   **Level:** 2/5

Nutritional Info *(Per Serving, based on kombucha and no optional additions)*: 160 kcal; 30g carbs; 4g protein; 2g fat; 6g fiber.

Ingredients

- **Liquid Base (Choose One):** 1 cup unflavored kombucha, 1 cup coconut water, 1 cup unsweetened almond milk
- **Main Ingredients:** 1 cup fresh or frozen cherries (pitted), 1/2 frozen banana, 1 teaspoon matcha powder, 1 teaspoon fresh lime juice, 1/2 teaspoon grated fresh ginger
- **Optional Sweetener:** 1 teaspoon raw honey or maple syrup
- **Optional Superfood Additions:** 1 tablespoon chia seeds, 1 teaspoon ground flaxseeds, 1 teaspoon MCT oil, 1 scoop vanilla or unflavored protein powder

Optional Variations:
- **Diabetic-Friendly:** Replace banana with 1/4 avocado for a lower glycemic option. Use unsweetened almond milk instead of kombucha. Avoid additional sweeteners.
- **Vegan:** Use plant-based protein powder and avoid honey.
- **Keto:** Remove banana and replace with 1/4 avocado. Use unsweetened almond milk and avoid sweeteners.
- **Pregnancy-Safe:** Ensure all ingredients are fresh and thoroughly washed. Use pasteurized kombucha or replace with coconut water.
- **Protein-Packed:** Add 1 tablespoon hemp seeds.

Serving Tip: Garnish with a few whole cherries or a sprinkle of matcha powder on top. Pair with a handful of raw walnuts or a small bowl of Greek yogurt for a balanced antioxidant-rich meal.

Instructions

1. If using fresh banana, freeze it ahead for a creamier texture. Rinse cherries and remove pits.

2. Add ingredients to the blender. Pour the liquid base first, followed by cherries, banana (or substitute), matcha powder, lime juice, and ginger. Sprinkle in any optional superfoods.

3. Start on low speed, then gradually increase to high for 1–2 minutes until smooth and creamy. Adjust consistency with more liquid if needed.

4. Pour into glasses and enjoy fresh.

---

07 Orange Cranberry Vitality Shake

Total: 5 mins   **Servings:** 2   **Level:** 2/5

Nutritional Info *(Per Serving, based on almond milk and no optional additions)*: 150 kcal; 32g carbs; 3g protein; 1.5g fat; 6g fiber.

Ingredients

- **Liquid Base (Choose One):** 1 cup unsweetened almond milk, 1 cup coconut water, or 1 cup fresh orange juice
- **Main Ingredients:** 1/2 cup fresh or frozen cranberries, 1/2 frozen banana, 1/2 teaspoon ground cinnamon, 1/4 teaspoon ground ginger (or 1/2 teaspoon fresh grated ginger), 1/4 teaspoon ground nutmeg, 1 teaspoon fresh lemon or orange zest
- **Optional Sweetener:** 1 teaspoon raw honey or maple syrup
- **Optional Superfood Additions:** 1 tablespoon chia seeds, 1 teaspoon ground flaxseeds, 1 scoop vanilla protein powder, 1 teaspoon MCT oil

Optional Variations:
- **Diabetic-Friendly:** Replace banana with 1/4 avocado. Use unsweetened almond milk. Avoid additional sweeteners.
- **Vegan:** Use plant-based protein powder and avoid honey.
- **Keto:** Remove banana and replace with 1/4 avocado. Use unsweetened almond milk and avoid sweeteners.
- **Pregnancy-Safe:** Ensure all ingredients are fresh and thoroughly washed. Use pasteurized orange juice or replace with coconut water.
- **Protein-Packed:** Add 1 tablespoon hemp seeds.

Serving Tip: Garnish with a sprinkle of cinnamon or orange zest for a festive touch. Pair with a small handful of almonds or walnuts for a balanced meal. Serve warm by blending with heated almond milk for a cozy, spiced winter drink.

Instructions

1. If using fresh banana, freeze it ahead for a creamier texture. Rinse cranberries well.

2. Add ingredients to the blender. Pour the liquid base first, followed by cranberries, banana (or substitute), cinnamon, ginger, nutmeg, and zest. Sprinkle in any optional superfoods.

3. Start blending on low speed, then gradually increase to high for 1–2 minutes until smooth and creamy. Adjust consistency with more liquid if needed.

4. Pour into glasses and enjoy fresh.

08 Pear and Green Tea Zen

🕐 **Total:** 5 mins   🍴 **Servings:** 2   📊 **Level:** 2/5

Nutritional Info *(Per Serving, based on green tea and no optional additions)*: 140 kcal; 32g carbs; 2g protein; 1g fat; 5g fiber.

Ingredients

- **Liquid Base (Choose One):** 1 cup brewed and cooled green tea, 1 cup unsweetened almond milk, or 1 cup coconut water
- **Main Ingredients:** 1 ripe pear, cored and chopped (skin on for extra fiber), 1/2 frozen banana, 1/2 teaspoon fresh grated ginger, 1 teaspoon fresh lemon juice, 1/2 teaspoon ground cinnamon
- **Optional Sweetener:** 1 teaspoon raw honey or maple syrup
- **Optional Superfood Additions:** 1 tablespoon chia seeds, 1 teaspoon ground flaxseeds, 1 scoop vanilla protein powder, 1 teaspoon matcha powder

Optional Variations:
- **Diabetic-Friendly:** Replace banana with 1/4 avocado. Use unsweetened almond milk and avoid additional sweeteners.
- **Vegan:** Use plant-based protein powder and avoid honey.
- **Keto:** Remove banana and replace with 1/4 avocado. Use unsweetened almond milk and avoid sweeteners.
- **Pregnancy-Safe:** Ensure all ingredients are fresh and thoroughly washed. Use decaffeinated green tea or replace with coconut water.
- **Protein-Packed:** Add 1 tablespoon hemp seeds.

🧑‍🍳 **Serving Tip:** Garnish with a sprinkle of matcha powder or chia seeds for an extra antioxidant kick. Pair with a handful of almonds or a light oat-based snack. Serve chilled over ice for a refreshing summer smoothie or warm by blending with heated almond milk for a cozy winter drink.

Instructions

1. Brew green tea in advance and allow it to cool completely. If using fresh banana, freeze it ahead for a creamier texture.

2. Add ingredients to the blender. Pour the liquid base first, followed by pear, banana (or substitute), ginger, lemon juice, and cinnamon. Sprinkle in any optional superfoods.

3. Start blending on low speed, then gradually increase to high for 1–2 minutes until smooth and creamy. Adjust consistency with more liquid if needed.

4. Pour into glasses and enjoy fresh.

---

09 Lychee Probiotic Vitality

🕐 **Total:** 5 mins   🍴 **Servings:** 2   📊 **Level:** 1/5

Nutritional Info *(Per Serving, based on kombucha and no optional additions)*: 150 kcal; 32g carbs; 3g protein; 1g fat; 5g fiber.

Ingredients

- **Liquid Base (Choose One):** 1 cup unflavored kombucha, 1 cup coconut water, or 1 cup unsweetened almond milk
- **Main Ingredients:** 3/4 cup fresh or canned lychees (drained if using canned), 1/2 cup frozen pineapple chunks, 1/2 cup cucumber, chopped, 1 teaspoon lime juice, 1/4 teaspoon grated fresh ginger
- **Optional Sweetener:** 1 teaspoon raw honey or maple syrup
- **Optional Superfood Additions:** 1 tablespoon chia seeds, 1 teaspoon spirulina powder, 1 teaspoon MCT oil, 1 scoop unflavored protein powder

Optional Variations:
- **Diabetic-Friendly:** Replace pineapple with 1/4 cup zucchini to lower sugar. Use unsweetened kombucha or coconut water. Avoid additional sweeteners.
- **Vegan:** Use coconut water or almond milk, and avoid honey. Choose plant-based protein powder.
- **Keto:** Remove pineapple and use 1/4 avocado for creaminess. Avoid additional sweeteners.
- **Pregnancy-Safe:** Ensure lychees are fresh and all ingredients are washed. Use pasteurized kombucha.
- **Protein-Packed:** Add 1 tablespoon hemp seeds.

🧑‍🍳 **Serving Tip:** Garnish with a few chia seeds or afresh mint leaf. Pair with a handful of raw almonds or a light coconut yogurt bowl for a well-balanced snack. For an extra refreshing touch, serve over ice or blend with crushed ice.

Instructions

1. If using fresh lychees, peel and remove seeds. Slice the cucumber and measure out the pineapple chunks.

2. Add ingredients to the blender. Pour the liquid base first, followed by lychees, pineapple, cucumber, lime juice, and ginger. Sprinkle in any optional superfoods.

3. Start blending on low speed, then gradually increase to high for 1–2 minutes until smooth and creamy. Adjust consistency with more liquid if needed.

4. Pour into glasses and enjoy immediately.

10 Strawberry Hibiscus Cooler

Total: 5 mins **Servings:** 2 **Level:** 1/5

Nutritional Info *(Per Serving, based on hibiscus tea and no optional additions)*: 140 kcal; 28g carbs; 3g protein; 1g fat; 6g fiber.

Ingredients

- **Liquid Base (Choose One):** 1 cup brewed and cooled hibiscus tea, 1 cup coconut water, or 1 cup unsweetened almond milk
- **Main Ingredients:** 1 cup fresh or frozen strawberries, 1/2 cup cucumber (chopped), 1 teaspoon fresh lime juice, 1/2 teaspoon grated fresh ginger
- **Optional Sweetener:** 1 teaspoon raw honey or maple syrup
- **Optional Superfood Additions:** 1 tablespoon chia seeds, 1 teaspoon spirulina powder, 1 teaspoon MCT oil, 1 scoop unflavored protein powder

Optional Variations:
- **Diabetic-Friendly:** Replace strawberries with 1/2 cup raspberries. Use unsweetened hibiscus tea or coconut water. Avoid additional sweeteners.
- **Vegan:** Use coconut water or almond milk, and avoid honey. Choose plant-based protein powder.
- **Keto:** Replace strawberries with 1/4 cup blackberries and avoid additional sweeteners.
- **Pregnancy-Safe:** Ensure all ingredients are fresh and washed. Use pasteurized coconut water if choosing this option.

> **Serving Tip:** Garnish with a fresh mint leaf or a few chia seeds. Serve with a handful of almonds or a coconut yogurt bowl. Enjoy chilled over ice for an even more refreshing experience!

Instructions

1. Brew hibiscus tea ahead and let it cool. Rinse strawberries and cucumber thoroughly.

2. Add ingredients to the blender. Pour the liquid base first, followed by strawberries, cucumber, lime juice, and ginger. Sprinkle in any optional superfoods.

3. Start blending on low speed, then gradually increase to high for 1–2 minutes until smooth and creamy. Adjust consistency with more liquid if needed.

4. Pour into glasses and enjoy immediately!

---

11 Passion Fruit Berry Bliss

Total: 5 mins **Servings:** 2 **Level:** 1/5

Nutritional Info *(Per Serving, based on coconut water and no optional additions)*: 150 kcal; 30g carbs; 3g protein; 3g fat; 8g fiber.

Ingredients

- **Liquid Base (Choose One):** 1 cup coconut water, 1 cup unsweetened almond milk, or 1 cup plain filtered water
- **Main Ingredients:** 1/2 cup fresh passion fruit pulp (about 2 passion fruits, seeds included for fiber), 1 cup fresh or frozen blueberries, 1 tablespoon chia seeds, 1 teaspoon fresh lime juice
- **Optional Sweetener:** 1 teaspoon raw honey or maple syrup
- **Optional Superfood Additions:** 1 tablespoon ground flaxseeds, 1 teaspoon spirulina powder

Optional Variations:
- **Diabetic-Friendly:** Reduce blueberries to 1/2 cup and replace with 1/4 cup raspberries for lower sugar. Use unsweetened almond milk or coconut water. Avoid additional sweeteners.
- **Vegan:** Use coconut water or almond milk, and avoid honey.
- **Keto:** Replace blueberries with 1/4 cup blackberries and avoid additional sweeteners. Add 1 teaspoon MCT oil.
- **Pregnancy-Safe:** Ensure all ingredients are fresh and washed. Use pasteurized coconut water if choosing this option.
- **Protein-Packed:** Add 1 scoop of plant-based protein powder or 1 tablespoon hemp seeds.

> **Serving Tip:** Garnish with a few extra chia seeds or a fresh mint sprig. Serve with a handful of raw almonds or a slice of whole-grain toast with almond butter for a balanced meal. Enjoy chilled over ice for a more refreshing experience!

Instructions

1. Scoop out the passion fruit pulp, ensuring seeds are included.

2. Add ingredients to the blender. Pour the liquid base first, followed by blueberries, passion fruit, lime juice, and chia seeds. Sprinkle in any optional superfoods.

3. Start on low speed, then gradually increase to high for 1–2 minutes until smooth and creamy. Adjust consistency with more liquid if needed.

4. Pour into glasses and enjoy immediately!

12 Sea Buckthorn Matcha Cream

Total: 5 mins   **Servings:** 2   **Level:** 2/5

Nutritional Info *(Per Serving, based on almond milk and no optional additions)*: 180 kcal; 28g carbs; 5g protein; 5g fat; 6g fiber.

Ingredients

- **Liquid Base (Choose One):** 1 cup unsweetened almond milk, 1 cup coconut water, 1 cup plain filtered water
- **·Main Ingredients:** 1/2 cup sea buckthorn juice, 1 teaspoon matcha powder, 1 cup frozen mango chunks, 1 cup fresh spinach leaves, 1/2 teaspoon pure vanilla extract
- **Optional Sweetener:** 1 teaspoon raw honey or maple syrup
- **Optional Superfood Additions:** 1 tablespoon chia seeds, 1 teaspoon ground flaxseeds, 1 scoop of protein powder

Optional Variations:
- **Diabetic-Friendly:** Reduce mango to 1/2 cup and replace with 1/4 cup zucchini. Use unsweetened almond milk and avoid sweeteners.
- **Vegan:** Use plant-based protein powder and avoid honey.
- **Keto:** Replace mango with 1/4 avocado for a lower-carb version. Use unsweetened almond milk and and avoid sweeteners. Add 1 teaspoon MCT oil.
- **Pregnancy-Safe:** Ensure all ingredients are fresh and washed. Use pasteurized sea buckthorn juice if choosing this option.
- **Protein-Packed:** Add 1 tablespoon hemp seeds.

Serving Tip: Garnish with a sprinkle of matcha powder or a few chia seeds. Serve alongside a handful of raw almonds or a slice of whole-grain toast with cashew butter. Enjoy chilled over ice for a more refreshing experience.

Instructions

1. If using fresh sea buckthorn berries, blend and strain to extract juice.

2. Add ingredients to the blender. Pour the liquid base first, followed by sea buckthorn juice, frozen mango, spinach, matcha powder, and vanilla extract. Sprinkle in any optional superfoods.

3. Start blending on low speed, then gradually increase to high for 1–2 minutes until smooth and creamy. Adjust consistency with more liquid if needed.

4. Pour into glasses and enjoy immediately!

---

13 Tamarind Berry Bliss

Total: 5 mins   **Servings:** 2   **Level:** 2/5

Nutritional Info *(Per Serving, based on almond milk and no optional additions)*: 180 kcal; 35g carbs; 4g protein; 4g fat; 8g fiber.

Ingredients

- **Liquid Base (Choose One):** 1 cup unsweetened almond milk, 1 cup coconut water, or 1 cup plain filtered water
- **Main Ingredients:** 2 tablespoons tamarind pulp, 1 cup mixed berries (blueberries, strawberries, raspberries)
- **Optional Sweetener:** 1 teaspoon raw honey or maple syrup
- **Optional Superfood Additions:** 1 tablespoon chia seeds, 1 teaspoon ground flaxseeds

Optional Variations:
- **Diabetic-Friendly:** Reduce mixed berries to 1/2 cup and replace with 1/4 avocado for lower sugar. Use unsweetened almond milk and avoid additional sweeteners.
- **Vegan:** Avoid honey and opt for maple syrup.
- **Keto:** Remove berries and replace with 1/4 avocado. Use unsweetened almond milk and avoid sweeteners. Add 1 teaspoon of MCT oil.
- **Pregnancy-Safe:** Ensure all ingredients are fresh and thoroughly washed. Avoid tamarind if experiencing acid reflux.
- **Protein-Packed:** Add 1 scoop of plant-based protein powder or 1 tablespoon hemp seeds.

Serving Tip: Garnish with a sprinkle of chia seeds or a few whole berries for extra texture. Serve with a handful of raw almonds or a side of coconut yogurt for a more filling meal. Enjoy chilled or over ice for an extra refreshing boost!

Instructions

1. If using whole tamarind pods, soak in warm water for 5–10 minutes, then remove seeds and strain the pulp.

2. Add ingredients to the blender. Pour the liquid base first, followed by tamarind pulp, mixed berries, honey (if using), and chia seeds. Add any optional superfoods.

3. Start blending on low speed, then gradually increase to high for 1–2 minutes until fully blended. Adjust consistency with more liquid if needed.

4. Pour into glasses and enjoy fresh!

14 Elderberry Lemongrass Elixir

Total: 5 mins   **Servings:** 2   **Level:** 2/5

Nutritional Info *(Per Serving, based on lemongrass tea and no optional additions):* 160 kcal; 30g carbs; 4g protein; 2g fat; 6g fiber.

Ingredients

- **Liquid Base (Choose One):** 1 cup brewed & cooled lemongrass tea, 1 cup unsweetened coconut milk, 1 cup coconut water
- **Main Ingredients:** 1/2 cup elderberry syrup(or 1/2 cup fresh elderberries), 1/2 cup frozen mango chunks, 1 teaspoon fresh lime juice
- **Optional Sweetener:** 1 teaspoon honey or maple syrup
- **Optional Superfood Additions:** 1 tablespoon chia seeds, 1 teaspoon ground flaxseeds, 1 scoop unflavored protein powder, 1 teaspoon MCT oil

Optional Variations:
- **Diabetic-Friendly:** Use unsweetened lemongrass tea and avoid sweeteners. Reduce mango to 1/4 cup and replace with 1/4 avocado.
- **Vegan:** Avoid honey and opt for maple syrup. Choose plant-based protein powder.
- **Keto:** Remove mango and replace with 1/4 avocado. Use unsweetened coconut milk and avoid sweeteners.
- **Pregnancy-Safe:** Ensure all ingredients are fresh and thoroughly washed. Use pasteurized elderberry syrup and avoid raw elderberries if unsure.
- **Protein-Packed:** Add 1 tablespoon hemp seeds.

Serving Tip: Garnish with a slice of lime or a few whole elderberries. Serve with a handful of raw nuts or coconut yogurt.

Instructions

1. Brew the lemongrass tea in advance and allow it to cool completely.

2. If using fresh elderberries, rinse them well. Slice the lime.

3. Add ingredients to the blender. Pour the liquid base first, followed by elderberry syrup (or fresh elderberries), frozen mango, and lime juice. Sprinkle in any optional superfoods.

4. Start blending on low speed, then gradually increase to high for 1-2 minutes until smooth and creamy. Adjust consistency with more liquid if needed.

5. Pour into glasses and enjoy immediately!

---

15 Gooseberry Coconut Chai Fusion

Total: 5 mins   **Servings:** 2   **Level:** 2/5

Nutritional Info *(Per Serving, based on coconut milk and no optional additions):* 190 kcal; 24g carbs; 4g protein; 9g fat; 6g fiber.

Ingredients

- **Liquid Base (Choose One):** 1 cup unsweetened almond milk, 1 cup coconut water, or 1 cup fresh orange juice
- **Main Ingredients:** 1/2 cup fresh or frozen cranberries, 1/2 frozen banana, 1/2 teaspoon ground cinnamon, 1/4 teaspoon ground ginger (or 1/2 teaspoon fresh grated ginger), 1/4 teaspoon ground nutmeg, 1 teaspoon fresh lemon or orange zest
- **Optional Sweetener:** 1 teaspoon raw honey or maple syrup
- **Optional Superfood Additions:** 1 tablespoon chia seeds, 1 teaspoon ground flaxseeds, 1 scoop vanilla protein powder, 1 teaspoon MCT oil

Optional Variations:
- **Diabetic-Friendly:** Replace banana with 1/4 avocado. Use unsweetened chai tea or almond milk and avoid sweeteners.
- **Vegan:** Avoid honey and opt for maple syrup. Choose plant-based protein powder.
- **Keto:** Remove banana and replace with 1/4 avocado. Use unsweetened coconut milk and avoid sweeteners.
- **Pregnancy-Safe:** Ensure all ingredients are fresh and well-washed. Use pasteurized coconut milk if choosing this option.
- **Protein-Packed:** Add 1 tablespoon hemp seeds.

Serving Tip: Garnish with a sprinkle of cinnamon or toasted coconut flakes. Serve alongside a handful of raw almonds or a spiced date energy ball. Enjoy chilled over ice for a more refreshing experience.

Instructions

1. Brew the chai tea in advance and let it cool completely.

2. If using fresh gooseberries, rinse them well and remove any stems. Slice the banana.

3. Add ingredients to the blender. Pour the liquid base first, followed by gooseberries, frozen banana (or substitute), cinnamon, cardamom, and ginger. Sprinkle in any optional superfoods.

4. Start blending on low speed, then gradually increase to high for 1-2 minutes until smooth and creamy. Adjust consistency with more liquid if needed.

5. Pour into glasses and enjoy immediately!

WHY THESE SMOOTHIES ARE EFFECTIVE

Antioxidant smoothies are more than just a delicious way to start your day—they are your body's natural defense against oxidative stress, inflammation, and premature aging. These carefully crafted blends are packed with high-antioxidant ingredients like berries, leafy greens, cacao, and superfoods to help neutralize free radicals, support cellular health, and boost overall vitality.

Let's explore why each of these powerhouse smoothies earns its place in your antioxidant arsenal.

1. Blueberry Antioxidant Vitality Blend
Blueberries are one of the most potent sources of anthocyanins, compounds known to combat oxidative stress and support brain function. Combined with spinach for iron and kombucha for gut-friendly probiotics, this smoothie is a powerhouse for cognitive health and digestion.

2. Raspberry Superfood Glow
Raspberries are loaded with ellagic acid, a polyphenol that helps fight inflammation and supports skin health. Cacao powder adds a boost of flavonoids for heart health, while almond butter provides healthy fats that enhance nutrient absorption.

3. Acai Turmeric Wellness Boost
Acai berries are famous for their exceptionally high antioxidant content, while turmeric and ginger reduce inflammation and boost immune function. Paired with pineapple for digestive enzymes, this smoothie is a tropical elixir for whole-body wellness.

4. Pomegranate Kiwi Lime Burst
Pomegranate seeds contain powerful polyphenols that protect skin cells from oxidative stress, while kiwi provides a hefty dose of vitamin C for collagen production. This smoothie is a skin-loving, immune-boosting delight.

5. Hibiscus Berry Antioxidant Power
Hibiscus tea is rich in anthocyanins and vitamin C, supporting cardiovascular health and reducing oxidative damage. Blackberries bring fiber and antioxidants, while ginger adds an anti-inflammatory kick.

6. Cherry Matcha Antioxidant Shield
Cherries provide melatonin for sleep support, while matcha delivers a slow-releasing caffeine boost with calming L-theanine. This blend is a perfect combination of energy and relaxation in one glass.

7. Orange Cranberry Vitality Shake
Cranberries are packed with proanthocyanidins that support urinary tract health, while orange provides an immune-boosting vitamin C punch. Spices like cinnamon and nutmeg add warmth and extra antioxidant benefits.

8. Pear and Green Tea Zen
Green tea is rich in catechins, which enhance metabolism and cellular repair. Paired with fiber-rich pear and ginger for digestion, this smoothie is a calming yet energizing blend for overall balance.

9. Lychee Probiotic Vitality
Lychee is packed with vitamin C and polyphenols, while kombucha introduces beneficial probiotics that support gut health. This combination promotes digestion, hydration, and a radiant complexion.

10. Strawberry Hibiscus Cooler
Hibiscus tea and strawberries work together to fight free radicals and inflammation. This cooling

blend is perfect for summer hydration and skin rejuvenation.

11. Passion Fruit Berry Bliss
Passion fruit contains piceatannol, a unique antioxidant that may support healthy aging. When paired with blueberries and chia seeds, this smoothie becomes a nutrient-dense powerhouse for skin and heart health.

12. Sea Buckthorn Matcha Cream
Sea buckthorn is one of the richest sources of vitamin C and omega fatty acids, supporting both skin elasticity and immune function. Matcha brings a gentle energy lift, while mango adds natural sweetness.

13. Tamarind Berry Bliss
Tamarind is high in polyphenols and tartaric acid, which fight oxidative damage and promote digestion. When blended with mixed berries and chia seeds, this smoothie delivers a tangy, fiber-rich boost.

14. Elderberry Lemongrass Elixir
Elderberries are widely used to strengthen the immune system, while lemongrass provides a refreshing, citrusy twist with antimicrobial benefits. This blend is a perfect choice for staying healthy year-round.

15. Gooseberry Coconut Chai Fusion
Gooseberries (amla) have an exceptionally high vitamin C content, supporting skin and immune health. Coconut milk and chai spices add a creamy, warming depth to this exotic antioxidant-rich smoothie.

The Science Behind the Benefits
- **Free Radical Defense:** Berries, hibiscus, and matcha provide polyphenols that neutralize oxidative stress.
- **Cellular Repair & Longevity:** Ingredients like pomegranate, green tea, and acai protect DNA and support healthy aging.
- **Inflammation Reduction:** Turmeric, ginger, and cacao combat chronic inflammation, reducing the risk of disease.
- **Immune Support:** Vitamin C-rich fruits like elderberry, sea buckthorn, and oranges strengthen immune defenses.
- **Brain & Heart Health:** Cherries, cacao, and lychee promote cognitive function and cardiovascular well-being.

A Delicious Way to Fight Oxidative Stress
These antioxidant smoothies prove that protecting your health can be as delicious as it is powerful. By incorporating these nutrient-dense blends into your daily routine, you're giving your body the best defense against aging, inflammation, and everyday stressors. Drink up and glow from the inside out!

ANTI-AGING
SMOOTHIES

---

01 Goji Berry Recharge

🕐 **Total:** 5 mins   🍴 **Servings:** 2   📶 **Level:** 2/5

Nutritional Info *(Per Serving, based on coconut water and no optional additions)*: 180 kcal; 35g carbs; 6g protein; 4g fat; 8g fiber.

Ingredients

- **Liquid Base (Choose One):** 1 cup coconut water, 1 cup unsweetened almond milk, or 1 cup Greek yogurt
- **Main Ingredients:** 1/4 cup dried goji berries (soaked in warm water for 5 minutes), 1 cup fresh or frozen strawberries, 1/2 cup freshly squeezed orange juice, 1 tablespoon chia seeds, 1/2 cup ice cubes (optional)
- **Optional Sweetener:** 1 teaspoon raw honey or maple syrup
- **Optional Superfood Additions:** 1 teaspoon MCT oil, 1 tablespoon ground flaxseeds, 1 scoop vanilla protein powder, 1/2 teaspoon spirulina powder

Optional Variations:
- **Diabetic-Friendly:** Replace orange juice with 1/4 cup unsweetened coconut milk. Use unsweetened almond milk as the base and omit sweeteners.
- **Vegan:** Use almond milk or coconut water instead of Greek yogurt. Choose plant-based protein powder and avoid honey.
- **Keto:** Replace orange juice with 1/4 avocado. Use almond milk as the base and avoid sweeteners.
- **Pregnancy-Safe:** Ensure all fruits are fresh and thoroughly washed. Use pasteurized juice and avoid unpasteurized ingredients.
- **Protein-Packed:** Add 1 tablespoon of hemp seeds.

🧑‍🍳 **Serving Tip:** Garnish with fresh blueberries or a sprinkle of chia seeds. Serve with a handful of raw almonds or a light avocado toast for a balanced meal.

Instructions

1. Soak the goji berries in warm water for 5 minutes to soften and enhance blending. Drain before use.

2. Add ingredients to the blender. Pour in the liquid base first, followed by strawberries, soaked goji berries, orange juice, and chia seeds. If using ice, add it last.

3. Start blending on low speed for 30 seconds, then gradually increase to high speed for about 1–2 minutes until smooth and creamy. Scrape down the sides if needed. Taste and adjust sweetness if necessary, adding a touch of honey or maple syrup.

4. Pour into glasses and serve immediately for the freshest taste.

02 Rosewater Fig Glow

Total: 5 mins   **Servings:** 2   **Level:** 2/5

Nutritional Info *(Per Serving, based on almond milk and no optional additions)*: 160 kcal; 30g carbs; 4g protein; 2g fat; 6g fiber.

Ingredients

- **Liquid Base (Choose One):** 1 cup unsweetened almond milk, 1 cup whole milk, or 1 cup Greek yogurt
- **Main Ingredients:** 3 fresh figs (stems removed and halved), 1/2 frozen banana, 1 teaspoon rosewater, 1 tablespoon chia seeds
- **Optional Sweetener:** 1 teaspoon raw honey or maple syrup
- **Optional Superfood Additions:** 1 scoop vanilla protein powder,1 teaspoon MCT oil, 1 tablespoon ground flaxseeds, 1/2 teaspoon collagen powder

Optional Variations:
- **Diabetic-Friendly:** Use unsweetened almond milk as the base, omit sweeteners, and replace banana with 1/4 avocado for creaminess with a lower glycemic load.
- **Vegan:** Use almond milk or coconut yogurt instead of Greek yogurt. Choose plant-based protein powder and avoid honey.
- **Keto:** Replace banana with 1/4 avocado. Use whole milk or almond milk as the base and omit sweeteners.
- **Pregnancy-Safe:** Ensure all ingredients are fresh and thoroughly washed. Opt for pasteurized dairy if using yogurt or milk.
- **Protein-Packed:** Add 1 tablespoon of hemp seeds for extra protein.

Serving Tip: Garnish with a drizzle of honey, a few fig slices, or a sprinkle of chia seeds. Serve with a handful of raw almonds or a whole-grain cracker with almond butter.

Instructions

1. Add ingredients to the blender. Pour in the liquid base first, followed by fresh figs, frozen banana, rosewater, and chia seeds. If using ice, add it last.

2. Start blending on low speed for 30 seconds, then gradually increase to high speed for about 1–2 minutes until smooth and creamy. Scrape down the sides if needed. Taste and adjust sweetness if necessary, adding a touch of honey or maple syrup.

3. Pour into glasses and serve immediately.

03 Cucumber Matcha Hydration

Total: 5 mins   **Servings:** 2   **Level:** 2/5

Nutritional Info *(Per Serving, based on almond milk and no optional additions)*: 150 kcal; 28g carbs; 4g protein; 3g fat; 5g fiber.

Ingredients

- **Liquid Base (Choose One):** 1 cup unsweetened almond milk,1 cup coconut water, or 1 cup dairy milk
- **Main Ingredients:** 1/2 large cucumber (peeled and chopped), 1 teaspoon matcha powder, 1/2 frozen banana, 1/2 cup ice cubes (optional)
- **Optional Sweetener:** 1 teaspoon raw honey or maple syrup
- **Optional Superfood Additions:** 1 tablespoon chia seeds, 1 teaspoon MCT oil, 1 scoop vanilla protein powder, 1/2 teaspoon spirulina powder

Optional Variations:
- **Diabetic-Friendly:** Replace banana with 1/4 cup frozen zucchini. Use unsweetened almond milk and omit sweeteners.
- **Vegan:** Use almond milk or coconut water instead of dairy milk. Choose plant-based protein powder and avoid honey.
- **Keto:** Replace banana with 1/4 avocado for a creamy texture and added healthy fats. Use unsweetened almond milk and omit sweeteners.
- **Pregnancy-Safe:** Ensure all ingredients are fresh and thoroughly washed. Choose pasteurized dairy if using milk.
- **Protein-Packed:** Add 1 tablespoon of hemp seeds.

Serving Tip: Garnish with a sprinkle of chia seeds or a dusting of matcha powder. Serve with a handful of raw almonds or a light toast with avocado for a balanced meal. For an extra cooling effect, blend in a few fresh mint leaves.

Instructions

1. Add ingredients to the blender. Pour in the liquid base first, followed by cucumber, frozen banana, matcha powder, and honey or maple syrup (if using). If adding ice cubes, put them in last.

2. Start blending on low speed for 30 seconds, then gradually increase to high speed for about 1–2 minutes until smooth and creamy. Scrape down the sides if needed. Taste and adjust sweetness if necessary, adding a touch of honey or maple syrup.

3. Pour into glasses and serve immediately.

04 Acai Berry Elixir

(clock) **Total:** 5 mins   (utensils) **Servings:** 2   (bars) **Level:** 2/5

Nutritional Info *(Per Serving, based on almond milk and no optional additions):* 190 kcal; 35g carbs; 5g protein; 5g fat; 8g fiber.

Ingredients

- **Liquid Base (Choose One):** 1 cup unsweetened almond milk, 1 cup coconut water, or 1 cup Greek yogurt
- **Main Ingredients:** 1 tablespoon acai powder, 1 cup mixed berries (blueberries, strawberries, raspberries, or blackberries), 1/2 frozen banana, 1 tablespoon ground flaxseeds
- **Optional Sweetener:** 1 teaspoon raw honey or maple syrup
- **Optional Superfood Additions:** 1 scoop vanilla protein powder, 1 teaspoon MCT oil, 1 tablespoon chia seeds, 1/2 teaspoon spirulina powder

Optional Variations:
- **Diabetic-Friendly:** Replace banana with 1/4 cup frozen zucchini. Use unsweetened almond milk and avoid sweeteners.
- **Vegan:** Use almond milk or coconut water instead of Greek yogurt. Choose plant-based protein powder and avoid honey.
- **Keto:** Remove banana and replace with 1/4 avocado for a creamy, low-carb alternative. Use unsweetened almond milk and omit sweeteners.
- **Pregnancy-Safe:** Ensure all ingredients are fresh and thoroughly washed. Choose pasteurized dairy if using yogurt.
- **Protein-Packed:** Add 1 tablespoon of hemp seeds.

(chef icon) **Serving Tip:** Garnish with a sprinkle of chia seeds or a few whole berries. Serve with a handful of raw nuts or a whole-grain granola bar. For an added boost, top with unsweetened coconut flakes or a drizzle of almond butter.

Instructions

1. Add ingredients to the blender. Pour in the liquid base first, followed by mixed berries, banana, acai powder, and ground flaxseeds.

2. Start blending on low speed for 30 seconds, then gradually increase to high speed for about 1–2 minutes until smooth and creamy. Scrape down the sides if needed. Taste and adjust sweetness if necessary, adding a touch of honey or maple syrup.

3. Pour into glasses and serve immediately.

---

05 Aloe Vera & Pineapple Shake

(clock) **Total:** 5 mins   (utensils) **Servings:** 2   (bars) **Level:** 2/5

Nutritional Info *(Per Serving, based on coconut water and no optional additions):* 130 kcal; 30g carbs; 2g protein; 1g fat; 4g fiber.

Ingredients

- **Liquid Base (Choose One):** 1 cup coconut water, 1 cup unsweetened almond milk, or 1 cup Greek yogurt
- **Main Ingredients:** 2 tablespoons fresh aloe vera gel, 1 cup fresh or frozen pineapple chunks, 1/2 frozen banana, 1/2 cup ice cubes
- **Optional Sweetener:** 1 teaspoon raw honey or maple syrup
- **Optional Superfood Additions:** 1 tablespoon chia seeds, 1 teaspoon MCT oil, 1 scoop collagen powder, 1/2 teaspoon turmeric powder

Optional Variations:
- **Diabetic-Friendly:** Replace banana with 1/4 cup frozen zucchini. Use unsweetened almond milk and omit sweeteners.
- **Vegan:** Use coconut water or almond milk instead of Greek yogurt. Choose plant-based protein powder and avoid honey.
- **Keto:** Remove banana and replace with 1/4 avocado for creaminess and healthy fats. Use unsweetened almond milk and avoid sweeteners.
- **Pregnancy-Safe:** Ensure all ingredients are fresh and thoroughly washed. Use pasteurized coconut water if available.
- **Protein-Packed:** Add 1 tablespoon of hemp seeds.

(chef icon) **Serving Tip:** Garnish with a sprinkle of chia seeds or a few coconut flakes. Serve with a handful of raw cashews or a light coconut-based snack for a tropical pairing. For an extra cooling effect, blend in a few fresh mint leaves.

Instructions

1. Prepare the aloe vera gel: If using fresh aloe vera, scoop the gel from a leaf and rinse thoroughly to remove any bitterness.

2. Add ingredients to the blender. Pour in the liquid base first, followed by pineapple chunks, frozen banana, and aloe vera gel. If using ice, add it last.

3. Start blending on low speed for 30 seconds, then gradually increase to high speed for about 1–2 minutes until smooth and creamy. Scrape down the sides if needed. Taste and adjust sweetness if necessary, adding a touch of honey or maple syrup.

4. Pour into glasses and serve immediately.

WHY THESE SMOOTHIES ARE EFFECTIVE

Aging is an inevitable process, but how we nourish our bodies can dramatically influence how gracefully we age. The smoothies in this chapter are designed to fight the underlying causes of aging —oxidative stress, collagen degradation, dehydration, and inflammation—while providing essential nutrients to support longevity, vitality, and radiant skin. These blends don't just offer a refreshing sip; they deliver a concentrated dose of powerful anti-aging compounds.

Let's explore how each of these smoothies contributes to a youthful, healthy glow from the inside out.

1. Goji Berry Recharge
Goji berries are packed with antioxidants, particularly carotenoids like beta-carotene and zeaxanthin, which protect the skin from oxidative stress and UV damage. Their high vitamin C content promotes collagen synthesis, helping maintain skin elasticity and reducing fine lines. Paired with vitamin-rich strawberries and hydrating coconut water, this smoothie supports both skin firmness and deep hydration.

2. Rosewater Fig Glow
Figs are a powerhouse of antioxidants, polyphenols, and fiber, all of which contribute to healthy digestion and radiant skin. They help neutralize free radicals that cause premature aging, while rosewater provides anti-inflammatory benefits, reducing redness and puffiness. The combination of omega-3-rich chia seeds and protein-packed almond milk makes this smoothie a nourishing choice for smooth, glowing skin.

3. Cucumber Matcha Hydration
Hydration is essential for maintaining youthful skin, and cucumber provides a natural source of water, silica, and antioxidants that keep the skin plump and clear. Matcha, with its high concentration of catechins, fights inflammation and free radical damage, preventing collagen breakdown. This blend is a powerhouse for hydration, detoxification, and skin repair.

4. Acai Berry Elixir
Acai berries contain some of the highest antioxidant levels of any fruit, particularly anthocyanins, which combat oxidative stress and reduce inflammation. Combined with mixed berries rich in vitamin C and fiber, this smoothie supports gut health, brain function, and vibrant skin. Flaxseeds provide a boost of omega-3s, helping to reduce dryness and promote skin elasticity.

5. Aloe Vera and Pineapple Shake
Aloe vera is well known for its skin-healing properties, but it also supports gut health, which plays a crucial role in nutrient absorption and overall vitality. The bromelain in pineapple works as a natural anti-inflammatory, reducing puffiness and improving digestion. Together, these ingredients make this smoothie a powerful detoxifier that helps maintain clear, hydrated skin.

The Science Behind the Benefits
Each smoothie in this chapter is designed to target the root causes of aging and promote overall wellness:
- **Antioxidant Defense:** Goji berries, acai, and matcha are packed with free-radical-fighting compounds that protect skin cells from premature aging.
- **Collagen Production:** Vitamin C-rich ingredients like strawberries, oranges, and pineapple help stimulate collagen formation, keeping skin firm and resilient.
- **Hydration & Detoxification:** Cucumber, aloe vera, and coconut water replenish moisture, flush out toxins, and maintain a youthful, dewy glow.
- **Inflammation Reduction:** Polyphenols in figs, catechins in green tea, and bromelain in pineapple work to soothe inflammation, reducing puffiness and redness.

- **Gut & Skin Connection:** Ingredients like chia seeds, flaxseeds, and aloe vera promote gut health, which in turn improves digestion, nutrient absorption, and skin clarity.

A Delicious Approach to Healthy Aging
Aging isn't just about wrinkles—it's about maintaining vitality, energy, and overall well-being. These smoothies provide a simple yet effective way to fuel your body with the right nutrients for long-lasting health. By incorporating them into your routine, you're giving your body and skin the support they need to stay radiant and strong for years to come.

MOOD-BOOSTING
SMOOTHIES

---

01 Spiced Blueberry Ashwagandha Bliss

Total: 5 mins   **Servings:** 2   **Level:** 1/5

Nutritional Info (Per Serving, based on almond milk and no optional additions): 180 kcal; 30g carbs; 5g protein; 6g fat; 7g fiber.

Ingredients

- **Liquid Base (Choose One):** 1 cup unsweetened almond milk, 1 cup oat milk, or 1 cup brewed and cooled chamomile tea
- **Main Ingredients:** 1 cup fresh or frozen blueberries, 1/2 frozen banana, 1/2 teaspoon ground cinnamon, 1/4 teaspoon ground nutmeg, 1/2 teaspoon ashwagandha powder
- **Optional Sweetener:** 1 teaspoon raw honey or maple syrup
- **Optional Superfood Additions:** 1 tablespoon chia seeds, 1 teaspoon ground flaxseeds, 1 scoop vanilla protein powder, 1/2 teaspoon maca powder

Optional Variations:
- **Diabetic-Friendly:** Replace banana with 1/4 cup frozen zucchini. Use unsweetened almond milk and omit sweeteners.
- **Vegan:** Choose plant-based protein powder and avoid honey.
- **Keto:** Remove banana and replace with 1/4 avocado. Use unsweetened almond milk and omit sweeteners.
- **Pregnancy-Safe:** Ensure all ingredients are fresh and thoroughly washed. Opt for pasteurized plant-based milk. Avoid ashwagandha (consult with a doctor before consuming adaptogens during pregnancy).
- **Protein-Packed:** Add 1 tablespoon of hemp seeds.

> **Serving Tip:** Garnish with a sprinkle of cinnamon or a few whole blueberries. Serve with a handful of raw almonds or a whole-grain granola bar. For an added boost, top with toasted coconut flakes or a drizzle of almond butter.

Instructions

1. Add ingredients to the blender. Pour in the liquid base first, followed by blueberries, frozen banana, cinnamon, nutmeg, and ashwagandha powder. If using ice cubes, add them last.

2. Start blending on low speed for 30 seconds, then gradually increase to high speed for about 1–2 minutes until smooth and creamy. Scrape down the sides if needed. Taste and adjust sweetness if necessary, adding a touch of honey or maple syrup.

3. Pour into glasses and serve immediately for the freshest taste.

02 Tamarind Peach Sunshine

Total: 5 mins **Servings:** 2 **Level:** 2/5

Nutritional Info *(Per Serving, based on coconut water and no optional additions)*: 160 kcal; 35g carbs; 3g protein; 1g fat; 5g fiber.

Ingredients

- **Liquid Base (Choose One):** 1 cup coconut water, 1 cup freshly squeezed orange juice, or 1 cup unsweetened almond milk
- **Main Ingredients:** 1 tablespoon tamarind pulp, 1 cup fresh or frozen peaches, 1/2 frozen banana, 1/2 cup ice cubes
- **Optional Sweetener:** 1 teaspoon raw honey or maple syrup
- **Optional Superfood Additions:** 1 tablespoon chia seeds, 1 teaspoon MCT oil, 1 scoop vanilla protein powder, 1/2 teaspoon turmeric powder

Optional Variations:
- **Diabetic-Friendly:** Replace banana with 1/4 cup frozen zucchini. Use unsweetened almond milk and avoid sweeteners.
- **Vegan:** Choose plant-based protein powder and avoid honey.
- **Keto:** Remove banana and replace with 1/4 avocado for a creamy, low-carb alternative. Use unsweetened almond milk and omit sweeteners.
- **Pregnancy-Safe:** Ensure all ingredients are fresh and thoroughly washed. Choose pasteurized orange juice if using.
- **Protein-Packed:** Add 1 tablespoon of hemp seeds.

Serving Tip: Garnish with a sprinkle of chia seeds or a few peach slices for extra texture. Serve with a handful of raw cashews or a light coconut-based snack for a tropical pairing.

Instructions

1. If using fresh tamarind pods, soak in warm water for 10 minutes, then strain out the fibers and seeds.

2. Add ingredients to the blender. Pour in the liquid base first, followed by peaches, frozen banana, and tamarind pulp. If using ice, add it last.

3. Start blending on low speed for 30 seconds, then gradually increase to high speed for about 1–2 minutes until smooth and creamy. Scrape down the sides if needed. Taste and adjust sweetness if necessary, adding a touch of honey or maple syrup.

4. Pour into glasses and serve immediately.

---

03 Blissful Brain Boost

Total: 5 mins **Servings:** 2 **Level:** 2/5

Nutritional Info *(Per Serving, based on almond milk and no optional additions)*: 220 kcal; 24g carbs; 6g protein; 12g fat; 6g fiber.

Ingredients

- **Liquid Base (Choose One):** 1 cup unsweetened almond milk, 1 cup oat milk, or 1 cup coconut water
- **Main Ingredients:** 1 tablespoon raw cacao powder, 1/2 ripe avocado, 1/2 frozen banana, 1/2 teaspoon ground turmeric, 1/4 teaspoon ground cinnamon
- **Optional Sweetener:** 1 teaspoon raw honey or maple syrup
- **Optional Superfood Additions:** 1 scoop vanilla or chocolate protein powder, 1 teaspoon MCT oil, 1 tablespoon chia seeds, 1/2 teaspoon maca powder

Optional Variations:
- **Diabetic-Friendly:** Replace banana with 1/4 cup frozen zucchini. Use unsweetened almond milk and avoid sweeteners.
- **Vegan:** Choose plant-based protein powder and avoid honey.
- **Keto:** Remove banana and replace with 1/4 more avocado. Use unsweetened almond milk and omit sweeteners.
- **Pregnancy-Safe:** Ensure all ingredients are fresh and thoroughly washed. Use pasteurized almond or oat milk if available. Avoid maca powder unless approved by a doctor.
- **Protein-Packed:** Add 1 scoop of protein powder or 1 tablespoon of hemp seeds.

Serving Tip: Garnish with a dusting of cacao powder or a sprinkle of cinnamon. Serve with a handful of raw almonds or a whole-grain granola bar. For an added crunch, top with unsweetened coconut flakes or cacao nibs.

Instructions

1. Add ingredients to the blender. Pour in the liquid base first, followed by cacao powder, avocado, frozen banana, turmeric, and cinnamon. If using ice, add it last.

2. Start blending on low speed for 30 seconds, then gradually increase to high speed for about 1–2 minutes until smooth and creamy. Scrape down the sides if needed. Taste and adjust sweetness if necessary, adding a touch of honey or maple syrup.

3. Pour into glasses and serve immediately.

04 Maca Mood Magic

Total: 5 mins   **Servings:** 2   **Level:** 1/5

Nutritional Info *(Per Serving, based on coconut milk and no optional additions)*: 210 kcal; 38g carbs; 4g protein; 8g fat; 7g fiber.

Ingredients

- **Liquid Base (Choose One):** 1 cup unsweetened coconut milk, 1 cup almond milk, or 1 cup plain water
- **Main Ingredients:** 1 cup mixed berries (blueberries, strawberries, raspberries), 1/2 frozen banana, 1 tablespoon maca powder, 1 tablespoon flaxseeds, 1/2 teaspoon vanilla extract
- **Optional Sweetener:** 1 teaspoon raw honey or maple syrup
- **Optional Superfood Additions:** 1 tablespoon chia seeds, 1 teaspoon MCT oil, 1 scoop vanilla protein powder

Optional Variations:
- **Diabetic-Friendly:** Replace banana with 1/4 cup frozen zucchini. Use unsweetened almond milk and avoid sweeteners.
- **Vegan:** Choose plant-based protein powder and avoid honey.
- **Keto:** Remove banana and replace with 1/4 avocado for a creamy, low-carb option. Use unsweetened almond milk and omit sweeteners.
- **Pregnancy-Safe:** Ensure all ingredients are fresh and thoroughly washed. Use pasteurized coconut milk if choosing this option.
- **Protein-Packed:** Add 1 tablespoon of hemp seeds.

Serving Tip: Garnish with a sprinkle of chia seeds or a few fresh berries for extra texture. Serve with a handful of raw almonds or a small piece of dark chocolate for an extra mood-enhancing boost.

Instructions

1. If using fresh berries, wash and pat dry. Freeze the banana ahead of time for a creamier texture.

2. Add ingredients to the blender. Pour the liquid base first, followed by mixed berries, frozen banana (or alternative), maca powder, flaxseeds, and vanilla extract. Add any optional superfoods.

3. Start blending on low speed for 30 seconds, then gradually increase to high speed for about 1–2 minutes until smooth and creamy. Adjust consistency with more liquid if needed.

4. Pour into glasses and serve immediately.

---

05 Tropical Joy Lift

Total: 5 mins   **Servings:** 2   **Level:** 1/5

Nutritional Info *(Per Serving, based on coconut water and no optional additions)*: 190 kcal; 42g carbs; 3g protein; 2g fat; 6g fiber.

Ingredients

- **Liquid Base (Choose One):** 1 cup coconut water, 1 cup unsweetened almond milk, or 1 cup plain filtered water
- **Main Ingredients:** 1/2 cup fresh passion fruit pulp (about 2 passion fruits), 1 cup fresh or frozen mango chunks, 1/2 frozen banana, 1 tablespoon maca powder
- **Optional Sweetener:** 1 teaspoon raw honey or maple syrup
- **Optional Superfood Additions:** 1 tablespoon chia seeds, 1 teaspoon MCT oil, 1 scoop vanilla or unflavored protein powder

Optional Variations:
- **Diabetic-Friendly:** Replace banana with 1/4 cup frozen zucchini. Use unsweetened almond milk and avoid sweeteners.
- **Vegan:** Choose plant-based protein powder and avoid honey.
- **Keto:** Remove banana and replace with 1/4 avocado. Use unsweetened almond milk and omit sweeteners.
- **Pregnancy-Safe:** Ensure all ingredients are fresh and thoroughly washed. Use pasteurized coconut water if choosing this option.
- **Protein-Packed:** Add 1 tablespoon of hemp seeds or 1/2 scoop of protein powder.

Serving Tip: Garnish with a sprinkle of chia seeds or a few fresh passion fruit seeds for extra texture. Serve with a handful of raw almonds or coconut flakes for a tropical, energy-boosting snack.

Instructions

1. Scoop out fresh passion fruit pulp and freeze the banana in advance for a smoother texture.

2. Add ingredients to the blender. Pour the liquid base first, followed by passion fruit, mango, banana (or alternative), and maca powder. Add any optional superfoods.

3. Start blending on low speed for 30 seconds, then gradually increase to high for 1–2 minutes until smooth and creamy. Adjust consistency with more liquid if needed.

4. Pour into glasses and drink immediately.

06 Banana Chai Delight

Total: 5 mins **Servings:** 2 **Level:** 1/5

Nutritional Info *(Per Serving, based on almond milk and no optional additions)*: 180 kcal; 36g carbs; 4g protein; 3g fat; 5g fiber.

Ingredients

- **Liquid Base (Choose One):** 1 cup unsweetened almond milk, 1 cup oat milk, or 1 cup coconut milk
- **Main Ingredients:** 1 large ripe banana (frozen for a creamier texture), 1 teaspoon ground cinnamon, 1/2 teaspoon ground cardamom, 1/4 teaspoon ground nutmeg
- **Optional Sweetener:** 1 teaspoon raw honey or maple syrup
- **Optional Superfood Additions:** 1 tablespoon chia seeds, 1 scoop vanilla protein powder, 1 teaspoon MCT oil, 1 teaspoon ground flaxseeds

Optional Variations:
- **Diabetic-Friendly:** Replace banana with 1/4 cup frozen zucchini. Use unsweetened almond milk and avoid sweeteners.
- **Vegan:** Choose plant-based protein powder and avoid honey.
- **Keto:** Replace banana with 1/4 avocado. Use unsweetened almond milk and omit sweeteners.
- **Pregnancy-Safe:** Ensure all ingredients are fresh and thoroughly washed. Choose pasteurized milk alternatives if needed.
- **Protein-Packed:** Add 1 tablespoon of hemp seeds.

Serving Tip: Sprinkle a dash of cinnamon on top for extra warmth. Serve with a handful of walnuts or a side of almond butter toast for a complete, mood-enhancing snack.

Instructions

1. Freeze the banana ahead of time for a thicker smoothie.

2. Add ingredients to the blender. Pour the liquid base first, followed by the banana, spices, and honey. Add any optional superfoods last.

3. Start blending on low speed for 30 seconds, then gradually increase to high for 1–2 minutes until smooth and creamy. Adjust consistency with more liquid if needed.

4. Pour into glasses and drink immediately.

---

07 Coconut Cherry Dream

Total: 5 mins **Servings:** 2 **Level:** 2/5

Nutritional Info *(Per Serving, based on coconut milk and no optional additions)*: 250 kcal; 35g carbs; 5g protein; 12g fat; 6g fiber.

Ingredients

- **Liquid Base (Choose One):** 1 cup unsweetened coconut milk, 1 cup almond milk, or 1 cup oat milk
- **Main Ingredients:** 1 cup fresh or frozen dark cherries, 1/2 frozen banana, 1 tablespoon almond butter
- **Optional Sweetener:** 1 teaspoon raw honey, maple syrup, or agave syrup
- **Optional Superfood Additions:** 1 tablespoon chia seeds, 1 teaspoon MCT oil, 1 scoop vanilla protein powder, 1/2 teaspoon cinnamon

Optional Variations:
- **Diabetic-Friendly:** Replace banana with 1/4 avocado. Use unsweetened coconut or almond milk and omit the honey.
- **Vegan:** Avoid honey and use maple syrup or agave. Choose plant-based protein if adding protein.
- **Keto:** Remove banana and replace with 1/4 avocado. Use unsweetened coconut milk and omit sweeteners.
- **Pregnancy-Safe:** Ensure all ingredients are fresh and thoroughly washed. Use pasteurized coconut milk if opting for store-bought.
- **Protein-Packed:** Add 1 tablespoon hemp seeds.

Serving Tip: Garnish with a sprinkle of chia seeds or a few extra cherries. Serve with a handful of raw cashews or a light coconut-based snack for a tropical pairing.

Instructions

1. If using fresh banana, freeze it ahead for a creamier texture.

2. Add the liquid base to the blender first, followed by cherries, frozen banana (or avocado), almond butter, and honey. Sprinkle in any optional superfoods.

3. Start blending on low speed, then gradually increase to high for 1–2 minutes until smooth and creamy. Adjust consistency with more liquid if needed.

4. Pour into glasses and drink immediately.

08 Chocolate Prune Shake

🕐 **Total:** 5 mins
(plus soaking time for prunes)

🍴 **Servings:** 2

📊 **Level:** 1/5

Nutritional Info *(Per Serving, based on almond milk and no optional additions)*: 190 kcal; 38g carbs; 4g protein; 5g fat; 7g fiber.

Ingredients

- **Liquid Base (Choose One):** 1 cup unsweetened almond milk, 1 cup oat milk, 1 cup coconut milk
- **Main Ingredients:** 1/2 cup prunes (soaked in warm water for 10 minutes, then drained), 1 tablespoon raw cacao powder, 1/2 frozen banana, 1 teaspoon pure maple syrup
- **Optional Sweetener:** 1 teaspoon honey or agave syrup
- **Optional Superfood Additions:** 1 tablespoon chia seeds, 1 teaspoon ground flaxseeds, 1 scoop vanilla or chocolate protein powder, 1/4 teaspoon cinnamon

Optional Variations:
- **Diabetic-Friendly:** Reduce prunes to 1/4 cup and replace banana with 1/4 avocado. Use unsweetened almond milk and skip sweeteners.
- **Vegan:** Choose plant-based protein powder and avoid honey.
- **Keto:** Remove banana and replace with 1/4 avocado. Reduce prunes to 1/4 cup and increase cacao for a deeper chocolate flavor.
- **Pregnancy-Safe:** Ensure all ingredients are fresh and thoroughly washed. Prunes are great for digestion!
- **Protein-Packed:** Add 1 tablespoon hemp seeds.

Serving Tip: Garnish with a sprinkle of cacao nibs or a dusting of cinnamon. Pair with a handful of almonds or a dark chocolate square for an indulgent yet balanced snack.

Instructions

1. Place prunes in warm water for 10 minutes, then drain.

2. Slice the banana if using fresh, and measure out cacao powder and sweetener.

3. Pour the liquid base into the blender first, followed by soaked prunes, frozen banana, cacao powder, and any optional superfoods.

4. Start blending on low speed, then gradually increase to high for 1–2 minutes until smooth and creamy. Adjust consistency with more liquid if needed.

5. Pour into glasses and drink immediately.

---

09 Ginger Peach Serenity

🕐 **Total:** 5 mins

🍴 **Servings:** 2

📊 **Level:** 1/5

Nutritional Info *(Per Serving, based on coconut water and no optional additions)*: 140 kcal; 35g carbs; 2g protein; 0.5g fat; 4g fiber.

Ingredients

- **Liquid Base (Choose One):** 1 cup coconut water, 1 cup freshly squeezed orange juice, 1 cup filtered water
- **Main Ingredients:** 1 cup fresh or frozen peach slices, 1/2 teaspoon grated fresh ginger, 1 teaspoon fresh lemon juice
- **Optional Sweetener:** 1 teaspoon raw honey or maple syrup
- **Optional Superfood Additions:** 1 tablespoon chia seeds, 1 teaspoon ground flaxseeds, 1 scoop plant-based protein powder, 1/4 teaspoon turmeric powder

Optional Variations:
- **Diabetic-Friendly:** Replace orange juice with 1/2 cup unsweetened almond milk and 1/2 cup water to reduce sugar. Avoid added sweeteners.
- **Vegan:** Ensure any added sweetener is plant-based.
- **Keto:** Replace orange juice with unsweetened almond milk and swap peaches for 1/4 avocado + a few drops of peach extract.
- **Pregnancy-Safe:** Ensure all ingredients are fresh and thoroughly washed. Avoid unpasteurized juice if store-bought.
- **Protein-Packed:** Add 1 tablespoon of hemp seeds.

Serving Tip: Garnish with a peach slice or a sprinkle of chia seeds. Serve with a handful of raw almonds or a coconut yogurt parfait for a light, energizing snack.

Instructions

1. Slice peaches if using fresh, and grate fresh ginger.

2. Pour the liquid base into the blender first, followed by peaches, grated ginger, lemon juice, and any optional superfoods.

3. Start blending on low speed, then gradually increase to high for 1–2 minutes until smooth and creamy. Adjust consistency with more liquid if needed.

4. Pour into glasses and drink immediately.

10 Passion Kiwi Coconut Refresher

Total: 5 mins **Servings:** 2 **Level:** 1/5

Nutritional Info *(Per Serving, based on coconut water and no optional additions):* 160 kcal; 38g carbs; 2g protein; 1g fat; 6g fiber.

Ingredients

- **Liquid Base (Choose One):** 1 cup coconut water, 1 cup unsweetened almond milk, or 1 cup filtered water
- **Main Ingredients:** 1/2 cup passion fruit pulp (about 2 passion fruits), 1 medium kiwi (peeled and sliced), 1/2 cup frozen pineapple chunks
- **Optional Sweetener:** 1 teaspoon raw honey or maple syrup
- **Optional Superfood Additions:** 1 tablespoon chia seeds, 1/2 teaspoon spirulina powder, 1 teaspoon ground flaxseeds, 1 scoop unflavored collagen or plant-based protein powder

Optional Variations:
- **Diabetic-Friendly:** Reduce pineapple to 1/4 cup and replace with 1/4 avocado. Use unsweetened coconut water and avoid added sweeteners.
- **Vegan:** Skip the honey and use maple syrup if additional sweetness is needed.
- **Keto:** Remove pineapple and replace with 1/4 avocado. Use unsweetened almond milk and avoid sweeteners.
- **Pregnancy-Safe:** Ensure all ingredients are fresh and thoroughly washed. Use pasteurized coconut water if store-bought.
- **Protein-Packed:** Add 1 tablespoon hemp seeds.

Serving Tip: Garnish with fresh passion fruit seeds, a kiwi slice, or a sprinkle of chia seeds. Serve with a handful of raw cashews or a coconut yogurt parfait topped with granola for a complete tropical-inspired snack.

Instructions

1. Scoop out passion fruit pulp, peel and slice the kiwi, and ensure the pineapple is frozen for an extra refreshing texture.

2. Pour the liquid base into the blender first, followed by passion fruit, kiwi, frozen pineapple, and honey. Sprinkle in any optional superfoods.

3. Start blending on low speed, then gradually increase to high for 1-2 minutes until smooth and creamy. Adjust consistency with more liquid if needed.

4. Pour into glasses and drink immediately.

---

11 Dragon Berry Coconut Cream

Total: 5 mins **Servings:** 2 **Level:** 1/5

Nutritional Info *(Per Serving, based on coconut milk and no optional additions):* 220 kcal; 35g carbs; 4g protein; 10g fat; 6g fiber.

Ingredients

- **Liquid Base (Choose One):** 1 cup unsweetened coconut milk, 1 cup oat milk, or 1 cup almond milk
- **Main Ingredients:** 1/2 cup dragon fruit (fresh or frozen), 1/2 cup mixed berries (strawberries, blueberries, raspberries), 1/2 frozen banana, 1 teaspoon vanilla extract
- **Optional Sweetener:** 1 teaspoon raw honey or maple syrup
- **Optional Superfood Additions:** 1 tablespoon chia seeds, 1 teaspoon MCT oil, 1 scoop vanilla protein powder, 1 teaspoon ground flaxseeds

Optional Variations:
- **Diabetic-Friendly:** Replace banana with 1/4 avocado. Use unsweetened almond or coconut milk and avoid added sweeteners.
- **Vegan:** Avoid honey and opt for maple syrup. Choose plant-based protein powder.
- **Keto:** Remove banana and replace with 1/4 avocado. Use unsweetened almond milk and avoid sweeteners.
- **Pregnancy-Safe:** Ensure all ingredients are fresh and thoroughly washed. Use pasteurized coconut milk if store-bought.
- **Protein-Packed:** Add 1 tablespoon hemp seeds.

Serving Tip: Garnish with shredded coconut, a few whole berries, or a sprinkle of chia seeds. Serve with a handful of almonds or a small coconut yogurt parfait topped with granola.

Instructions

1. Slice dragon fruit, measure out berries, and ensure the banana is frozen for optimal creaminess.

2 Pour the liquid base into the blender first, followed by dragon fruit, berries, banana (or substitute), and vanilla extract. Sprinkle in any optional superfoods.

3. Start blending on low speed, then gradually increase to high for 1-2 minutes until smooth and creamy. Adjust consistency with more liquid if needed.

4. Pour into glasses and drink immediately.

12 Fig and Maca Zen Blend

Total: 5 mins   **Servings:** 2   **Level:** 1/5

Nutritional Info *(Per Serving, based on coconut milk and no optional additions)*: 250 kcal; 38g carbs; 6g protein; 10g fat; 7g fiber.

Ingredients

- **Liquid Base (Choose One):** 1 cup unsweetened coconut milk, 1 cup almond milk, 1 cup oat milk
- **Main Ingredients:** 2 dried or fresh figs (stems removed), 1/4 avocado, 1/2 cup frozen mango, 1 teaspoon maca powder, 5 fresh mint leaves, 1 teaspoon fresh lime juice
- **Optional Sweetener:** 1 teaspoon raw honey or maple syrup
- **Optional Superfood Additions:** 1 tablespoon chia seeds, 1 teaspoon ground flaxseeds, 1 teaspoon MCT oil, 1 scoop vanilla protein powder

Optional Variations:
- **Diabetic-Friendly:** Replace mango with 1/4 cup zucchini. Use unsweetened almond milk and avoid added sweeteners.
- **Vegan:** Avoid honey and opt for maple syrup. Choose plant-based protein powder.
- **Keto:** Replace mango with 1/4 avocado. Use unsweetened almond milk and avoid sweeteners.
- **Pregnancy-Safe:** Ensure all ingredients are fresh and thoroughly washed. Use pasteurized almond or coconut milk if store-bought.
- **Protein-Packed:** Add 1 tablespoon hemp seeds.

Serving Tip: Garnish with a few crushed almonds or a sprig of fresh mint. Serve with a handful of walnuts or a small bowl of coconut yogurt topped with cinnamon for a complete mood-boosting experience.

Instructions

1. Remove stems from figs, slice avocado, and measure out other ingredients.

2. Add the liquid base to the blender first, followed by figs, avocado, frozen mango, maca powder, mint leaves, and lime juice. Sprinkle in any optional superfoods.

3. Start blending on low speed, then gradually increase to high for 1–2 minutes until smooth and creamy. Adjust consistency with more liquid if needed.

4. Pour into glasses and drink immediately.

---

13 Tranquili-Tea Tonic

Total: 5 mins   **Servings:** 2   **Level:** 1/5

Nutritional Info *(Per Serving, based on almond milk and no optional additions)*: 220 kcal; 34g carbs; 5g protein; 7g fat; 6g fiber.

Ingredients

- **Liquid Base (Choose One):** 1 cup unsweetened almond milk, 1 cup oat milk, or 1 cup coconut milk
- **Main Ingredients:** 1 ripe pear, cored and chopped, 1/2 frozen banana, 1/2 teaspoon ground cardamom, 1 teaspoon ashwagandha powder, 1 tablespoon almond butter
- **Optional Sweetener:** 1 teaspoon raw honey or maple syrup
- **Optional Superfood Additions:** 1 tablespoon chia seeds, 1 teaspoon flaxseeds, 1 scoop vanilla protein powder, 1/2 teaspoon cinnamon, 1/2 teaspoon maca powder

Optional Variations:
- **Diabetic-Friendly:** Replace banana with 1/4 avocado. Use unsweetened almond or oat milk and avoid added sweeteners.
- **Vegan:** Avoid honey and opt for maple syrup. Choose plant-based protein powder.
- **Keto:** Remove banana and replace with 1/4 avocado. Use unsweetened almond or coconut milk.
- **·Pregnancy-Safe:** Ensure all ingredients are fresh and thoroughly washed.
- **Protein-Packed:** Add 1 tablespoon hemp seeds.

Serving Tip: Garnish with a dusting of cinnamon or a few crushed nuts. Serve alongside a handful of raw walnuts.

Instructions

1. Slice the pear and freeze the banana ahead of time for a smoother texture.

2. Add the liquid base to the blender first, followed by pear, frozen banana (or avocado), cardamom, ashwagandha powder, and almond butter. Sprinkle in any optional superfoods.

3. Start blending on low speed, then gradually increase to high for 1–2 minutes until smooth and creamy. Adjust consistency with more liquid if needed.

4. Pour into glasses and drink immediately.

14 Mindful Chocolate Green Power

Total: 5 mins **Servings:** 2 **Level:** 1/5

Nutritional Info *(Per Serving, based on almond milk and no optional additions)*: 260 kcal; 32g carbs; 7g protein; 12g fat; 6g fiber.

Ingredients

- **Liquid Base (Choose One):** 1 cup unsweetened almond milk, 1 cup oat milk, or 1 cup coconut milk
- **Main Ingredients:** 1 frozen banana, 1 tablespoon raw cacao powder, 1/2 teaspoon spirulina powder, or 1 tablespoon almond butter
- **Optional Sweetener:** 1 teaspoon raw honey or maple syrup
- **Optional Superfood Additions:** 1 teaspoon chia seeds, 1 teaspoon flaxseeds, 1 scoop vanilla or chocolate protein powder, 1 teaspoon MCT oil

Optional Variations:
- **Diabetic-Friendly:** Replace banana with 1/4 avocado and add a few drops of stevia instead of sweeteners.
- **Vegan:** Avoid honey and opt for maple syrup. Choose plant-based protein powder.
- **Keto:** Remove banana and replace with 1/4 avocado. Use unsweetened almond or coconut milk.
- **Pregnancy-Safe:** Ensure all ingredients are fresh and thoroughly washed.
- **Protein-Packed:** Add 1 tablespoon hemp seeds.

Serving Tip: Garnish with a sprinkle of cacao nibs or shredded coconut. Serve with a handful of raw almonds or a square of dark chocolate for an extra indulgence.

Instructions

1. If using fresh banana, freeze it ahead for a creamier texture.

2. Add the liquid base to the blender first, followed by the frozen banana (or avocado), cacao powder, spirulina powder, and almond butter. Sprinkle in any optional superfoods.

3. Start blending on low speed, then gradually increase to high for 1–2 minutes until smooth and creamy. Adjust consistency with more liquid if needed.

4. Pour into glasses and drink immediately.

15 Tropical Matcha Happiness

Total: 5 mins **Servings:** 2 **Level:** 1/5

Nutritional Info *(Per Serving, based on coconut milk and no optional additions)*: 220 kcal; 38g carbs; 4g protein; 7g fat; 5g fiber.

Ingredients

- **Liquid Base (Choose One):** 1 cup unsweetened coconut milk, 1 cup almond milk, or 1 cup coconut water
- **Main Ingredients:** 1 cup fresh or frozen pineapple chunks, 1/2 frozen banana, 1 teaspoon matcha powder, 1 teaspoon fresh lime juice
- **Optional Sweetener:** 1 teaspoon raw honey or maple syrup
- **Optional Superfood Additions:** 1 tablespoon chia seeds, 1 teaspoon MCT oil, 1 scoop vanilla protein powder, 1/2 teaspoon ground flaxseeds

Optional Variations:
- **Diabetic-Friendly:** Replace banana with 1/4 avocado. Use unsweetened almond milk and omit sweeteners.
- **Vegan:** Avoid honey and opt for maple syrup. Choose plant-based protein powder.
- **Keto:** Remove banana and replace with 1/4 avocado. Use unsweetened coconut milk and omit sweeteners.
- **Pregnancy-Safe:** Ensure all ingredients are fresh and thoroughly washed.
- **Protein-Packed:** Add 1 tablespoon hemp seeds.

Serving Tip: Garnish with a sprinkle of chia seeds or a dusting of matcha powder. Serve with a handful of raw almonds or coconut flakes for a tropical pairing.

Instructions

1. If using fresh banana, freeze it ahead for a creamier texture.

2. Add the liquid base to the blender first, followed by pineapple, frozen banana (or avocado), matcha powder, and lime juice. Sprinkle in any optional superfoods.

3. Start blending on low speed, then gradually increase to high for 1–2 minutes until smooth and creamy. Adjust consistency with more liquid if needed.

4. Pour into glasses and drink immediately.

WHY THESE SMOOTHIES ARE EFFECTIVE

Mood isn't just about emotions—it's deeply connected to nutrition, gut health, hormone balance, and brain chemistry. The smoothies in this chapter are formulated with ingredients that naturally enhance serotonin and dopamine levels, stabilize blood sugar, reduce stress-related inflammation, and provide sustained energy. Whether you need an uplift, mental clarity, or relaxation, these blends work harmoniously with your body to support emotional well-being.

1. Spiced Blueberry Ashwagandha Bliss
Blueberries are rich in flavonoids that help reduce stress and improve cognitive function, while ashwagandha, an adaptogen, balances cortisol levels, easing anxiety and tension. The combination of warming spices like cinnamon and nutmeg also enhances circulation and supports digestion, making this smoothie a calming yet invigorating choice.

2. Tamarind Peach Sunshine
Peaches contain natural mood-boosting compounds, while tamarind provides gut-supporting polyphenols that promote serotonin production. Coconut water replenishes electrolytes and prevents fatigue, making this a refreshing blend that lifts spirits and maintains stable energy levels throughout the day.

3. Blissful Brain Boost
Raw cacao stimulates endorphin release, providing a natural "chocolate high" while also enhancing blood flow to the brain. Avocado supplies healthy fats to support neurotransmitter function, while turmeric fights inflammation, helping to prevent brain fog and mental sluggishness.

4. Maca Mood Magic
Maca root is well known for its ability to balance hormones and improve mood, energy, and endurance. Combined with antioxidant-rich berries and flaxseeds, this smoothie supports emotional stability and provides a steady release of energy, making it ideal for busy mornings or pre-workout fuel.

5. Tropical Joy Lift
Passion fruit is loaded with serotonin-boosting compounds that enhance relaxation and mood regulation, while mango provides vitamin B6, a key nutrient in neurotransmitter production. The addition of maca root supports adrenal function, reducing the effects of stress and fatigue.

6. Banana Chai Delight
This creamy blend features bananas, a natural source of tryptophan, which converts into serotonin, improving mood and sleep quality. Warming spices like cinnamon and nutmeg boost circulation and support digestion, making this a comforting and grounding smoothie.

7. Coconut Cherry Dream
Cherries contain anthocyanins that help regulate sleep-wake cycles and reduce oxidative stress, while coconut milk provides healthy fats that support brain function. Almond butter adds protein and magnesium, essential for relaxation and nervous system health.

8. Chocolate Prune Shake
Prunes are rich in fiber and antioxidants that support gut health, while cacao provides mood-enhancing flavonoids. The combination of these ingredients helps improve digestion and stabilizes blood sugar, leading to a calmer, more balanced mood.

9. Ginger Peach Serenity
Ginger has anti-inflammatory properties that reduce stress and anxiety, while peaches contribute

antioxidants and vitamin C, which support brain health. The touch of lemon juice adds brightness and refreshes the senses, making this a perfect pick-me-up.

10. Passion Kiwi Coconut Refresher
Passion fruit and kiwi are rich in vitamin C, which reduces stress hormones and supports adrenal health. Coconut water replenishes electrolytes, preventing dehydration-related fatigue and irritability. This smoothie is a light, tropical way to elevate your mood.

11. Dragon Berry Coconut Cream
Dragon fruit and berries are packed with antioxidants that fight oxidative stress, while coconut milk provides nourishing fats for brain health. This combination helps protect against mood swings and supports skin hydration, making it a beauty-boosting blend as well.

12. Fig and Maca Zen Blend
Figs contain natural sugars and fiber that provide steady energy, while maca root supports hormonal balance and reduces stress-related fatigue. Mint adds a refreshing element, making this smoothie a great choice for both relaxation and revitalization.

13. Tranquili-Tea Tonic
Ashwagandha and cardamom work together to reduce cortisol levels and promote relaxation. Pear provides natural sweetness and hydration, while almond butter adds magnesium to further support a calm nervous system. This blend is designed for unwinding after a long day.

14. Mindful Chocolate Green Power
Cacao and spirulina deliver powerful antioxidants that enhance cognitive function, while banana provides a natural energy boost. Almond butter contributes essential fatty acids that nourish the brain, making this smoothie a perfect blend for focus and productivity.

15. Tropical Matcha Happiness
Matcha is a natural source of L-theanine, an amino acid that promotes relaxation while enhancing mental clarity. Combined with pineapple's vitamin C and lime's refreshing zing, this smoothie delivers a balanced energy boost without the crash of coffee.

The Science Behind the Benefits
These smoothies are designed to enhance mental well-being by targeting the biological pathways that regulate mood and stress:
- **Neurotransmitter Balance:** Ingredients like cacao, maca, and passion fruit naturally support serotonin and dopamine production, improving emotional stability and overall happiness.
- **Cortisol Regulation:** Adaptogens such as ashwagandha and maca help control stress hormones, reducing feelings of anxiety and fatigue.
- **Stable Energy Levels:** Healthy fats from avocado, flaxseeds, and MCT oil prevent energy crashes and sustain cognitive performance.
- **Gut-Brain Connection:** Fiber-rich ingredients like chia seeds, figs, and tamarind support gut health, which plays a crucial role in serotonin production and mood regulation.
- **Inflammation Reduction:** Turmeric, cacao, and cinnamon work to lower inflammation, which has been linked to depression and cognitive decline.

Sip Your Way to a Brighter Mood
Happiness isn't just a state of mind—it's a state of health. These smoothies are carefully designed to enhance mental well-being, whether you need relaxation, focus, or an uplifting boost. By incorporating them into your daily routine, you're giving your body the nutrients it needs to stay calm, energized, and resilient, making every day a little brighter.

STRESS-RELIEF
SMOOTHIES

---

01 Chamomile Lavender Dream

🕐 **Total:** 5 mins 🍴 **Servings:** 2 📶 **Level:** 2/5

Nutritional Info *(Per Serving, based on chamomile tea and no optional additions):* 140 kcal; 30g carbs; 3g protein; 3g fat; 4g fiber.

Ingredients

- **Liquid Base (Choose One):** 1 cup brewed chamomile tea (chilled), 1 cup unsweetened almond milk, 1 cup oat milk
- **Main Ingredients:** 1/2 teaspoon fresh or dried lavender buds, 1/2 frozen banana, 1/2 teaspoon vanilla extract, 1/2 cup ice cubes
- **Optional Sweetener:** 1 teaspoon raw honey or maple syrup
- **Optional Superfood Additions:** 1 scoop vanilla protein powder, 1 tablespoon chia seeds, 1 teaspoon ground flaxseeds, 1 teaspoon MCT oil

Optional Variations:
- **Diabetic-Friendly:** Replace banana with 1/4 cup frozen zucchini. Use unsweetened almond milk and avoid sweeteners.
- **Vegan:** Avoid honey and opt for maple syrup. Choose plant-based protein powder.
- **Keto:** Remove banana and replace with 1/4 avocado. Use unsweetened almond milk and omit sweeteners.
- **Pregnancy-Safe:** Ensure all ingredients are fresh and thoroughly washed. Avoid excessive lavender consumption and consult a healthcare provider before use.
- **Protein-Packed:** Add 1 tablespoon of hemp seeds.

🧑‍🍳 **Serving Tip:** Garnish with a sprinkle of dried lavender buds or a drizzle of honey for extra relaxation. Serve with a handful of raw almonds or a whole-grain granola bar for a balanced snack. For an added touch, warm the smoothie slightly and enjoy as a comforting nighttime beverage.

Instructions

1. Brew the chamomile tea and let it cool completely.

2. Add the liquid base to the blender first, followed by lavender buds, frozen banana, honey, and vanilla extract. If using ice, add it last.

3. Blend on low speed for 30 seconds, then gradually increase to high speed for about 1–2 minutes until smooth and creamy. Scrape down the sides if needed. Taste and adjust sweetness if necessary, adding a touch of honey or maple syrup.

4. Pour into glasses and serve immediately.

02 Reishi Cacao Comfort

Total: 5 mins   **Servings:** 2   **Level:** 2/5

Nutritional Info *(Per Serving, based on almond milk and no optional additions):* 170 kcal; 28g carbs; 4g protein; 5g fat; 6g fiber.

Ingredients

- **Liquid Base (Choose One):** 1 cup unsweetened almond milk, 1 cup oat milk, or 1 cup coconut milk
- **Main Ingredients:** 1 teaspoon reishi mushroom powder, 1 tablespoon raw cacao powder, 1/2 frozen banana, 1/2 teaspoon cinnamon, 1/2 cup ice cubes (optional, for a refreshing chill)
- **Optional Sweetener:** 1 teaspoon raw honey or maple syrup
- **Optional Superfood Additions:** 1 scoop chocolate or vanilla protein powder, 1 tablespoon chia seeds, 1 teaspoon MCT oil, 1/2 teaspoon ashwagandha powder

Optional Variations:
- **Diabetic-Friendly:** Replace banana with 1/4 cup frozen zucchini. Use unsweetened almond milk and avoid sweeteners.
- **Vegan:** Avoid honey and opt for maple syrup. Choose plant-based protein powder.
- **Keto:** Replace banana with 1/4 avocado. Use unsweetened almond milk and omit sweeteners.
- **Pregnancy-Safe:** Ensure all ingredients are fresh and thoroughly washed. Avoid reishi mushroom and ashwagandha unless approved by a doctor.
- **Protein-Packed:** Add 1 tablespoon of hemp seeds.

Serving Tip: Garnish with a dusting of cacao powder or a sprinkle of cinnamon for extra depth of flavor. Serve with a handful of raw almonds or a small piece of dark chocolate for a stress-relieving snack. For an added warming effect, slightly heat the smoothie and enjoy it as a cozy beverage.

Instructions

1. Add the liquid base to the blender first, followed by reishi powder, cacao powder, frozen banana, cinnamon, and honey (if using). If adding ice, put it in last.

2. Blend on low speed for 30 seconds, then gradually increase to high speed for about 1–2 minutes until smooth and creamy. Scrape down the sides if needed. Taste and adjust sweetness if necessary, adding a touch of honey or maple syrup.

3. Pour into glasses and serve immediately.

---

03 Zen Garden Refresh

Total: 5 mins   **Servings:** 2   **Level:** 2/5

Nutritional Info *(Per Serving, based on chamomile tea and no optional additions):* 140 kcal; 28g carbs; 4g protein; 4g fat; 6g fiber.

Ingredients

- **Liquid Base (Choose One):** 1 cup brewed chamomile tea (chilled), 1 cup unsweetened coconut water, 1 cup almond milk
- **Main Ingredients:** 1 cup fresh arugula, 1 large kiwi, peeled and sliced, 1 tablespoon fresh lime juice, 1 tablespoon raw pumpkin seeds, 1/2 cup ice cubes (optional, for a refreshing chill)
- **Optional Sweetener:** 1 teaspoon raw honey or maple syrup
- **Optional Superfood Additions:** 1 scoop unflavored or vanilla protein powder, 1 tablespoon chia seeds, 1/2 teaspoon spirulina powder, 1 teaspoon MCT oil

Optional Variations:
- **Diabetic-Friendly:** Replace honey with a few drops of liquid stevia or omit sweeteners. Use unsweetened coconut water or chamomile tea as the base.
- **Vegan:** Use coconut water or chamomile tea instead of dairy-based liquids. Choose plant-based protein powder if adding protein. Avoid honey.
- **Keto:** Remove kiwi and replace with 1/4 avocado. Use unsweetened almond milk and omit sweeteners.
- **Pregnancy-Safe:** Ensure all ingredients are fresh and thoroughly washed. Opt for pasteurized almond milk or coconut water.
- **Protein-Packed:** Add 1 tablespoon of hemp seeds.

Serving Tip: Garnish with a few pumpkin seeds or a slice of kiwi. Serve with a handful of almonds or a light whole-grain cracker with avocado. Enjoy chilled over ice for a refreshing, detoxifying boost.

Instructions

1. Brew the chamomile tea and let it cool completely.

2. Add the liquid base to the blender first, followed by arugula, kiwi, lime juice, pumpkin seeds, and honey (if using). If adding ice, put it in last.

3. Blend on low speed for 30 seconds, then gradually increase to high speed for about 1–2 minutes until smooth and creamy. Scrape down the sides if needed. Taste and adjust sweetness if necessary, adding a touch of honey or lime juice.

4. Pour into glasses and serve immediately.

04 Black Sesame Blueberry Bliss

Total: 5 mins   **Servings:** 2   **Level:** 2/5

Nutritional Info *(Per Serving, based on almond milk and no optional additions)*: 190 kcal; 30g carbs; 5g protein; 7g fat; 6g fiber.

Ingredients

- **Liquid Base (Choose One):** 1 cup unsweetened almond milk,1 cup oat milk, or 1 cup coconut milk
- **Main Ingredients:** 1 tablespoon black sesame seeds, 1 cup fresh or frozen blueberries,1/2 frozen banana, 1/2 teaspoon ground cardamom, 1/2 cup ice cubes (optional, for a refreshing chill)
- **Optional Sweetener:** 1 teaspoon raw honey or maple syrup
- **Optional Superfood Additions:** 1 scoop vanilla or chocolate protein powder, 1 tablespoon chia seeds, 1 teaspoon MCT oil, 1/2 teaspoon cinnamon

Optional Variations:
- **Diabetic-Friendly:** Replace banana with 1/4 cup frozen zucchini. Use unsweetened almond milk and avoid sweeteners.
- **Vegan:** Choose plant-based protein powder and avoid honey.
- **Keto:** Remove banana and replace with 1/4 avocado. Use unsweetened almond milk and omit sweeteners.
- **Pregnancy-Safe:** Ensure all ingredients are fresh and thoroughly washed. Opt for pasteurized almond or oat milk.
- **Protein-Packed:** Add 1 tablespoon of hemp seeds.

Serving Tip: Garnish with a sprinkle of toasted black sesame seeds or a few whole blueberries for extra texture. Serve with a handful of raw walnuts or a dark chocolate square for a luxurious pairing. Enjoy slightly warmed for a comforting, rich drink on cooler days.

Instructions

1. Add the liquid base to the blender first, followed by black sesame seeds, blueberries, frozen banana, and cardamom. If using ice, add it last.

2. Blend on low speed for 30 seconds, then gradually increase to high speed for about 1–2 minutes until smooth and creamy. Scrape down the sides if needed. Taste and adjust sweetness if necessary, adding a touch of honey or maple syrup.

3. Pour into glasses and serve immediately.

05 Holy Basil Berry Delight

Total: 5 mins   **Servings:** 2   **Level:** 1/5

Nutritional Info *(Per Serving, based on coconut milk and no optional additions)*: 180 kcal; 28g carbs; 3g protein; 7g fat; 5g fiber.

Ingredients

- **Liquid Base (Choose One):** 1 cup unsweetened coconut milk, 1 cup almond milk, 1 cup coconut water
- **Main Ingredients:** 1/2 cup fresh holy basil leaves, 1 cup fresh or frozen strawberries, 1/2 frozen banana, 1/2 cup ice cubes
- **Optional Sweetener:** 1 teaspoon raw honey or maple syrup
- **Optional Superfood Additions:** 1 scoop vanilla protein powder, 1 tablespoon chia seeds, 1 teaspoon ground flaxseeds, 1 teaspoon MCT oil

Optional Variations:
- **Diabetic-Friendly:** Replace banana with 1/4 cup frozen zucchini. Use unsweetened almond milk and omit sweeteners.
- **Vegan:** Choose plant-based protein powder and avoid honey.
- **Keto:** Remove banana and replace with 1/4 avocado. Use unsweetened coconut milk and omit sweeteners.
- **Pregnancy-Safe:** Ensure all ingredients are fresh and thoroughly washed. Avoid excessive holy basil consumption and consult a healthcare provider before use.
- **Protein-Packed:** Add 1 tablespoon of hemp seeds.

Serving Tip: Garnish with a few whole basil leaves or a slice of strawberry for an elegant touch. Serve with a handful of almonds or a light granola bar for a balanced snack. Enjoy slightly chilled or over ice for an extra-refreshing boost.

Instructions

1. Add the liquid base to the blender first, followed by holy basil leaves, strawberries, frozen banana, and honey (if using). If adding ice, put it in last.

2. Blend on low speed for 30 seconds, then gradually increase to high speed for about 1–2 minutes until smooth and creamy. Scrape down the sides if needed. Taste and adjust sweetness if necessary, adding a touch of honey or maple syrup.

3. Pour into glasses and serve immediately.

06 Spicy Ashwagandha Chai

Total: 5 mins **Servings:** 2 **Level:** 2/5

Nutritional Info (Per Serving, based on almond milk and no optional additions): 170 kcal; 32g carbs; 4g protein; 3g fat; 5g fiber.

Ingredients

- **Liquid Base (Choose One):** 1 cup unsweetened almond milk, 1 cup oat milk, 1 cup coconut milk
- **Main Ingredients:** 1/2 teaspoon ashwagandha powder, 1/2 teaspoon ground cinnamon, 1/4 teaspoon ground cardamom, 1/4 teaspoon ground nutmeg. 1/2 frozen banana, 1/2 cup ice cubes (optional, for a refreshing chill)
- **Optional Sweetener:** 1 teaspoon raw honey or maple syrup
- **Optional Superfood Additions:** 1 scoop vanilla or unflavored protein powder, 1 teaspoon MCT oil, 1 tablespoon chia seeds, 1/2 teaspoon turmeric

Optional Variations:
- **Diabetic-Friendly:** Replace banana with 1/4 cup frozen zucchini. Use unsweetened almond milk and omit sweeteners.
- **Vegan:** Choose plant-based protein powder and avoid honey.
- **Keto:** Remove banana and replace with 1/4 avocado. Use unsweetened almond milk and omit sweeteners.
- **Pregnancy-Safe:** Ensure all ingredients are fresh and thoroughly washed. Avoid ashwagandha unless approved by a healthcare provider.
- **Protein-Packed:** Add 1 tablespoon of hemp seeds.

Serving Tip: Garnish with a cinnamon sprinkle or nutmeg dusting for an extra warming touch. Serve with a handful of raw almonds or a piece of dark chocolate for a balanced snack. Enjoy slightly warmed for a cozy, latte-like experience.

Instructions

1. Add the liquid base to the blender first, followed by ashwagandha powder, cinnamon, cardamom, nutmeg, frozen banana, and honey (if using). If adding ice, put it in last.

2. Blend on low speed for 30 seconds, then gradually increase to high speed for about 1-2 minutes until smooth and creamy. Scrape down the sides if needed. Taste and adjust sweetness if necessary, adding a touch of honey or maple syrup.

3. Pour into glasses and serve immediately for the freshest taste.

---

07 Matcha Rhodiola Blend

Total: 5 mins **Servings:** 2 **Level:** 2/5

Nutritional Info (Per Serving, based on coconut milk and no optional additions): 180 kcal; 28g carbs; 3g protein; 7g fat; 4g fiber.

Ingredients

- **Liquid Base (Choose One):** 1 cup unsweetened coconut milk, 1 cup almond milk, 1 cup coconut water
- **Main Ingredients:** 1 teaspoon matcha powder, 1/2 teaspoon Rhodiola powder, 1 cup frozen pineapple chunks, 1 tablespoon fresh lime juice, 1/2 cup ice cubes (optional, for a refreshing chill)
- **Optional Sweetener:** 1 teaspoon raw honey or maple syrup
- **Optional Superfood Additions:** 1 scoop vanilla protein powder, 1 tablespoon chia seeds, 1 teaspoon MCT oil, 1/2 teaspoon turmeric

Optional Variations:
- **Diabetic-Friendly:** Replace pineapple with 1/4 cup frozen zucchini. Use unsweetened coconut milk and avoid sweeteners.
- **Vegan:** Choose plant-based protein powder and avoid honey.
- **Keto:** Replace pineapple with 1/4 avocado for a creamy, low-carb alternative. Use unsweetened coconut milk and omit sweeteners.
- **Pregnancy-Safe:** Ensure all ingredients are fresh and thoroughly washed. Avoid Rhodiola unless approved by a healthcare provider.
- **Protein-Packed:** Add 1 tablespoon of hemp seeds.

Serving Tip: Garnish with a sprinkle of matcha powder or a lime wedge. Serve with a handful of raw cashews or a coconut-based energy ball. Enjoy chilled for an energizing and refreshing experience.

Instructions

1. Pour the liquid base into the blender first, followed by matcha powder, Rhodiola powder, frozen pineapple, and lime juice. If using ice, add it last.

2. Blend on low speed for 30 seconds, then gradually increase to high speed for about 1-2 minutes until smooth and creamy. Scrape down the sides if needed. Taste and adjust sweetness if necessary, adding a touch of honey or maple syrup.

3. Pour into glasses and serve immediately.

08 Spirulina Coconut Cooler

Total: 5 mins   **Servings:** 2   **Level:** 2/5

Nutritional Info *(Per Serving, based on coconut milk and no optional additions)*: 170 kcal; 26g carbs; 4g protein; 6g fat; 4g fiber.

Ingredients

- **Liquid Base (Choose One):** 1 cup unsweetened coconut milk, 1 cup coconut water, 1 cup almond milk
- **Main Ingredients:** 1/2 teaspoon spirulina powder, 1 cup frozen pineapple chunks, 1 tablespoon fresh lime juice, 8–10 fresh mint leaves, 1/2 cup ice cubes (optional, for a refreshing chill)
- **Optional Sweetener:** 1 teaspoon raw honey or maple syrup
- **Optional Superfood Additions:** 1 scoop vanilla protein powder, 1 tablespoon chia seeds, 1 teaspoon MCT oil, 1/2 teaspoon turmeric

Optional Variations:
- **Diabetic-Friendly:** Replace pineapple with 1/4 cup frozen zucchini. Use unsweetened coconut milk and avoid sweeteners.
- **Vegan:** Choose plant-based protein powder and avoid honey.
- **Keto:** Replace pineapple with 1/4 avocado. Use unsweetened coconut milk and omit sweeteners.
- **Pregnancy-Safe:** Ensure all ingredients are fresh and thoroughly washed. Avoid spirulina unless approved by a healthcare provider.
- **Protein-Packed:** Add 1 tablespoon of hemp seeds.

Serving Tip: Garnish with a few fresh mint leaves or a lime wedge. Serve with a handful of raw cashews or a coconut-based energy ball. Enjoy chilled for a deeply hydrating and detoxifying experience.

Instructions

1. Add the liquid base to the blender first, followed by spirulina powder, frozen pineapple, lime juice, fresh mint leaves, and honey (if using). If adding ice, put it in last.

2. Start blending on low speed for 30 seconds, then gradually increase to high speed for about 1–2 minutes until smooth and creamy. Scrape down the sides if needed. Taste and adjust sweetness if necessary, adding a touch of honey or maple syrup.

3. Pour into glasses and serve immediately for the freshest taste.

---

09 Tulsi Pineapple Infusion

Total: 5 mins   **Servings:** 2   **Level:** 1/5

Nutritional Info *(Per Serving, based on coconut water and no optional additions)*: 160 kcal; 30g carbs; 4g protein; 5g fat; 5g fiber.

Ingredients

- **Liquid Base (Choose One):** 1 cup coconut water, 1 cup unsweetened almond milk, 1 cup brewed and chilled green tea
- **Main Ingredients:** 1 cup fresh kale leaves (stems removed), 1/2 cup fresh holy basil (tulsi) leaves, 1 cup frozen pineapple chunks, 1 tablespoon fresh lime juice, 1 tablespoon raw pumpkin seeds, 1/2 cup ice cubes (optional, for a refreshing chill)
- **Optional Sweetener:** 1 teaspoon raw honey or maple syrup
- **Optional Superfood Additions:** 1 scoop vanilla or unflavored protein powder, 1 tablespoon chia seeds, 1 teaspoon MCT oil, 1/2 teaspoon spirulina powder

Optional Variations:
- **Diabetic-Friendly:** Replace pineapple with 1/4 cup frozen zucchini. Use unsweetened coconut water and omit sweeteners.
- **Vegan:** Choose plant-based protein powder and avoid honey.
- **Keto:** Replace pineapple with 1/4 avocado. Use unsweetened coconut water and omit sweeteners.
- **Pregnancy-Safe:** Avoid excessive tulsi consumption unless approved by a healthcare provider.
- **Protein-Packed:** Add 1 tablespoon of hemp seeds.

Serving Tip: Garnish with a few fresh tulsi leaves or a slice of lime. Serve with a handful of nuts or a light chia pudding. Enjoy over ice for an even more cooling effect.

Instructions

1. Add the liquid base to the blender first, followed by kale, holy basil leaves, frozen pineapple, lime juice, and pumpkin seeds. If using ice, put it in last.

2. Blend on low speed for 30 seconds, then gradually increase to high speed for about 1–2 minutes until smooth and creamy. Scrape down the sides if needed. Taste and adjustsweetness if necessary, adding a touch of honey or maple syrup.

3. Pour into glasses and serve immediately.

10 Sacred Basil Citrus Soother

Total: 5 mins | **Servings:** 2 | **Level:** 2/5

Nutritional Info *(Per Serving, based on orange juice and no optional additions)*: 150 kcal; 28g carbs; 4g protein; 4g fat; 5g fiber.

Ingredients

- **Liquid Base (Choose One):** 1 cup freshly squeezed orange juice, 1 cup coconut water, or 1 cup unsweetened almond milk
- **Main Ingredients:** 1 cup Swiss chard leaves (stems removed), 1/2 cup fresh holy basil (tulsi) leaves, 1 tablespoon raw pumpkin seeds, 1/2 teaspoon fresh ginger (grated), 1/2 cup ice cubes (optional, for a refreshing chill)
- **Optional Sweetener:** 1 teaspoon raw honey or maple syrup
- **Optional Superfood Additions:** 1 scoop vanilla or unflavored protein powder, 1 tablespoon chia seeds, 1 teaspoon MCT oil, 1/2 teaspoon turmeric

Optional Variations:
- **Diabetic-Friendly:** Replace orange juice with 1/2 cup unsweetened coconut water and 1/2 cup filtered water. Use unsweetened almond milk and avoid sweeteners.
- **Vegan:** Choose plant-based protein powder. Use maple syrup instead of honey.
- **Keto:** Replace orange juice with 1/4 avocado and use unsweetened almond milk or coconut water. Omit sweeteners.
- **Pregnancy-Safe:** Avoid excessive tulsi consumption unless approved by a healthcare provider.
- **Protein-Packed:** Add 1 tablespoon of hemp seeds.

Serving Tip: Garnish with a sprinkle of chia seeds or a thin slice of orange. Serve with a handful of raw almonds or a whole-grain toast with almond butter. Enjoy slightly chilled for an ultra-refreshing and revitalizing drink.

Instructions

1. Add the liquid base to the blender first, followed by Swiss chard, holy basil leaves, pumpkin seeds, grated ginger. If using ice, put it in last.

2. Blend on low speed for 30 seconds, then gradually increase to high speed for about 1–2 minutes until smooth and creamy. Scrape down the sides if needed. Taste and adjust sweetness if necessary, adding a touch of honey or maple syrup.

3. Pour into glasses and serve immediately.

---

11 Passion Fruit and Lemongrass Elixir

Total: 5 mins | **Servings:** 2 | **Level:** 2/5

Nutritional Info *(Per Serving, based on lemongrass tea and no optional additions)*: 140 kcal; 32g carbs; 2g protein; 1g fat; 5g fiber.

Ingredients

- **Liquid Base (Choose One):** 1 cup brewed lemongrass tea, chilled, 1 cup coconut water, 1 cup unsweetened almond milk
- **Main Ingredients:** 1/2 cup passion fruit pulp, 1 cup frozen mango chunks 1/2 cup ice cubes
- **Optional Sweetener:** 1 teaspoon raw honey or maple syrup
- **Optional Superfood Additions:** 1 scoop vanilla protein powder, 1 tablespoon chia seeds, 1 teaspoon MCT oil, 1/2 teaspoon turmeric

Optional Variations:
- **Diabetic-Friendly:** Replace mango with 1/4 cup frozen zucchini. Use unsweetened coconut water and avoid sweeteners.
- **Vegan:** Choose plant-based protein powder. Use maple syrup instead of honey.
- **Keto:** Replace mango with 1/4 avocado. Use unsweetened coconut water and omit sweeteners.
- **Pregnancy-Safe:** Ensure all ingredients are fresh and thoroughly washed. Avoid unpasteurized passion fruit pulp.
- **Protein-Packed:** Add 1 tablespoon of hemp seeds.

Serving Tip: Garnish with a few passion fruit seeds or a slice of lime. Serve with a handful of cashews or a coconut-based energy ball for a balanced snack. Enjoy chilled for a light, refreshing, and revitalizing elixir.

Instructions

1. Brew the lemongrass tea in advance and let it cool completely.

2. Add the liquid base to the blender first, followed by passion fruit pulp, frozen mango, and ice (if using).

3. Blend on low speed for 30 seconds, then gradually increase to high speed for about 1–2 minutes until smooth and creamy. Scrape down the sides if needed. Taste and adjust sweetness if necessary, adding a touch of honey or maple syrup.

4. Pour into glasses and serve immediately.

12 Lavender Love Splash

🕐 **Total:** 5 mins   🍴 **Servings:** 2   📶 **Level:** 2/5

Nutritional Info *(Per Serving, based on lavender tea and no optional additions):* 120 kcal; 28g carbs; 1g protein; 0.5g fat; 3g fiber.

Ingredients

- **Liquid Base (Choose One):** 1 cup brewed lavender tea, chilled, 1 cup coconut water, 1 cup unsweetened almond milk
- **Main Ingredients:** 1 ½ cups fresh watermelon chunks, 1 teaspoon rose water, 1 tablespoon fresh lime juice, 8–10 fresh mint leaves, 1/2 cup ice cubes
- **Optional Sweetener:** 1 teaspoon raw honey or maple syrup
- **Optional Superfood Additions:** 1 scoop vanilla protein powder, 1 tablespoon chia seeds, 1 teaspoon MCT oil, 1/2 teaspoon turmeric

Optional Variations:
- **Diabetic-Friendly:** Replace watermelon with 1/2 cup frozen zucchini. Use unsweetened lavender tea or coconut water and avoid sweeteners.
- **Vegan:** Choose plant-based protein powder. Use maple syrup instead of honey.
- **Keto:** Replace watermelon with 1/4 avocado. Use unsweetened coconut water and omit sweeteners.
- **Pregnancy-Safe:** Avoid excessive lavender and rose water consumption unless approved by a healthcare provider.
- **Protein-Packed:** Add 1 tablespoon of hemp seeds.

🧑‍🍳 **Serving Tip:** Garnish with a sprig of fresh mint or edible rose petals. Serve with a handful of almonds or a coconut-based energy ball. Enjoy chilled for a deeply hydrating and stress-relieving experience.

Instructions

1. Brew the lavender tea in advance and let it cool completely.

2. Add the liquid base to the blender first, followed by watermelon chunks, rose water, lime juice, fresh mint leaves, and ice (if using).

3. Blend on low speed for 30 seconds, then gradually increase to high speed for about 1–2 minutes until smooth and creamy. Scrape down the sides if needed. Taste and adjust sweetness if necessary, adding a touch of honey or maple syrup.

4. Pour into glasses and serve immediately.

---

13 Butterfly Pea Harmony

🕐 **Total:** 5 mins   🍴 **Servings:** 2   📶 **Level:** 2/5

Nutritional Info *(Per Serving, based on butterfly pea flower and no optional additions):* 130 kcal; 28g carbs; 3g protein; 2g fat; 6g fiber.

Ingredients

- **Liquid Base (Choose One):** 1 cup brewed butterfly pea flower tea, chilled, 1 cup coconut water, 1 cup unsweetened almond milk
- **Main Ingredients:** 1 cup frozen pineapple chunks, 1 tablespoon chia seeds, 1 tablespoon fresh lemon juice, 1/2 cup ice cubes (optional, for extra refreshment)
- **Optional Sweetener:** 1 teaspoon raw honey or maple syrup
- **Optional Superfood Additions:** 1 scoop vanilla protein powder, 1 teaspoon MCT oil, 1 teaspoon ground flaxseeds, 1/2 teaspoon spirulina powder

Optional Variations:
- **Diabetic-Friendly:** Replace pineapple with 1/4 cup frozen zucchini. Use unsweetened coconut water and avoid sweeteners.
- **Vegan:** Choose plant-based protein powder. Use maple syrup instead of honey.
- **Keto:** Replace pineapple with 1/4 avocado. Use unsweetened coconut water and omit sweeteners.
- **Protein-Packed:** Add 1 tablespoon of hemp seeds.

🧑‍🍳 **Serving Tip:** Garnish with a sprinkle of chia seeds or a twist of lemon peel. Serve with a handful of raw cashews or a coconut-based energy ball. Enjoy over ice for an ultra-refreshing and vibrant experience.

Instructions

1. Brew the butterfly pea flower tea in advance and let it cool completely.

2. Add the liquid base to the blender first, followed by frozen pineapple, chia seeds, lemon juice, and ice (if using).

3. Blend on low speed for 30 seconds, then gradually increase to high speed for about 1–2 minutes until smooth and creamy. Scrape down the sides if needed. Taste and adjust sweetness if necessary, adding a touch of honey or maple syrup.

4. Pour into glasses and serve immediately.

14 Corn and Basil Mellow Mix

🕐 **Total:** 5 mins   🍴 **Servings:** 2   📊 **Level:** 2/5

Nutritional Info *(Per Serving, based on coconut water and no optional additions)*: 160 kcal; 35g carbs; 4g protein; 2g fat; 4g fiber.

Ingredients

- **Liquid Base (Choose One):** 1 cup coconut water, 1 cup unsweetened almond milk, 1 cup oat milk
- **Main Ingredients:** 1/2 cup cooked sweet corn kernels, 1/2 cup fresh basil leaves, 1 cup frozen pineapple chunks, 1 tablespoon fresh lime juice, 1/2 cup ice cubes
- **Optional Sweetener:** 1 teaspoon raw honey or maple syrup
- **Optional Superfood Additions:** 1 scoop vanilla protein powder, 1 tablespoon chia seeds, 1 teaspoon MCT oil, 1/2 teaspoon turmeric

Optional Variations:
- **Diabetic-Friendly:** Replace pineapple with 1/4 cup frozen zucchini. Use unsweetened coconut water and avoid sweeteners.
- **Vegan:** Choose plant-based protein powder. Use maple syrup instead of honey.
- **Keto:** Remove sweet corn and replace with 1/4 avocado. Use unsweetened coconut water and omit sweeteners.
- **Pregnancy-Safe:** Ensure all ingredients are fresh and thoroughly washed. Use pasteurized coconut water if available.
- **Protein-Packed:** Add 1 tablespoon of hemp seeds.

> **Serving Tip:** Garnish with a basil leaf or a sprinkle of corn kernels. Serve with a handful of almonds or a whole-grain cracker. Enjoy slightly chilled or over ice for a refreshing and revitalizing experience.

Instructions

1. Add the liquid base to the blender first, followed by cooked sweet corn, fresh basil leaves, frozen pineapple, lime juice, and ice (if using).

2. Blend on low speed for 30 seconds, then gradually increase to high speed for about 1-2 minutes until smooth and creamy. Scrape down the sides if needed. Taste and adjust sweetness if necessary, adding a touch of honey or maple syrup.

3. Pour into glasses and serve immediately.

15 Pink Lotus Relaxation Drink

🕐 **Total:** 5 mins   🍴 **Servings:** 2   📊 **Level:** 2/5

Nutritional Info *(Per Serving, based on coconut water and no optional additions)*: 150 kcal; 32g carbs; 2g protein; 1g fat; 5g fiber.

Ingredients

- **Liquid Base (Choose One):** 1 cup coconut water, 1 cup unsweetened almond milk, 1 cup chilled herbal tea (such as chamomile or lemongrass)
- **Main Ingredients:** 2 tablespoons fresh aloe vera gel, 1 cup pink dragon fruit (diced), 1/2 cup frozen mango chunks, 1 tablespoon fresh lime juice, 1/2 cup ice cubes (optional, for extra refreshment)
- **Optional Sweetener:** 1 teaspoon raw honey or maple syrup
- **Optional Superfood Additions:** 1 scoop vanilla protein powder, 1 tablespoon chia seeds, 1 teaspoon MCT oil, 1/2 teaspoon spirulina

Optional Variations:
- **Diabetic-Friendly:** Replace mango with 1/4 cup frozen zucchini. Use unsweetened coconut water and avoid sweeteners.
- **Vegan:** Choose plant-based protein powder. Use maple syrup instead of honey.
- **Keto:** Replace mango with 1/4 avocado. Use unsweetened coconut water and omit sweeteners.
- **Pregnancy-Safe:** Avoid unprocessed aloe vera gel unless confirmed safe by a healthcare provider.
- **Protein-Packed:** Add 1 tablespoon of hemp seeds.

> **Serving Tip:** Garnish with a slice of dragon fruit or a few chia seeds. Serve with a handful of raw cashews or a coconut-based energy ball. Enjoy chilled for a refreshing, hydrating, and rejuvenating experience.

Instructions

1. If using fresh aloe, scoop out the gel and rinse it thoroughly to remove any bitterness.

2. Add the liquid base to the blender first, followed by dragon fruit, frozen mango, fresh aloe vera gel, and lime juice. If using ice, add it last.

3. Blend on low speed for 30 seconds, then gradually increase to high speed for about 1-2 minutes until smooth and creamy. Scrape down the sides if needed. Taste and adjust sweetness if necessary, adding a touch of honey or maple syrup.

4. Pour into glasses and serve immediately.

WHY THESE SMOOTHIES ARE EFFECTIVE

Each smoothie in this collection has been formulated to deliver targeted benefits that enhance mood, reduce stress, and support overall emotional well-being. These recipes incorporate adaptogens, calming herbs, and nutrient-dense ingredients to regulate cortisol levels, improve serotonin production, and provide a steady source of energy without the spikes and crashes associated with caffeine and sugar. By nourishing both the mind and body, these smoothies serve as a natural way to boost resilience, increase relaxation, and maintain balanced energy throughout the day.

Here's why each of these blends is a powerhouse for mental and emotional wellness:

1. Spiced Blueberry Ashwagandha Bliss
This smoothie combines the antioxidant power of blueberries with the adaptogenic benefits of ashwagandha, a renowned herb for reducing stress and improving mood. The addition of cinnamon and nutmeg enhances circulation and provides natural warmth, while bananas contribute potassium to support brain function and nerve health.

2. Tamarind Peach Sunshine
A tangy, tropical blend of tamarind and peaches, this smoothie is loaded with vitamin C, which plays a crucial role in neurotransmitter synthesis, helping to stabilize mood. Tamarind supports digestion and gut health, which is directly linked to emotional well-being, while peaches offer natural sweetness and hydration.

3. Blissful Brain Boost
Raw cacao in this smoothie provides a rich dose of flavonoids and magnesium, both essential for reducing stress and enhancing cognitive function. Turmeric and cinnamon work as anti-inflammatory agents, protecting brain cells, while avocado adds healthy fats for sustained energy and mental clarity.

4. Maca Mood Magic
Maca root has been traditionally used to balance hormones, improve endurance, and uplift mood. Paired with antioxidant-packed berries and flaxseeds, this smoothie promotes hormonal harmony and delivers a natural boost in energy without caffeine.

5. Tropical Joy Lift
Passion fruit and mango create a vibrant, mood-enhancing blend rich in vitamin B6, which aids in serotonin production. The addition of maca powder supports adrenal health, helping the body adapt to stress more efficiently.

6. Banana Chai Delight
Bananas provide natural tryptophan, a precursor to serotonin, while chai spices like cinnamon, nutmeg, and cardamom promote relaxation and circulation. The cozy, spiced profile of this smoothie makes it a soothing choice for easing tension and calming the nervous system.

7. Coconut Cherry Dream
Cherries are a natural source of melatonin, making this smoothie a great choice for supporting healthy sleep cycles. Almond butter adds protein and healthy fats to stabilize blood sugar levels, preventing mood swings and energy crashes.

8. Chocolate Prune Shake
Raw cacao's mood-enhancing properties combine with fiber-rich prunes to support gut health, which directly influences emotional well-being. This blend also provides natural sweetness and a deep, comforting flavor.

9. Ginger Peach Serenity
Ginger's anti-inflammatory properties help reduce stress-related inflammation in the body, while peaches and lemon juice provide a refreshing, uplifting flavor. This smoothie is ideal for easing tension and promoting relaxation.

10. Passion Kiwi Coconut Refresher
High in vitamin C and hydration-boosting ingredients, this smoothie helps regulate cortisol levels and combat fatigue. Kiwi and passion fruit are known to support immune health and improve mood by reducing oxidative stress.

11. Dragon Berry Coconut Cream
Dragon fruit is packed with antioxidants that protect brain health, while berries provide polyphenols that support cognitive function. The creamy texture, enhanced by coconut milk, makes this blend both indulgent and soothing.

12. Fig and Maca Zen Blend
Figs contribute natural fiber and prebiotics that support gut-brain communication, while maca powder works as an adaptogen to balance mood and enhance vitality. Mint adds a refreshing touch, promoting digestion and mental clarity.

13. Tranquili-Tea Tonic
A blend of calming herbs, ashwagandha, and pear, this smoothie provides gentle adaptogenic support while helping to stabilize blood sugar levels. Cardamom and cinnamon enhance circulation and digestion, promoting a grounded, peaceful state.

14. Mindful Chocolate Green Power
This energizing blend of cacao, spirulina, and banana delivers a balanced combination of antioxidants, healthy fats, and minerals that combat fatigue and promote mental sharpness. Spirulina's detoxifying properties also help reduce oxidative stress, which can impact mood.

15. Tropical Matcha Happiness
Matcha is a natural source of L-theanine, an amino acid known to enhance relaxation and focus simultaneously. Paired with pineapple and lime, this smoothie delivers a refreshing, uplifting experience with a boost of steady energy.

The Science Behind Mood-Boosting Smoothies
These smoothies work because they address the biological and psychological factors that contribute to emotional well-being:
- **Neurotransmitter Support:** Ingredients like bananas, cacao, and matcha enhance serotonin and dopamine production, promoting a stable, happy mood.
- **Adaptogens for Stress Management:** Ashwagandha, maca, and reishi mushroom help the body adapt to stress and regulate cortisol levels.
- **Blood Sugar Stability:** Healthy fats from coconut, almond butter, and avocado prevent energy crashes and mood swings.
- **Gut-Brain Connection:** Fiber-rich ingredients like figs, prunes, and chia seeds support a healthy microbiome, which influences mood and cognitive function.
- **Anti-Inflammatory Properties:** Turmeric, ginger, and cinnamon reduce inflammation, which is linked to anxiety and depression.

A Delicious Way to Elevate Your Mood
These smoothies aren't just functional—they're a joyful, sensory experience. Whether you want to lift your spirits or unwind after a long day, these blends offer an easy and delicious way to feel your best. Incorporating them into your routine'll fuel your body and mind with ingredients that promote long-term emotional resilience and vitality.

HEALTHY DESSERT
SMOOTHIES

---

01 Dark Chocolate Berry Blend

🕐 **Total:** 5 mins   🍴 **Servings:** 2   📶 **Level:** 2/5

Nutritional Info *(Per Serving, based on almond milk and no optional additions)*: 220 kcal; 38g carbs; 5g protein; 7g fat; 8g fiber.

Ingredients

- **Liquid Base (Choose One):** 1 cup unsweetened almond milk, 1 cup oat milk, or 1 cup coconut milk
- **Main Ingredients:** 1 tablespoon unsweetened dark cocoa powder, 1 frozen banana, 1/2 cup fresh or frozen mixed berries, 1 tablespoon ground flaxseeds, 1/2 teaspoon vanilla extract, 1/2 cup ice cubes (optional, for a refreshing chill)
- **Optional Sweetener:** 1 teaspoon raw honey or maple syrup
- **Optional Superfood Additions:** 1 scoop chocolate or vanilla protein powder, 1 tablespoon chia seeds, 1 teaspoon MCT oil, 1/2 teaspoon cinnamon

Optional Variations:
- **Diabetic-Friendly:** Replace banana with 1/4 cup frozen zucchini. Use unsweetened almond milk and avoid sweeteners.
- **Vegan:** Use plant-based protein powder. Choose maple syrup instead of honey.
- **Keto:** Replace banana with 1/4 avocado. Use unsweetened almond or coconut milk and omit sweeteners.
- **Pregnancy-Safe:** Ensure all ingredients are fresh and thoroughly washed. Choose pasteurized plant-based milk if available.
- **Protein-Packed:** Add 1 tablespoon of hemp seeds.

> **Serving Tip:** GGarnish with a sprinkle of dark chocolate shavings or cacao nibs. Serve with a handful of almonds or a piece of dark chocolate. Enjoy slightly chilled for a rich, dessert-like experience.

Instructions

1. Freeze the banana in advance for a creamier texture.

2. Add the liquid base to the blender first, followed by cocoa powder, frozen banana, mixed berries, flaxseeds, and vanilla extract. If using ice, put it in last.

3. Blend on low speed for 30 seconds, then gradually increase to high speed for about 1–2 minutes until smooth and creamy. Scrape down the sides if needed. Taste and adjust sweetness if necessary, adding a touch of honey or maple syrup.

4. Pour into glasses and serve immediately.

02 Strawberry Cheesecake Smoothie

Total: 5 mins   **Servings:** 2   **Level:** 2/5

Nutritional Info *(Per Serving, based on almond milk and no optional additions)*: 210 kcal; 32g carbs; 8g protein; 5g fat; 4g fiber.

Ingredients

- **Liquid Base (Choose One):** 1 cup unsweetened almond milk, 1 cup oat milk, or 1 cup dairy milk
- **Main Ingredients:** 1 cup frozen strawberries, 1/2 cup plain Greek yogurt, 1/2 teaspoon vanilla extract, 1/2 cup ice cubes (optional, for a thicker texture), 1 tablespoon graham cracker crumbs (optional, for an authentic cheesecake feel)
- **Optional Sweetener:** 1 teaspoon raw honey or maple syrup
- **Optional Superfood Additions:** 1 scoop vanilla protein powder, 1 tablespoon chia seeds, 1 teaspoon MCT oil, 1/2 teaspoon ground cinnamon

Optional Variations:
- **Diabetic-Friendly:** Replace honey with a few drops of liquid stevia or omit sweeteners. Use unsweetened almond milk and avoid graham cracker crumbs.
- **Vegan:** Use coconut yogurt or plant-based Greek yogurt. Choose plant-based milk and protein powder. Replace honey with maple syrup.
- **Keto:** Replace strawberries with raspberries. Use unsweetened almond or coconut milk and omit sweeteners and graham crackers.
- **Pregnancy-Safe:** Use pasteurized dairy products.
- **Protein-Packed:** Add 1 tablespoon of hemp seeds.

> **Serving Tip:** Garnish with a few fresh strawberry slices or a light dusting of graham cracker crumbs. Serve with a handful of almonds or a piece of dark chocolate.

Instructions

1. Freeze strawberries in advance.

2. Add the liquid base to the blender first, followed by frozen strawberries, Greek yogurt, vanilla extract, honey (if using), and ice (if using).

3. Blend on low speed for 30 seconds, then gradually increase to high speed for about 1-2 minutes until smooth and creamy. Scrape down the sides if needed. Taste and adjust sweetness if necessary, adding a touch of honey or maple syrup.

4. Pour into glasses and serve immediately. If using, sprinkle graham cracker crumbs on top for a true cheesecake feel.

---

03 Gingerbread Smoothie

Total: 5 mins   **Servings:** 2   **Level:** 2/5

Nutritional Info *(Per Serving, based on almond milk and no optional additions)*: 210 kcal; 40g carbs; 6g protein; 4g fat; 6g fiber.

Ingredients

- **Liquid Base (Choose One):** 1 cup unsweetened almond milk, 1 cup oat milk, or 1 cup coconut milk
- **Main Ingredients:** 1 frozen banana, 1 tablespoon molasses, 1/4 cup rolled oats, 1/2 teaspoon ground ginger, 1/2 teaspoon ground cinnamon, 1/4 teaspoon ground nutmeg, 1/2 teaspoon vanilla extract, 1/2 cup ice cubes (optional, for a refreshing chill)
- **Optional Sweetener:** 1 teaspoon raw honey or maple syrup
- **Optional Superfood Additions:** 1 scoop vanilla protein powder, 1 tablespoon chia seeds, 1 teaspoon MCT oil, 1/2 teaspoon ground cloves

Optional Variations:
- **Diabetic-Friendly:** Replace banana with 1/4 cup frozen zucchini. Use unsweetened almond milk and avoid sweeteners.
- **Gluten-Free:** Make sure to use certified gluten-free oats or replace oats with 2 tablespoons of cooked quinoa.
- **Vegan:** Use plant-based protein powder. Choose maple syrup instead of honey.
- **Keto:** Replace banana with 1/4 avocado. Use unsweetened almond or coconut milk and omit sweeteners.
- **Pregnancy-Safe:** Use pasteurized plant-based milk if available.
- **Protein-Packed:** Add 1 tablespoon of hemp seeds.

> **Serving Tip:** Garnish with a sprinkle of cinnamon or crushed gingerbread cookie crumbs. Serve with a handful of walnuts or a small oat bar. Enjoy slightly chilled for a warm, spiced holiday-inspired experience.

Instructions

1. Freeze the banana in advance for a creamier texture.

2. Add the liquid base to the blender first, followed by frozen banana, molasses, oats, ginger, cinnamon, nutmeg, vanilla extract, and ice (if using).

3. Blend on low speed for 30 seconds, then gradually increase to high speed for about 1-2 minutes until smooth and creamy. Scrape down the sides if needed. Taste and adjust sweetness if necessary, adding a touch of molasses or maple syrup if needed.

4. Pour into glasses and serve immediately.

04 Red Velvet Smoothie

Total: 5 mins   **Servings:** 2   **Level:** 2/5

Nutritional Info *(Per Serving, based on oat milk and no optional additions)*: 190 kcal; 35g carbs; 8g protein; 4g fat; 6g fiber.

Ingredients

- **Liquid Base (Choose One):** 1 cup unsweetened almond milk, 1 cup oat milk, or 1 cup coconut milk
- **Main Ingredients:** 1/2 cup cooked beetroot (chopped), 1 tablespoon cacao powder, 1/2 cup plain Greek yogurt, 1 frozen banana, 1/2 teaspoon vanilla extract, 1/2 cup ice cubes (optional, for a refreshing chill)
- **Optional Sweetener:** 1 teaspoon raw honey or maple syrup
- **Optional Superfood Additions:** 1 scoop chocolate or vanilla protein powder, 1 tablespoon chia seeds, 1 teaspoon MCT oil, 1/2 teaspoon cinnamon

Optional Variations:
- **Diabetic-Friendly:** Replace banana with 1/4 cup frozen zucchini. Use unsweetened almond milk and avoid sweeteners.
- **Vegan:** Swap Greek yogurt for a dairy-free alternative. Choose maple syrup instead of honey. Use plant-based protein powder.
- **Keto:** Replace banana with 1/4 avocado. Use unsweetened almond or coconut milk and omit sweeteners.
- **Pregnancy-Safe:** Ensure all ingredients are fresh and thoroughly washed. Use pasteurized yogurt if consuming dairy.
- **Protein-Packed:** Add 1 scoop of protein powder or 1 tablespoon of hemp seeds.

Serving Tip: Garnish with a sprinkle of cacao powder or dark chocolate shavings. Serve with a handful of almonds or a piece of dark chocolate.

Instructions

1. Freeze the banana in advance for a creamier texture.

2. Add the liquid base to the blender first, followed by cooked beetroot, cacao powder, Greek yogurt, frozen banana, vanilla extract, honey (if using), and ice (if using).

3. Blend on low speed for 30 seconds, then gradually increase to high speed for about 1–2 minutes until smooth and creamy. Scrape down the sides if needed. Taste and adjust sweetness if necessary, adding a touch more honey or maple syrup if needed.

4. Pour into glasses and serve immediately.

---

05 Vanilla Pear Cream Delight

Total: 5 mins   **Servings:** 2   **Level:** 2/5

Nutritional Info *(Per Serving, based on butterfly pea flower and no optional additions)*: 220 kcal; 38g carbs; 7g protein; 6g fat; 5g fiber.

Ingredients

- **Liquid Base (Choose One):** 1 cup oat milk, 1 cup almond milk, or 1 cup coconut milk
- **Main Ingredients:** 1 ripe pear (cored and diced), 1/2 cup plain Greek yogurt, 1 frozen banana, 1/2 teaspoon pure vanilla extract, 1 tablespoon almond butter, 1/2 cup ice cubes (optional, for a refreshing texture)
- **Optional Sweetener:** 1 teaspoon raw honey or maple syrup
- **Optional Superfood Additions:** 1 scoop vanilla protein powder, 1 tablespoon chia seeds, 1 teaspoon MCT oil, 1/2 teaspoon cinnamon

Optional Variations:
- **Diabetic-Friendly:** Replace banana with 1/4 cup frozen zucchini. Use unsweetened almond or oat milk. Avoid sweeteners.
- **Vegan:** Use plant-based Greek-style yogurt and protein powder. Choose maple syrup instead of honey.
- **Keto:** Replace banana with 1/4 avocado. Use unsweetened almond or coconut milk and omit sweeteners.
- **Pregnancy-Safe:** Ensure all ingredients are fresh and thoroughly washed. Use pasteurized yogurt if consuming dairy.
- **Protein-Packed:** Add 1 tablespoon of hemp seeds.

Serving Tip: Garnish with a sprinkle of cinnamon or crushed almonds. Serve with a handful of walnuts or a light oat biscuit.

Instructions

1. Freeze the banana in advance for a creamier texture.

2. Add the liquid base to the blender first, followed by diced pear, Greek yogurt, frozen banana, vanilla extract, almond butter, maple syrup, and ice (if using).

3. Blend on low speed for 30 seconds, then gradually increase to high speed for about 1–2 minutes until smooth and creamy. Scrape down the sides if needed. Taste and adjust sweetness if necessary, adding a touch more maple syrup if needed.

4. Pour into glasses and serve immediately.

06 Pineapple Upside-Down Cake Smoothie

Total: 5 mins   **Servings:** 2   **Level:** 2/5

Nutritional Info (Per Serving, based on almond milk and no optional additions): 180 kcal; 32g carbs; 7g protein; 4g fat; 3g fiber.

Ingredients

- **Liquid Base (Choose One):** 1 cup unsweetened almond milk, 1 cup oat milk, or 1 cup coconut milk
- **Main Ingredients:** 1 cup fresh or frozen pineapple chunks, 1/2 cup plain Greek yogurt, 1/2 teaspoon vanilla extract, 1/2 cup ice cubes (optional, for a refreshing chill)
- **Optional Sweetener:** 1 teaspoon raw honey or maple syrup
- **Optional Superfood Additions:** 1 scoop vanilla protein powder, 1 tablespoon chia seeds, 1 teaspoon MCT oil, 1/2 teaspoon cinnamon

Optional Variations:
- **Diabetic-Friendly:** Replace pineapple with 1/4 cup frozen zucchini. Use unsweetened almond milk and omit sweeteners.
- **Vegan:** Swap Greek yogurt for a dairy-free alternative. Choose maple syrup instead of honey. Use plant-based protein powder.
- **Keto:** Replace pineapple with 1/4 avocado. Use unsweetened almond or coconut milk and omit sweeteners.
- **Pregnancy-Safe:** Ensure all ingredients are fresh and thoroughly washed. Use pasteurized yogurt if consuming dairy.
- **Protein-Packed:** Add 1 tablespoon of hemp seeds.

Serving Tip: Garnish with a sprinkle of cinnamon or a few crushed walnuts. Serve with a small piece of grilled pineapple or a handful of almonds.

Instructions

1. Freeze pineapple in advance for a creamier texture.

2. Add the liquid base to the blender first, followed by pineapple chunks, Greek yogurt, vanilla extract, maple syrup, and ice (if using).

3. Blend on low speed for 30 seconds, then gradually increase to high speed for about 1–2 minutes until smooth and creamy. Scrape down the sides if needed. Taste and adjust sweetness if necessary, adding a touch more maple syrup if needed.

4. Pour into glasses and serve immediately.

---

07 Tiramisu-Inspired Smoothie

Total: 5 mins   **Servings:** 2   **Level:** 2/5

Nutritional Info (Per Serving, based on almond milk and no optional additions): 190 kcal; 30g carbs; 8g protein; 5g fat; 4g fiber.

Ingredients

- **Liquid Base (Choose One):** 1/2 cup brewed espresso (chilled), 1/2 cup unsweetened almond milk, or 1/2 cup oat milk (naturally sweet and creamy)
- **Main Ingredients:** 1/2 cup plain Greek yogurt, 1 frozen banana, 1 tablespoon unsweetened cacao powder, 1/2 teaspoon vanilla extract, 1/2 cup ice cubes (optional, for a frothy texture)
- **Optional Sweetener:** 1 teaspoon raw honey or maple syrup
- **Optional Superfood Additions:** 1 scoop vanilla or chocolate protein powder, 1 tablespoon chia seeds, 1 teaspoon MCT oil, 1/2 teaspoon cinnamon

Optional Variations:
- **Diabetic-Friendly:** Replace banana with 1/4 cup frozen zucchini. Use unsweetened almond milk and omit sweeteners.
- **Vegan:** Swap Greek yogurt for a dairy-free alternative. Choose maple syrup instead of honey. Use plant-based protein powder.
- **Keto:** Replace banana with 1/4 avocado for a creamy, low-carb alternative. Use unsweetened almond milk and omit sweeteners.
- **Pregnancy-Safe:** Ensure all ingredients are fresh and thoroughly washed. Use decaf espresso if avoiding caffeine.
- **Protein-Packed:** Add 1 tablespoon of hemp seeds.

Serving Tip: Garnish with a dusting of cacao powder or a sprinkle of finely ground coffee beans. Serve with a small biscotti or a few almonds. Enjoy slightly chilled for a true coffeehouse-style dessert smoothie.

Instructions

1. Freeze the banana in advance for a creamier texture.

2. Brew and chill the espresso in advance for a smooth and refreshing taste.

3. Add the liquid base to the blender first, followed by Greek yogurt, frozen banana, cacao powder, vanilla extract, and ice (if using).

4. Blend on low speed for 30 seconds, then gradually increase to high speed for about 1–2 minutes until smooth and creamy. Scrape down the sides if needed. Taste and adjust sweetness if necessary, adding a touch of honey or maple syrup.

5. Pour into glasses and serve immediately.

08 Key Lime Pie Smoothie

Total: 5 mins   **Servings:** 2   **Level:** 2/5

Nutritional Info *(Per Serving, based on coconut milk and no optional additions)*: 210 kcal; 32g carbs; 7g protein; 8g fat; 3g fiber.

Ingredients

- **Liquid Base (Choose One):** 1 cup unsweetened almond milk, 1 cup oat milk, or 1 cup coconut milk
- **Main Ingredients:** 1/2 cup cooked beetroot (chopped), 1 tablespoon cacao powder, 1/2 cup plain Greek yogurt, 1 frozen banana, 1/2 teaspoon vanilla extract, 1/2 cup ice cubes (optional, for a refreshing chill)
- **Optional Sweetener:** 1 teaspoon raw honey or maple syrup
- **Optional Superfood Additions:** 1 scoop chocolate or vanilla protein powder, 1 tablespoon chia seeds, 1 teaspoon MCT oil, 1/2 teaspoon cinnamon

Optional Variations:
- **Diabetic-Friendly:** Replace banana with 1/4 cup frozen zucchini. Use unsweetened almond or coconut milk and avoid sweeteners.
- **Vegan:** Swap Greek yogurt for a dairy-free alternative. Choose maple syrup instead of honey. Use plant-based protein powder.
- **Keto:** Replace banana with 1/4 avocado. Use unsweetened coconut milk and omit sweeteners.
- **Pregnancy-Safe:** Ensure all ingredients are fresh and thoroughly washed. Use pasteurized yogurt if consuming dairy.
- **Protein-Packed:** Add 1 tablespoon of hemp seeds.

Serving Tip: Garnish with a thin lime slice or a sprinkle of lime zest. Serve with a handful of nuts or a small coconut energy ball.

Instructions

1. Freeze the banana in advance for a creamier texture.

2. Add the liquid base to the blender first, followed by lime juice, frozen banana, Greek yogurt, vanilla extract, and ice (if using).

3. Blend on low speed for 30 seconds, then gradually increase to high speed for about 1-2 minutes until smooth and creamy. Scrape down the sides if needed. Taste and adjust sweetness if necessary, adding a touch of honey or maple syrup.

4. Pour into glasses and serve immediately. If using, sprinkle graham cracker crumbs on top for a true Key Lime Pie experience.

---

09 Peanut Butter Brownie Smoothie

Total: 5 mins   **Servings:** 2   **Level:** 2/5

Nutritional Info *(Per Serving, based on almond milk flower and no optional additions)*: 280 kcal; 38g carbs; 8g protein; 12g fat; 6g fiber.

Ingredients

- **Liquid Base (Choose One):** 1 cup unsweetened almond milk, 1 cup oat milk, or 1 cup dairy milk
- **Main Ingredients:** 1 tablespoon peanut butter, 1 tablespoon raw cacao powder, 1 frozen banana, 1/2 cup ice cubes (optional, for a thicker texture)
- **Optional Sweetener:** 1 teaspoon raw honey or maple syrup
- **Optional Superfood Additions:** 1 scoop chocolate or vanilla protein powder, 1 tablespoon chia seeds, 1 teaspoon MCT oil, 1/2 teaspoon cinnamon

Optional Variations:
- **Diabetic-Friendly:** Replace banana with 1/4 cup frozen zucchini or 1/4 avocado. Use unsweetened almond milk and avoid sweeteners.
- **Vegan:** Use plant-based milk and protein powder. Choose maple syrup instead of honey.
- **Keto:** Replace banana with 1/4 avocado and avoid sweeteners.
- **Pregnancy-Safe:** Ensure all ingredients are fresh and thoroughly washed. Use pasteurized plant-based milk if available.
- **Protein-Packed:** Add 1 tablespoon of hemp seeds.

Serving Tip: Garnish with a drizzle of peanut butter or a sprinkle of cacao nibs. Serve with a handful of nuts or a piece of dark chocolate.

Instructions

1. Freeze the banana in advance for a creamier texture.

2. Add the liquid base to the blender first, followed by peanut butter, raw cacao powder, frozen banana, and honey (if using). If using ice, put it in last.

3. Blend on low speed for 30 seconds, then gradually increase to high speed for about 1-2 minutes until smooth and creamy. Scrape down the sides if needed. Taste and adjust sweetness if necessary, adding a touch of honey or maple syrup.

4. Pour into glasses and serve immediately.

10 Salted Caramel Date Smoothie

Total: 5 mins **Servings:** 2 **Level:** 2/5

Nutritional Info (Per Serving, based on almond milk and no optional additions): 250 kcal; 42g carbs; 6g protein; 9g fat; 5g fiber.

Ingredients

- **Liquid Base (Choose One):** 1 cup unsweetened almond milk, 1 cup oat milk, or 1 cup coconut milk
- **Main Ingredients:** 3 Medjool dates (pitted), 1 tablespoon almond butter, 1/2 teaspoon vanilla extract, a pinch of sea salt, 1/2 cup ice cubes (optional, for a thicker texture)
- **Optional Sweetener:** 1 teaspoon raw honey or maple syrup
- **Optional Superfood Additions:** 1 scoop vanilla or unflavored protein powder, 1 tablespoon chia seeds, 1 teaspoon MCT oil, 1/2 teaspoon ground cinnamon

Optional Variations:

- **Diabetic-Friendly:** Replace dates with 1/2 banana or 1/4 cup steamed and frozen cauliflower. Use unsweetened almond milk and avoid additional sweeteners.
- **Vegan:** Use plant-based protein powder. Choose maple syrup instead of honey if adding sweetener.
- **Keto:** Replace dates with 1/4 avocado and avoid sweeteners.
- **Pregnancy-Safe:** Ensure all ingredients are fresh and thoroughly washed. Use pasteurized plant-based milk if available.
- **Protein-Packed:** Add 1 tablespoon of hemp seeds.

Serving Tip: Garnish with a sprinkle of sea salt or a drizzle of almond butter. Serve with a handful of nuts or a small square of dark chocolate.

Instructions

1. Add the liquid base to the blender first, followed by Medjool dates, almond butter, vanilla extract, sea salt, and ice (if using).

2. Blend on low speed for 30 seconds, then gradually increase to high speed for about 1-2 minutes until smooth and creamy. Scrape down the sides if needed. Taste and adjust sweetness if necessary, adding a touch of honey or maple syrup.

3. Pour into glasses and serve immediately.

WHY THESE SMOOTHIES ARE EFFECTIVE

Dessert smoothies are the perfect way to indulge in rich, satisfying flavors while nourishing your body with wholesome ingredients. These blends are designed to provide the pleasure of a decadent treat while incorporating nutrient-dense elements that support energy, digestion, and overall well-being. Each smoothie in this collection offers a unique combination of natural sweetness, fiber, healthy fats, and plant-based proteins to help curb cravings, stabilize blood sugar, and satisfy your sweet tooth without guilt.

Here's why these dessert smoothies are not just delicious but also incredibly beneficial:

1. Dark Chocolate Berry Blend
A powerhouse of antioxidants, this smoothie combines dark cocoa with berries to protect against oxidative stress while satisfying chocolate cravings. Flaxseeds provide fiber and omega-3s, supporting brain health and digestion.

2. Strawberry Cheesecake Smoothie
Greek yogurt delivers protein and probiotics for gut health, while strawberries bring in vitamin C for skin and immune support. Graham cracker crumbs (optional) add a nostalgic cheesecake touch without the added sugar of traditional desserts.

3. Gingerbread Smoothie
Molasses is rich in iron and B vitamins, making this a great energizing treat. Warming spices like cinnamon and ginger aid digestion, boost metabolism, and give this smoothie a comforting holiday-inspired flavor.

4. Red Velvet Smoothie

Beets provide natural sweetness, antioxidants, and nitric oxide for improved blood flow and endurance. Paired with cacao powder, it creates a deep, rich flavor while supporting heart and brain health.

5. Vanilla Pear Cream Delight

This smoothie balances natural sweetness from ripe pears with the creamy texture of almond butter and Greek yogurt. Pears are high in fiber and antioxidants, promoting digestion and long-lasting satiety.

6. Pineapple Upside-Down Cake Smoothie

Pineapple's bromelain enzyme aids digestion, while Greek yogurt delivers protein and probiotics. The vanilla and cinnamon combination creates a dessert-like taste without added sugars.

7. Tiramisu-Inspired Smoothie

Chilled espresso adds a natural energy boost, while cacao powder and Greek yogurt create a rich, creamy flavor. This smoothie is perfect for a coffee lover's treat, providing sustained energy without refined sugar.

8. Key Lime Pie Smoothie

Lime juice is loaded with vitamin C and antioxidants, supporting immunity and digestion. Coconut milk adds healthy fats for a creamy, indulgent texture, mimicking the flavors of a classic pie.

9. Peanut Butter Brownie Smoothie

Peanut butter provides plant-based protein and healthy fats, while cacao powder delivers antioxidants and a deep chocolate flavor. This smoothie satisfies chocolate cravings while stabilizing blood sugar levels.

10. Salted Caramel Date Smoothie

Medjool dates bring natural caramel-like sweetness along with fiber, potassium, and magnesium. Almond butter adds healthy fats and protein, creating a rich, dessert-like experience that also nourishes your body.

The Science Behind Healthy Dessert Smoothies

These smoothies work because they focus on:

- **Natural Sweeteners:** Dates, bananas, and berries provide sweetness while offering fiber and nutrients, unlike refined sugar.
- **Protein & Healthy Fats:** Greek yogurt, nuts, and seeds help slow sugar absorption, keeping you satisfied longer.
- **Antioxidant-Rich Ingredients:** Cocoa, berries, and spices combat oxidative stress and inflammation.
- **Digestive Support:** Enzymes from pineapple, probiotics from yogurt, and fiber from fruits and seeds promote gut health.

Guilt-Free Indulgence That Nourishes

These smoothies prove that dessert can be both delicious and nutritious. By replacing processed ingredients with whole foods, you can satisfy your cravings while fueling your body with essential nutrients. Whether you're in the mood for a rich chocolate treat, a fruity delight, or a spiced comfort drink, these recipes offer a healthier way to indulge—without the sugar crash.

TROUBLESHOOTING SMOOTHIES: A QUICK REFERENCE GUIDE

Even the best of us occasionally end up with a smoothie that's too thick, too thin, or just plain uninspiring. Don't worry—most smoothie mishaps are easy to fix with a few simple tweaks. Below, you'll find solutions to common problems, and specific hacks to elevate your blends from meh to magnificent.

1. Problem: The Smoothie Is Too Thick
A smoothie that refuses to pour or feels like pudding might sound decadent, but it's frustrating when you aim for something drinkable.

How to Fix It:
- **Add More Liquid:** Start with 2 tablespoons of water, almond milk, or your preferred liquid base. Blend and gradually add more until it reaches your desired consistency.
- **Let It Sit:** If your smoothie is overloaded with frozen ingredients, let it sit at room temperature for 2–3 minutes before re-blending. This helps soften frozen fruits or veggies for easier blending.
- **Blend in Intervals:** Stop the blender, scrape down the sides, and pulse a few times to break down thicker chunks.

Hacks for Next Time:
- Stick to a **2:1 ratio of liquid to frozen ingredients**. For example, if you're using 1 cup of frozen fruit, start with 2 cups of liquid.
- To maintain flavor and prevent over-thickening, freeze liquids (like almond milk or tea) in ice cube trays instead of plain ice.

2. Problem: The Smoothie Is Too Thin
Nobody likes a watery, uninspiring smoothie that tastes more like juice. A smoothie should have some body—a satisfying, creamy texture that coats the tongue without being overly thick.

How to Fix It:
- **Add Creamy Ingredients:** Blend in half a banana, 1/4 avocado, or a dollop of Greek yogurt for instant thickness.
- **Use Dry Additions:** Toss in 2–3 tablespoons of rolled oats, chia seeds, or flaxseeds. Let the smoothie sit for 1–2 minutes after blending to allow these ingredients to absorb liquid.
- **Frozen Boost:** Add a handful of frozen fruit, frozen cauliflower, or ice cubes for quick thickening.

Hacks for Next Time:
- Start with less liquid than you think you need and add gradually as you blend. You can always thin out a smoothie, but thickening it takes extra effort.
- Keep **pre-frozen smoothie packs** (frozen fruit, greens, and portioned creamy ingredients) in your freezer to ensure every blend starts with a thick base.

3. Problem: The Smoothie Tastes Bland
A bland smoothie can be a major letdown, especially when it looks colorful and inviting. This often happens when flavors aren't balanced or if the ingredients lack variety.

How to Fix It:
- **Brighten It Up:** Add a splash of lemon, lime, or orange juice for a tangy kick. Citrus is a flavor lifeline that instantly revives dull blends.
- **Boost with Spices:** A pinch of cinnamon, nutmeg, or ginger can elevate flavors and add warmth.

For tropical smoothies, try cardamom or turmeric.

- **Sweeten Strategically:** If it's too neutral, blend in a Medjool date, 1/2 a ripe banana, or a teaspoon of honey or maple syrup.

Hacks for Next Time:
- Every smoothie should include a "star ingredient" with a bold flavor. Examples: ripe mango, pineapple, cocoa powder, or fresh mint.
- For last-minute adjustments, keep a **flavor enhancer toolkit** nearby, including vanilla extract, sea salt, citrus zest, and spices.

4. Problem: The Smoothie Is Too Sweet
A cloyingly sweet smoothie can feel like dessert gone wrong. Overly ripe bananas, too much fruit, or sweetened liquids are often to blame.

How to Fix It:
- **Balance It Out:** Add a handful of spinach, kale, or frozen zucchini to neutralize sweetness while boosting nutrients.
- **Introduce Tart Elements:** Blend in frozen raspberries, cranberries, or a splash of unsweetened cranberry or lemon juice.
- **Dilute It:** Add more liquid (preferably unsweetened or plain) and re-blend. You can also toss in a handful of ice cubes for a quick refresh.

Hacks for Next Time:
- Use ripe bananas sparingly—half is often enough to sweeten an entire smoothie.
- Pair naturally sweet fruits (like mangoes or dates) with tart fruits (like kiwi or citrus) to maintain balance.

5. Problem: The Smoothie Is Too Tart
While tart smoothies can feel refreshing, an overly sour blend can be off-putting. This usually happens when tart fruits are overloaded or unbalanced acidic ingredients are included.

How to Fix It:
- **Sweeten Gradually:** To soften the tartness, add a ripe banana, Medjool date, or a drizzle of honey. Start small and taste as you go.
- **Cream It Up:** Blend in Greek yogurt, avocado, or unsweetened nut milk to mellow out sharp flavors.
- **Balance with Salt:** A small pinch of salt can neutralize excessive acidity and bring out natural sweetness.

Hacks for Next Time:
- Stick to a **2:1 ratio of sweet to tart fruits.** For example, pair 2 cups of mango or banana with 1 cup of raspberries or kiwi.
- Use a neutral liquid base like almond milk or coconut water instead of citrus-heavy juices.

6. Problem: The Smoothie Is Gritty or Grainy
Unblended seeds, fibrous greens, or certain protein powders often cause a gritty smoothie. The texture can make it feel more like a chore than a treat.

How to Fix It:
- **Blend Longer:** Run your blender for an additional 30–60 seconds, especially if using fibrous ingredients like kale or chia seeds.
- **Soak Beforehand:** Pre-soak chia seeds, flaxseeds, or oats in liquid for 5–10 minutes before blending. This softens their texture.

- **Switch Up Protein Powder:** Some powders dissolve better than others. Opt for high-quality, finely milled options like collagen peptides.

Hacks for Next Time:
- Invest in a high-speed blender for silky-smooth results, especially if you frequently use seeds, nuts, or greens.
- Chop fibrous ingredients (like kale stems or celery) into smaller pieces before blending.

7. Problem: The Smoothie Separates Quickly
Layering or separation often indicates that the ingredients didn't fully emulsify, leaving a watery base and floating solids.

How to Fix It:
- **Re-blend It:** Add a small amount of yogurt, avocado, or banana to act as an emulsifier and re-blend.
- **Use Ice Cubes:** Re-blend with a handful of ice to redistribute ingredients and thicken the mixture.

Hacks for Next Time:
- Combine creamy and fibrous ingredients for better texture retention (e.g., spinach + yogurt or avocado + berries).
- Avoid over-blending, as excess heat from the blender can cause separation.

8. Problem: The Smoothie Has a "Weird" Aftertaste
Sometimes, a single overpowering ingredient—like overly bitter greens or an earthy superfood—can dominate the flavor profile.

How to Fix It:
- **Mask It:** Add bold flavors like cocoa powder, vanilla extract, or nut butter to cover up unpleasant aftertastes.
- **Dilute and Balance:** Blend in more liquid and a neutral ingredient like banana or cucumber to tone down the intensity.
- **Add Sweetness or Spice:** A small amount of honey, cinnamon, or ginger can neutralize strong aftertastes.

Hacks for Next Time:
- Taste greens or herbs before adding them—some older or bitter produce can affect flavor.
- Use strong-flavored superfoods like spirulina sparingly (start with 1/4 teaspoon).

9. Problem: The Smoothie Is Warm
Warm smoothies are rarely appetizing and often result from over-blending or using room-temperature ingredients.

How to Fix It:
- **Cool It Down:** Add a handful of ice cubes or frozen fruit and re-blend.
- **Chill Beforehand:** If you don't have frozen ingredients on hand, refrigerate your smoothie for 15 minutes before drinking.

Hacks for Next Time:
- Keep fruits like bananas or mangoes pre-frozen to instantly cool your smoothie without diluting it.
- Avoid blending for too long, as heat from the blender motor can warm up your drink.

Quick Reference Hacks
   1. Always Taste as You Go: Adjust sweetness, tartness, or spice while blending to avoid major fixes later.

2. Prep for Success: Pre-freeze portioned fruits, veggies, and liquid cubes for consistently cold, creamy smoothies.

3. Embrace Contrast: Balance rich, creamy ingredients with bright, refreshing ones for a more dynamic flavor.

Smoothies are forgiving, so don't stress over small missteps. With these troubleshooting tips and hacks, you'll be equipped to tackle any blending hiccup and create a smoothie that's as delicious as it is satisfying.

EXTRA BONUS

I hope you enjoy the Healthy Smoothie Recipe Book. But before you close it, pick up your gift!

Please scan this QR code to get the Bonus Book. It's a PDF where you'll find:

- 10 additional anti-aging smoothies recipes
- Formula to create your own signature smoothies with a potent anti-aging punch
- Full-color photos of every recipe from this book

Thank you for choosing my book!
Rosemary Brook

Printed in Dunstable, United Kingdom